CARMINE'S FAMILY-STYLE COOKBOOK

Catherine,

Michael Rini

"eat well"!

CARMINE'S™

FAMILY-STYLE COOKBOOK

*More than 100 Classic Italian Dishes
to Make at Home*

MICHAEL RONIS WITH MARY GOODBODY

ST. MARTIN'S PRESS ❄ NEW YORK

CARMINE'S FAMILY-STYLE COOKBOOK. Copyright © 2008 by Carmine's Broadway Feast Corporation. All rights reserved. Printed in the United States of America. For information, address St. Martin's Press, 175 Fifth Avenue, New York, N.Y. 10010.

www.stmartins.com

Photographs copyright © 2008 by Alex Martinez
Book design and composition by Gretchen Achilles
Production Manager: Cheryl Mamaril

Library of Congress Cataloging-in-Publication Data

Ronis, Michael.
    Carmine's family-style cookbook : more than 100 classic Italian dishes to make at home / Michael Ronis with Mary Goodbody.—1st ed.
        p. cm.
    ISBN-13: 978-0-312-37536-2
    ISBN-10: 0-312-37536-0
    1. Cookery, Italian.   2. Carmine's Restaurants.   I. Goodbody, Mary.   II. Title.
    TX723.R543   2008
    641.5945—dc22   2008024267

First Edition: October 2008

10 9 8 7 6 5 4 3 2 1

In loving memory of Artie Cutler
whose passion for food
and visionary spirit
created the Carmine's experience

CONTENTS

INTRODUCTION

When you are at Carmine's, there are happy people around you and everyone is smiling.

—ALICE CUTLER, PRESIDENT AND PARTNER

The intoxicating aromas of garlic, olive oil, and tomatoes waft through the front door of Carmine's so that from the moment you enter, you find yourself salivating. As you are led to your table, waiters pass by carrying trays loaded with large platters of hot antipasti, crisp Caesar salad, garlic bread oozing butter, pasta with white clam sauce, steak Contadina, and eggplant Parmesan. Dizzy with anticipation for the meal ahead, you suddenly are distracted by the sight of a gigantic ice cream dessert—aptly named, you later discover, the Titanic—on its way to a happy group at a nearby table. Everywhere you look, customers look well fed, happy, and relaxed. This is going to be some meal!

Laughter fills the air, bubbling into the room and dancing off the walls as it mingles with cheerful conversation and the gloriously inviting scents emanating from the constantly swinging kitchen doors. The tables are spacious, the lighting muted, the wood paneling dark, and the warm-toned beige walls are filled with black-and-white photographs of Italian families and well-known Italian Americans. Everything is designed to evoke the past and the great culinary heritage Italian immigrants brought to our shores, but nothing is actually old or outmoded.

This is the Carmine's experience. It's this experience that you can bring home to your family when you prepare the recipes on the following pages. Our food is a synthesis of what Italians, many from Southern Italy, brought

with them to New York when they passed through Ellis Island on their way to a better life. It is food rich with tomato sauces, fresh herbs, garlic, olive oil, seafood, pasta, sausages, cheese, and lots of love.

It's Italian!

OUR STYLE OF ITALIAN FOOD

Let's face it. When most Americans think about Italian food, it is dishes such as ours—stuffed mushrooms; pasta with broccoli, sausage, and tomatoes; shrimp scampi; and veal Marsala—that spark the taste buds. Everyone loves spicy meatballs and a good marinara sauce, and everyone loves bubbling hot lasagna—and it's been decades since these foods have been considered "foreign." On the contrary, they are all-American family favorites.

Perhaps this is no surprise. Italians began emigrating to the United States during the second half of the nineteenth century, with a concentration arriving after 1880. In the beginning, most were single men from Southern Italy, where overcrowding and poverty chased them from home, and most planned to return to Italy once they made some money. In fact, the Italians were dubbed "birds of passage" because they were considered migratory workers who traveled back and forth from one continent to the other. This also explains why so few went into farming, preferring the relatively high wages and numerous but transitory jobs in the cities—although they painstakingly cultivated small urban gardens. Because of the structure and importance of Italian family life, when wives and children finally emigrated, the women tended to stay home or to work in small family businesses rather than sign on as domestic or factory workers. This meant that they were around to cook simple, thrifty meals that reminded everyone in the household of home.

What were these meals? Pasta was easy to make with flour and eggs and cost very little. Tomatoes grew well during American summers and were ideal for canning. Cow's milk was plentiful and could be made into simple fresh cheeses such as mozzarella and ricotta. Pork was not too costly, and the fattier cuts could be cured into salami. Most Americans in those days didn't grow garlic, bell peppers, or zucchini, but that didn't stop the Italians from planting their gardens with these and other vegetables. Nor did they refrain from making wine and grappa in city basements.

When these Italian home cooks prepared meals, economy was always an issue. They braised inexpensive cuts of meat long and slow to tenderize them with tantalizingly delicious results. If they ran out of meat or cheese, resourceful cooks used bread crumbs to add texture to pasta. They stuffed garden-grown peppers with mixtures bolstered with bread cubes, garlic and herbs, and thrifty amounts of meat or chicken. They filled sheets of pasta with creative combinations of vegetables and cheese for ravioli.

From these humble beginnings great traditions were born in the kitchens of Lower Manhattan, Boston's North End, and South Philly. Sunday afternoons were family days when everyone, from the oldest great-grandmother to the youngest baby, got together to eat and drink, tell stories of the old country, and admire the growing families flourishing in America. Women began cooking their red sauce long before church on Sunday morning, and as soon as they got home from Mass they made the pasta, which they cut into various shapes as they gossiped around the kitchen table. The men sliced off hunks of salami and hard cheese to sustain them until the late-afternoon meal was served, and the kids raced up and down the front stoops, calling to their cousins as they played street games.

This is the experience we strive to re-create at Carmine's. Every day is Sunday afternoon for us, and everyone is always welcome. The food is fresh, hot, and redolent of garlic, basil, and olive oil. We pile platters with fresh salads, steaming, just-cooked pasta bathed in heady red sauce, perfectly seasoned chicken and steak, and glorious vegetables. All of our dishes are served family-style, and all of our dishes are made to order. You might swear

ALICE CUTLER

there's a little old Italian grandmother in the kitchen stirring pots and adding a pinch of this, a sprinkling of that to make your meal so perfect!

The dishes in this book are wonderful for everyday family meals or for large parties. We can't think of a better way to set a buffet table for a casual family get-together or a more formal dinner party than with platters of Cold Roasted Figs with Gorgonzola, Prosciutto Bits, Grapes, and Balsamic Glaze, our famous Chicken Wings Scarpariello-Style with Gorgonzola Dipping Sauce, perfectly cooked Porterhouse Steak Contadina, and Slow-Roasted Lamb Shoulder Chops with Vegetable Orzo Risotto, followed by Carmine's Tiramisu. Now that's a party!

So, with a smile on your face, a smear of tomato sauce on your apron, and *Carmine's Family-Style Cookbook* in your kitchen, you and your loved ones can sit down to a hearty, great-tasting meal of the beloved dishes from our restaurant. It's likely these will quickly become your signature dishes, too.

OUR BEGINNINGS AND OUR FUTURE

Long before he opened the first Carmine's in August of 1990 on New York's Upper West Side, Artie Cutler had been tossing around the idea for a family-style Italian restaurant. His interest was fueled when he attended a friend's wedding held in a suburban backyard where old-fashioned, hearty Italian food, served family-style, filled the guests' plates and helped turn the party into a splendidly boisterous celebration. Artie responded to the warmth and happiness of the occasion as well as its utter lack of pretension. Mostly, he recognized how happily the wedding guests responded to the "real food" and liberal portions. With this in mind, he sharpened his vision for a restaurant that would allow Manhattan's chic yuppies to unwind, a restaurant that would attract their parents and their children as well.

Two years after the first Carmine's opened its doors on Broadway and 91st Street, Artie opened another restaurant on 44th Street just west of Broadway.

"People told him he was nuts," his wife, Alice Cutler, remembers. Times Square had not yet gone through its transformation, and no one thought a restaurant right smack in its heart was a good idea—no one but Artie. He believed the area would very soon become desirable again, says Alice, who now is at the helm of the business. He was right, of course. The 44th Street Carmine's is our busiest and best-known location, and a great favorite with tourists from the United States and all over the world.

Clearly, Artie believed in teamwork, and Alice and her partners carry on that tradition today. "As a company, we are like a big family," she says. "A lot of employees have been here for a long time and the restaurant becomes a home away from home. We still have waiters who started with us when we opened the first Carmine's in 1990." One of the happiest examples of Carmine's dedication to upward mobility is Luis Javier, the talented executive chef at 44th Street, who started eighteen years ago as a salad chef. "To see Luis grow from within the company has been a pleasure," says Alice.

A tight-knit group of like-minded people, most of whom worked with Artie, work at the New York–based Alicart Restaurant Group, directed by CEO and partner Jeffrey Bank. Alicart operates the four Carmine's restaurants as well as Virgil's BBQ, Gabriela's Mexican, and Artie's Delicatessen. The first two Carmine's are in Manhattan. The others are in the Tropicana Hotel and Casino in Atlantic City, New Jersey; and at the Atlantis on Paradise Island in the Bahamas. There are others in the works. Jeffrey currently has expansion plans on the drawing boards for restaurants in Garden City, Long Island, New York; Las Vegas, Nevada; Washington, D.C.; and Orlando, Florida. In reality, Carmine's could go anywhere.

Carmine's Family-Style Cookbook was put together with the same enthusiasm, attention to detail, and great affection as the restaurants. If we do say so ourselves, we think it's going to be just as big a hit! We hope its pages will soon be stained with red sauce, dribbles of olive oil, and sticky fingerprints, all happy accidents as you discover our recipes. We trust you will find them as rewarding, delicious, and as mouthwatering as we do.

Welcome to Carmine's!

THE HEART AND SOUL OF CARMINE'S

"Artie loved to eat, and he loved to gamble," says Alice Cutler. He also believed a business with a one-word name was easy for customers to remember, so he took the first name of one of his favorite harness-racing drivers for the restaurant. When the New York State Restaurant Association named Artie Restaurateur of the Year in 1996, Alice recalls, he joked about what a "lucky" man he was because the restaurant business was a "perfect fit" for someone who had a passion for food and liked to gamble. He was a risk taker, his wife says, but Artie was a risk taker with a keen business sense and impeccable

instincts. Jeffrey Bank recalls Artie's mantra: "The best deals are the ones you walk away from."

When he started building his restaurant empire in the 1980s and lacked a formal office, Artie did most of his business from a bench in the meridian that runs through the center of Broadway on the Upper West Side. After he died, Alice bought that bench at Broadway and 90th Street and put a plaque on it that reads IN MEMORY OF ARTIE, "BUBBA" CUTLER (ARTIE'S FIRST OFFICE).

From those early days, Artie had a vision of what made a restaurant work. His legacy is reflected in our big, sprawling, boisterous Italian American restaurants where day after day and night after night hundreds of New Yorkers and out-of-towners sit down to huge portions of great food meant to be shared. "The simplicity of the concept makes it work," explains Gary Bologna, a partner and our chief operating officer, who has been with Carmine's since 1997. "It's about good service, great food, and family style."

This is all Artie Cutler. Without his vision, his remarkable energy, and his generosity of spirit, Carmine's would not exist. Those of us who worked with him miss him very much.

CARMINE'S KITCHEN

We love food, and we love to see people enjoying it, digging into platters piled high with freshly cooked pasta, rich red sauces, tender clams, and perfectly cooked meat and sausage. We appreciate cutting-edge cuisine, but that's not us. Instead, we are true to what we call "grandmother's cooking." Our food is the food you might have eaten on Sunday afternoon if you were part of a typical Italian American family in the Bronx or Brooklyn. Because we are from the city, we think of this as New York Italian, but we know most of our dishes are instantly recognizable in other parts of the country, too, and particularly where there is a concentration of Italian Americans.

Carmine's is big and can be noisy, and the number of people who dine

with us every day is impressive, with well over 1.3 million customers a year. The sheer volume leads some to assume that high quality cannot be sustained, but nothing could be further from the truth. Alice, our president, readily admits that many of our first-time customers are "blown away" when they taste our food. "Some come in with low expectations," she says, but with the first mouthful, any doubt is dispelled.

Running the kitchen on a classic European model is the brainchild of partner and founding chef Michael Ronis. As a classically trained chef, it never occurred to him to organize our kitchens any other way, and so the sauces are finished just before serving, no pasta is cooked until an order is placed, and the hero sandwiches are assembled right before they are carried to the customer. Even after eighteen years, which translates to lots of success and practice, the same close attention is given to all our food. For instance, Glenn Rolnick, corporate executive chef and partner, makes sure that popular dishes such as Penne alla Vodka are consistent from restaurant to restaurant so that customers are never disappointed. Since our food is fresh and nothing is held over, it's been easy to adapt our recipes for your home kitchen.

We wouldn't dream of doing anything differently.

CARMINE'S WINE CELLAR AND BAR

The wine we pour at Carmine's runs the gamut from earthy and gutsy to crisp and refreshing. Our wine list boasts approximately 120 labels, with bottles that are sophisticated enough for anyone who walks through our doors without being precious, esoteric, or expensive. As with our food, our wine is high in quality and a good value.

Our customers love our magnums, and with good reason. A magnum is 1.5 liters, or equal to two "normal-sized" 750 ml wine bottles. It's a big, bold bottle that never looks out of place on one of our spacious tables, where the platters are piled high and diners happily serve themselves as they sip their wine. Both our red magnum and our white magnum are festooned with the handsome Carmine's label, and both are bottled for us in central Italy. They don't hold "just any old wine"—not by a long shot! The wines are from a cooperative in Abruzzo called Casal Bordino, where the wine is made expressly for us from carefully selected grapes grown nearby and then bottled and shipped to us, all according to our precise specifications.

James Yacyshyn, our beverage director, travels to Abruzzo at least once a year to oversee the process, taste new varietals, and make sure the wine we buy meets our standards as well as the demanding tastes of our customers. There, with the deep blue Adriatic Sea lying at the feet of Casal Bordino and warm breezes wafting from the coastline up to the mountains, the sun-drenched vineyards are cool and pleasant. In this breathtaking setting, James tastes some of the finest wines in the world and makes sure they find their way to our cellars.

Our red magnum is a Monte Pulciano d'Abruzzo, which is a dry, medium-to full-bodied, ruby red pour with nuances of black cherry and licorice. Needless to say, it marries well with our red sauces and red meat dishes, as well as chicken and veal.

Our white magnum is a Trebbiano d'Abruzzo, which is a dry, crisp, light-to medium-bodied, soft golden wine with hints of apple. It's a perfect match for our seafood dishes, fried foods, salads, and lighter meat offerings such as chicken and veal. This is the wine we cook with most frequently, adhering to the adage that you should never cook with a wine you would not drink.

The wine program got off the ground in a big way in 1994 when Robert Castleberry came on board as Carmine's first beverage director. Robert was passionate about wine and was considered one of the finest connoisseurs in the city. Originally, Robert bought our wines from a California vineyard, but in time he turned to Italy to fill our growing need. He found the Casal Bordino cooperative and worked with them to establish our magnum wines.

Robert also expanded our wine list so that it became more global, in

keeping with the times. James has refined the list further, and today you can order wines from Italy and California but also from France, Greece, Spain, South America, New Zealand, and Australia. Our mission is to offer wines that drink well with our food—and while we think we meet that mission every day, we always work to make the list better. James also developed two more private-label wines for us: Chianti Classico and Pinot Grigio. Both are exceptionally popular with our customers.

Our attitude about wine is one that translates to the home. We don't try to impress with our wine, yet in the end we always do because we serve good, honest wines that complement the food but never take a backseat to it. In Italy, wine is considered food and is a natural part of the meal. We subscribe to the same principle.

In addition to wine, we serve a lot of cocktails, and you will probably not be astonished to learn that they tend to be oversized. Our martinis are legendary, as is our frozen cosmopolitan, which has become something of a signature drink. While the bar scene is lively, it's evocative of an old-time bar where traditional drinks are the order of the day. We also cater to contemporary tastes with any number of modern rum drinks, flavored vodkas, and Italian liqueurs.

Carmine's is a family restaurant. The food is our primary concern, but we understand the role wine and spirits play in any celebration, whether it's in a restaurant or at home. Our bartenders are hired for their ability to deliver a good experience to the customer without letting anyone overdo it, which is probably pretty much your attitude when you entertain guests in your own home!

OUR LOVE AFFAIR WITH CARMINE'S

We take care of our guests. It's apparent from the minute you walk in until the time you leave. Carmine's is loud, and it's a place for a good time. Since the restaurant opened its doors in August of 1990, review after review has praised the food. Even cynical New York foodies rave about it. "Trendy New Yorkers happily [eat] veal parmigiana, meatballs and spaghetti and 'garlic bread' instead of 'bruschetta.' The taste is right on . . . we never really had a place like this in the old neighborhood," wrote Arthur Schwartz in the *Daily News* when the first restaurant opened.

"Carmine's is everything that New York's Italian restaurants have been trying to get away from," cheerfully declared Moira Hodgson in the *New York Times* around the same time. "Red food . . . Chopped garlic and marinara

sauce . . . It's the sort of place you always hope to discover on City Island or Little Italy but that always lets you down. . . . Carmine's is a brilliant conceit," she continued, saying it had been "a long time since I had antipasto like this."

The drumbeat has not slackened over the years. Fodor's online travel site talks about the "mountains of such popular, toothsome items as fried calamari, linguine with white clam sauce, chicken parmigiana, and veal saltimbocca," and warns readers they will "inevitably order too much, but most of the food tastes just as wonderful the next day."

In a December 2000 roundup of restaurants handpicked for celebrations, the *New York Times* listed Carmine's, saying it was "not subtle or sophisticated cuisine but party food intended for boisterous groups who want to shovel it in while enjoying the convivial atmosphere."

In a review on Frommer's Web site, the writer describes the dining room at Carmine's as "vast enough to deserve its own zip code . . . [yet] remarkably [the kitchen] turns out better pasta and entrees than most twenty-table Italian restaurants." Customers writing on restaurant blogs have called the food "incredible" with "simple Italian recipes just done well . . . [that] seem new, leaving all past experiences in its dust."

We bask in this praise but never become complacent. We get up every day knowing that today our most important job is to keep the restaurant humming so that the kitchen turns out consistently delicious food with just the right attitude to keep our customers happy and well fed. With our recipes at your fingertips, you will be able to keep your loved ones equally happy and well fed. When you find a recipe for only two servings, remember that you can easily double or triple it. On the other hand, we often load up a table with three, four, or more dishes, which explains why some recipes do not serve a lot of people; when served all together, there is lots of food!

We hope our love affair with Carmine's will become yours!

1.
APPETIZERS,
SOUPS, AND SALADS

We never cut corners. Everything is done by hand; in fact, nineteen years ago we used to peel two cases of garlic a day.

STUFFED EGGPLANT ROLLITINI ❧ SPIEDINI ALLA ROMANO ❧ BAKED CLAMS ❧ STUFFED ARTICHOKE ❧ SAUSAGE-STUFFED MUSHROOMS ❧ TOMATO, MOZZARELLA, BASIL, RED ONION, AND ASSORTED OLIVES ❧ CHICKEN WINGS SCARPARIELLO-STYLE WITH GORGONZOLA DIPPING SAUCE ❧ COLD ROASTED FIGS WITH GORGONZOLA, PROSCIUTTO BITS, GRAPES, AND BALSAMIC GLAZE ❧ ROASTED PEPPERS AND MOZZARELLA WITH ANCHOVY ❧ PASTA E FAGIOLI SOUP ❧ RED ZUPPA DI CLAMS ❧ WHITE ZUPPA DI CLAMS ❧ RED ZUPPA DI MUSSELS ❧ WHITE ZUPPA DI MUSSELS ❧ RUSTIC LENTIL SOUP ❧ GARLIC BREAD AND GARLIC BREAD PARMIGIANA ❧ CARMINE'S FAMOUS CAESAR SALAD ❧ CARMINE'S SALAD ❧ BOSTON LETTUCE SALAD WITH RICOTTA SALATA AND ROASTED VEGETABLES ❧ MISTI SALAD WITH FALL FRUITS AND WALNUTS ❧ CHOPPED GRILLED CHICKEN SALAD ❧ GRILLED PORTOBELLO SALAD

STUFFED EGGPLANT ROLLITINI

This holds a favored place on our hot antipasti platter, but it also can be served as a light meal. The key to these rollitini is fresh ricotta and a firm, smooth, unblemished eggplant. The flavor combinations are reminiscent of lasagna, but without the noodles!

Serves 4 to 5

1 MEDIUM-SIZED EGGPLANT

1 CUP ALL-PURPOSE FLOUR

5 LARGE EGGS

2 CUPS VEGETABLE OIL

2½ CUPS FRESH WHOLE MILK RICOTTA

1 CUP COARSELY GRATED MOZZARELLA

5 TABLESPOONS GRATED ROMANO CHEESE

2 TABLESPOONS CHOPPED FLAT-LEAF PARSLEY

KOSHER SALT AND FRESHLY GROUND BLACK PEPPER

4 TO 4½ CUPS CARMINE'S MARINARA SAUCE, PAGE 288

1. Cut the ends off the eggplant and discard them. Peel the eggplant and then cut it lengthwise into fifteen ¼-inch-thick slices.

2. Spread the flour on a large plate. Whisk 4 of the eggs in a shallow bowl.

3. In a heavy saucepan or high-sided skillet, heat the oil over high heat until a deep-frying thermometer registers 325°F.

4. Coat both sides of each slice of eggplant with flour and shake off any excess. Dip the eggplant in the egg mixture to coat both sides and let any excess drip off. Work with a few slices at a time.

5. Using tongs, submerge 3 to 4 eggplant slices in the hot oil. Do not crowd the pan. Fry the eggplant for about 3 minutes on each side or until it is golden brown. Remove the eggplant with a slotted spoon, drain it on paper towels, and set it aside to cool to room temperature. Repeat with the remaining eggplant.

6. Preheat the oven to 375°F.

7. In a large bowl, mix together the ricotta, the mozzarella, ¼ cup of the grated Romano cheese, the remaining egg, and the parsley. Season the mixture to taste with salt and pepper.

8. Lay the eggplant slices lengthwise on a work surface. Put about 2 tablespoons of the cheese mixture on each slice, about 2 inches from the end. Roll the end of the eggplant over the cheese and continue rolling to the other end into rollitini.

9. Spread 3 cups of marinara sauce on the bottom of a shallow casserole large enough to hold the rollitini in one layer. Arrange the rollitini on the sauce and pour the remaining 1 to 1½ cups of sauce over them to cover the eggplant completely. Sprinkle them with the remaining tablespoon of Romano cheese.

10. Place the casserole on a sheet pan and transfer it to the oven. Bake the rollitini for 50 minutes or until they are heated through, bubbling, and lightly browned.

11. Remove the rollitini from the oven and let them rest for 20 minutes to settle before serving.

SPIEDINI ALLA ROMANO

This dish was inspired by Rita Cavallaro, whose son Tom, a friend of Alice and Artie's, introduced us to her and, by association, to this superdelicious, indulgent treat. When we began working on our own version of spiedini, we started with great peasant bread and the freshest mozzarella we could find. The spiedini is as much about the ingredients as the cooking method, and the result is crispy, golden brown bread and melting, stringy cheese provocatively flavored with shallots, capers, and fresh basil.

Serves 4

8 TABLESPOONS PLUS 1 TEASPOON UNSALTED BUTTER

1 SHALLOT, PEELED AND FINELY CHOPPED

4 ANCHOVY FILLETS, DRAINED AND COARSELY CHOPPED

¼ CUP WHITE WINE

¾ CUP CHICKEN STOCK, PAGE 306

1 TABLESPOON TINY NONPAREIL CAPERS, DRAINED

5 LARGE BASIL LEAVES, SLICED

1 TEASPOON CHOPPED FLAT-LEAF PARSLEY

SALT AND FRESHLY GROUND BLACK PEPPER

1 SMALL, ROUND LOAF DAY-OLD OR SLIGHTLY STALE RUSTIC, FARM-STYLE BREAD

2 GARLIC CLOVES, PEELED AND HALVED

1-POUND BALL FRESH MOZZARELLA

1. In a small sauté pan, heat 1 teaspoon of the butter over medium heat. When it sizzles, add the shallots and cook them for about 2 minutes or until they are lightly browned. Add the anchovies and rub them into the shallots with the back of a fork. Stir them for about 1 minute longer.

2. Add the wine and cook the mixture for about 30 seconds until it is heated through. Add the chicken stock, increase the heat to medium-high, bring the sauce to a boil, and cook it rapidly for 1 minute.

Continued

3. Reduce the heat to medium and add the remaining butter, a tablespoon at a time, whisking the sauce after each addition until it thickens and all the butter is incorporated.

4. Stir in the capers, basil, and parsley. Season the sauce to taste with salt and pepper. Set it aside, covered, to keep warm.

5. Preheat the oven to 500°F.

6. Cut a slice about 1 inch thick off each end of the loaf to square it. (Reserve the slices for croutons or bread crumbs.) Cut the loaf into five ½-inch-thick slices. Trim any crust from the bread and then cut each slice so that it measures 4 by 2½ inches.

7. Lightly toast the bread slices in a toaster, a toaster oven, or the oven. While they are warm, rub both sides with the garlic halves.

8. Cut the mozzarella into four ½-inch-thick slices cut to fit on top of the bread. Stack the bread and cheese, beginning and ending with the bread, so that you end up with a tall sandwich with 5 slices of bread and 4 slices of cheese.

9. Spear the sandwich with an 8-inch wooden skewer. Push the skewer all the way through so it will hold the spiedini in place as it cooks.

10. Transfer the spiedini to a shallow pan and bake it in the preheated oven for about 15 minutes, or until the bread is crisp and the cheese melts. Using tongs, turn the dish holding the spiedini at least twice, so that the bread browns on all sides and the cheese melts evenly.

11. Transfer the spiedini to a serving platter, remove the skewer, pour the sauce over the sandwich, and serve. You can cut it before serving or let everyone cut his or her own pieces.

ANTIPASTI

LITERALLY, "ANTI" MEANS "BEFORE"—ANTIPASTI IS SERVED BEFORE THE MEAL, OR BEFORE THE PASTA DISH THAT USUALLY STARTS A TRADITIONAL ITALIAN MEAL. AT CARMINE'S, CUSTOMERS ORDER ANY NUMBER OF ANTIPASTI AND SOMETIMES MAKE A WHOLE MEAL OF THEM, SAMPLING ONE PLATE AFTER ANOTHER. ANOTHER WORD FOR ANTIPASTI IN THIS COUNTRY IS "APPETIZER," BUT THEY ARE SO MUCH MORE. ANTIPASTI CAN MEAN A MAGNIFICENT PLATTER OF ITALIAN HAMS AND SALAMI, CHEESES, AND VINEGAR PEPPERS. OR IT CAN BE AN ASSORTMENT OF HOT DISHES SUCH AS STUFFED ARTICHOKES, CLAMS, STUFFED MUSHROOMS, AND SAUSAGES. THE BEST THING ABOUT ANTIPASTI IS HOW CREATIVE YOU CAN BE ASSEMBLING THE PLATTERS WITH YOUR FAVORITES TO TEMPT YOUR GUESTS.

BAKED CLAMS

When you start with fresh, fresh clams, you can't go wrong with this appetizer, particularly because it's made with our fresh bread crumbs, which truly make it special. The fresh crumbs are nicely seasoned with garlic and cheese. Baked clams are always among the most popular appetizers in any Italian restaurant, and Carmine's is no exception. Taste them and you will know why!

Serves 2 to 3

12 LITTLENECK CLAMS, RINSED AND SCRUBBED

1 CUP BOTTLED CLAM JUICE

¾ CUP CARMINE'S BREAD CRUMBS, PAGE 283

1 TABLESPOON FINELY CHOPPED GARLIC

1 TABLESPOON GRATED ROMANO CHEESE

1 TABLESPOON OLIVE OIL

2 LEMONS, HALVED

1. Preheat the oven to 400°F.

2. Open the clams and loosen the muscle underneath the clam meat. Discard the top shell and leave the clam and its juice in the bottom shell.

3. Place the clams in a shallow baking pan or on an ovenproof platter and spoon about 4 teaspoons of clam juice over each one. It's OK if the juice spills over.

4. Press about 1 teaspoon of the bread crumbs on top of each clam with your fingers. Sprinkle an additional ½ teaspoon of bread crumbs on each clam. Scatter the garlic around the clams.

5. Sprinkle the grated cheese over the clams and then drizzle them with olive oil.

6. Transfer the pan to the oven and bake the clams for about 15 minutes or until the bread-crumb topping is crispy.

7. Turn on the broiler and broil the clams for 2 to 3 minutes or until browned.

8. Serve the clams with the lemon halves and with any extra sauce spooned over them.

STUFFED ARTICHOKE

After some trial and error, we discovered that the best way to cook an artichoke is in enough chicken broth—never water—to nearly cover it. Of course, up until this Eureka! moment our stuffed artichokes were much loved, but when we put our discovery into practice, it made all the difference between artichokes that were just a few bites short of perfect and delectable, tender, out-of-this-world stuffed artichokes. The bread crumbs are equally crucial: Use firm, fresh white bread for the crumbs, such as Arnold's or Pepperidge Farm, never stale brown bread or dried crumbs from a cardboard can. Speaking of the crumbs, they will naturally float out from the artichoke leaves when you add the broth, but never mind. It's the way it's meant to be.

Serves 2 to 3

STUFFING	ARTICHOKE
10 SLICES WHITE BREAD, COARSELY TORN	1 LARGE GLOBE ARTICHOKE (ABOUT 1 POUND)
4 FRESH BASIL LEAVES, SLICED	LEMON QUARTER
1 TABLESPOON MINCED SPANISH ONION	3 CUPS CHICKEN STOCK, PAGE 306
1½ TEASPOONS MINCED GARLIC	¼ CUP OLIVE OIL
1 TEASPOON CHOPPED FLAT-LEAF PARSLEY	GRATED ROMANO CHEESE, FOR SPRINKLING, OPTIONAL
½ TEASPOON DRIED OREGANO	
GENEROUS ¼ CUP GRATED ROMANO CHEESE	

TO MAKE THE STUFFING

1. In the bowl of a food processor fitted with a metal blade, chop the bread slices to coarse crumbs. Add the basil, onions, garlic, parsley, and oregano. Pulse to mix the ingredients and continue processing until the crumbs are coarsely ground and about the size of grains of rice. Add the cheese, pulse the stuffing for 2 seconds, and then transfer it to a bowl. Set it aside.

TO PREPARE THE ARTICHOKE

1. Cut the stem close to the base of the artichoke so that the artichoke can sit flat.

Discard the stem. Hold the artichoke on its side on a cutting board and, using a serrated knife, cut off the first 3 inches from the top of the artichoke.

2. Open up the artichoke with your hands to expose as much of the heart as possible. With a soup spoon, cut into the thistle that sits on top of the heart and remove the inedible thistle, or choke.

3. Fill a bowl with water and squeeze the lemon quarter into it. Rinse the artichoke and then submerge it in the acidulated water to keep it from darkening. Lift the artichoke from the water and turn it upside down to drain. Using scissors, cut ¾ inch off the pointy end of each leaf on the artichoke. Return the artichoke to the water.

TO STUFF THE ARTICHOKE

1. Remove the artichoke from the water. Let the artichoke drain for several minutes on several layers of paper towels until it is well drained.

2. Work from the bottom row of leaves up to the top of the artichoke. Push the bread-crumb mixture into each leaf, stuffing them so that they come partially away from the artichoke without separating from it. When the first row is filled, work on the second row, until the entire artichoke is stuffed. Finally, put several spoonfuls of stuffing into the center of the artichoke on top of the heart.

TO COOK THE ARTICHOKE

1. Transfer the artichoke to a pot that easily holds it so that it can sit upright without tipping.

2. Pour the chicken stock into another pan and warm it over medium-high heat. When it is warm, carefully pour it into the saucepan with the artichoke. Try not to knock out too much of the stuffing. Drizzle the olive oil over the top of the artichoke so that all the leaves and stuffing are moistened.

3. Bring the liquid to a simmer over medium heat. Do not let the stock boil. Cover the pan with aluminum foil or a lid and cook the artichoke for about 45 minutes or until the leaves are easy to pull off and the artichoke is very tender.

4. Lift the artichoke from the pot and transfer it to a platter. Spoon some of the broth around it and sprinkle it with some more cheese, if desired.

SAUSAGE-STUFFED MUSHROOMS

Vinegar peppers are the secret weapon that propels this appetizer right into the stratosphere! The mushrooms are incredibly popular as a passed hors d'oeuvres for catered private parties and are equally favored at the table. For the best results, start with only well-made Italian fennel sausage and smooth, fleshy mushrooms. As Alice says, when you try these your taste buds start to dance!

Serves 4 to 6

14 LARGE WHITE MUSHROOMS, EACH ABOUT 2 INCHES WIDE

¼ CUP PLUS 2 TABLESPOONS OLIVE OIL

3 OUNCES FENNEL SAUSAGE, CASING REMOVED

1 CUP FINELY CHOPPED GREEN PEPPERS (1 LARGE OR 2 SMALL)

1 TABLESPOON CHOPPED GARLIC

¾ CUP CARMINE'S BREAD CRUMBS, PAGE 283

1 CUP CHICKEN STOCK, PAGE 306

2 TABLESPOONS GRATED ROMANO CHEESE

3 LARGE SWEET VINEGARED RED OR GREEN CHERRY PEPPERS, OR A MIXTURE OF BOTH, CHOPPED

1. Wipe the mushrooms clean and remove the stems. Set aside the 10 best and largest mushroom caps. Finely chop the remaining 4 mushroom caps and all the stems. Transfer them to a small bowl and set them aside.

2. In a large sauté pan, heat ¼ cup of the olive oil over medium-high heat. When the oil is hot, add the sausage and cook it for 4 to 5 minutes or until it is nicely browned. As it cooks, break the sausage apart with a wooden spoon.

3. Add the green peppers, garlic, and chopped mushrooms, increase the heat to high, and cook the mixture, stirring, for about 8 to 10 minutes or until it is browned and tender and the liquid from the mushrooms has evaporated.

4. Add the bread crumbs and chicken stock. Reduce the heat to medium and stir in the cheese. Add the pickled peppers and remove the mixture from the heat.

5. Spread the mixture on a platter, allow it to cool slightly, and then transfer it to the refrigerator for 15 to 20 minutes or until it has cooled completely.

Continued

6. Preheat the oven to 400°F.

7. Stuff each of the reserved mushroom caps with 1 to 1½ tablespoons of the sausage mixture. Set the stuffed mushrooms in a casserole and drizzle them with the remaining 2 tablespoons of olive oil. Bake them for 15 to 20 minutes or until the mushroom caps are tender. Transfer the mushrooms to a plate, spoon any remaining pan juices over them, and serve.

HANDMADE MOZZARELLA

IF YOU HAVE EVER WONDERED WHY THE TEXTURE OF DIFFERENT MOZZA-RELLAS VARIES SO GREATLY, IT IS PROBABLY BECAUSE SOME ARE MACHINE MADE AND OTHERS ARE HANDMADE. MOZZARELLA IS A FRESH CHEESE, WHICH MEANS IT IS NOT AGED AS ARE BLUE CHEESES, CHEDDARS, AND OTHER SEMISOFT AND FIRM CHEESES. (PARMIGIANO-REGGIANO, FOR EXAMPLE, IS ONE OF ITALY'S MOST PRIZED AGED CHEESES.) MOZZARELLA IS MADE FROM COW'S MILK—OR, IN SOME INSTANCES, BUFFALO MILK FROM THE LARGE HERDS OF WATER BUFFALO THAT THRIVE IN SOUTHERN ITALY. WITH TODAY'S EFFICIENT TRANSPORTATION, IT IS POSSIBLE TO BUY FRESHLY MADE IMPORTED BUFFALO MOZZARELLA IN THE UNITED STATES JUST HOURS AFTER IT'S MADE. ON THE OTHER HAND, DOMESTIC CHEESE MAKERS PRODUCE TENDER, DELICIOUS HANDMADE MOZZARELLA RIGHT HERE.

ALL MOZZARELLA IS MADE WHEN THE MILK'S WHEY (LIQUID) IS SEPARATED FROM ITS CURD (SOLID) BY "COOKING" IT IN HOT WATER. THE CURD MUST BE REMOVED FROM THE HOT WATER AT THE RIGHT TIME—DETERMINED BY A SKILLED CHEESE MAKER—AND THEN PULLED OR TURNED UNTIL IT REACHES THE PROPER CONSISTENCY. WHEN THIS PROCESS IS LEFT TO MACHINES, THE CHEESE CAN BE RUBBERY, ALTHOUGH, OF COURSE, SOME MASS-PRODUCED CHEESES ARE QUITE GOOD. THE PULLED CHEESE IS FORMED INTO BALLS AND MAY BE SALTED OR LEFT UNSALTED. THESE ARE THE LARGE OR SMALL PIECES OF FRESH MOZZARELLA WE BUY IN SUPERMARKETS, ITALIAN MARKETS, OR SPECIALTY SHOPS, USUALLY PACKED IN WATER IN SMALL PLASTIC TUBS TO KEEP THEM MOIST AND FRESH.

TOMATO, MOZZARELLA, BASIL, RED ONION, AND ASSORTED OLIVES

This salad may sound ordinary, but when you have the best mozzarella and juicy, garden-ripe tomatoes, as well as plump Kalamata and green olives, and golden, fruity olive oil, the ordinary becomes magical. We use mozzarella handmade for us in Brooklyn, which is as good as it gets, but you may want to try buffalo mozzarella imported from Italy. With modern-day transport, this cheese is very fresh, tender, and pleasantly salty. Mozzarella crafted from the milk of Italy's herds of water buffalo is the soft cheese of choice in Italy.

Serves 2 to 3

2 LARGE RIPE TOMATOES

¼ TEASPOON DRIED OREGANO

SALT AND FRESHLY GROUND BLACK PEPPER

1 RED ONION, PEELED AND SLICED INTO THIN RINGS

FIVE 1-OUNCE BALLS FRESH MOZZARELLA, HALVED

6 TO 7 FRESH BASIL LEAVES, THINLY SLICED

6 LARGE GREEN OLIVES, PITTED

6 BLACK OLIVES, SUCH AS KALAMATA OR GAETA, PITTED

2 TABLESPOONS EXTRA-VIRGIN OLIVE OIL

1 TABLESPOON RED WINE VINEGAR

1. Cut each tomato into 4 to 5 slices and place them on a platter.

2. Sprinkle the oregano over the tomatoes and season them to taste with salt and pepper. Scatter the onion rings over the tomatoes and place the mozzarella balls, cut sides down, on top of the onions. Sprinkle the basil and scatter the olives over the mozzarella.

3. In a small bowl, whisk together the olive oil and vinegar. Season the dressing to taste with salt and pepper. Drizzle it over the salad and serve.

CHICKEN WINGS SCARPARIELLO-STYLE WITH GORGONZOLA DIPPING SAUCE

These are made with the same flavorings as our world-famous Chicken Scarpariello. We introduced the wings when we were trying to attract the Monday Night Football *crowd. Our customers went berserk! You will, too. It's easy to find chicken wings already jointed and halved.*

Serves 2 to 4

CHICKEN

8 WHOLE CHICKEN WINGS, CUT INTO 16 DRUMSTICKS AND WINGS, TIPS REMOVED AND DISCARDED

1 CUP VEGETABLE OIL

4 TABLESPOONS UNSALTED BUTTER

6 CLOVES GARLIC, PEELED AND CRUSHED

JUICE OF 1 OR 2 LEMONS

ABOUT 8 DASHES TABASCO OR ANOTHER HOT PEPPER SAUCE

½ TEASPOON CHOPPED FRESH SAGE

½ TEASPOON CHOPPED FRESH ROSEMARY

½ TEASPOON CHOPPED FRESH OREGANO

PINCH OF CRUSHED RED PEPPER FLAKES

PINCH OF CAYENNE

SALT AND FRESHLY GROUND BLACK PEPPER

½ CUP CHICKEN STOCK, PAGE 306

1 SMALL FENNEL BULB, TRIMMED

MARINADE

2 LEMONS, HALVED

2 TABLESPOONS OLIVE OIL

2 TABLESPOONS COARSELY CHOPPED GARLIC

½ TEASPOON CHOPPED FRESH ROSEMARY

½ TEASPOON CHOPPED FRESH OREGANO

½ TEASPOON CHOPPED FRESH SAGE LEAVES

PINCH OF CAYENNE PEPPER

SALT AND FRESHLY GROUND BLACK PEPPER

Continued

GORGONZOLA DIPPING SAUCE

¾ CUP MAYONNAISE

4 TO 6 OUNCES GORGONZOLA CHEESE, CRUMBLED

¼ CUP HEAVY CREAM OR SOUR CREAM

2 TABLESPOONS FINELY CHOPPED CELERY WITH LEAVES

I TABLESPOON FINELY CHOPPED SPANISH ONION

I TEASPOON HOT PEPPER SAUCE SUCH AS TABASCO, OR MORE TO TASTE

½ TEASPOON FINELY CHOPPED GARLIC

TO MARINATE THE CHICKEN

1. In a large shallow glass, ceramic, or other nonreactive dish, mix together the juice of the 2 lemons, the squeezed lemon halves, the olive oil, garlic, rosemary, oregano, sage, and cayenne, and salt and pepper to taste.

2. Add the chicken wings to the marinade and turn them several times in the mixture to coat them. Distribute the lemon halves around the chicken so that the juice and natural oils in the rind will perfume the chicken. Cover the dish and refrigerate it for 8 hours or overnight.

3. Lift the wings from the marinade and let them drain on several layers of paper towels. Pat them with more towels to remove any excess marinade.

TO COOK THE CHICKEN

1. Preheat the oven to 425°F.

2. Pour the vegetable oil into a deep 8- to 10-inch skillet and heat it over medium-high heat for about 3 minutes or until the oil is almost smoking. Using tongs, carefully put as many chicken wings as possible into the skillet. Make sure they do not overlap or crowd each other. Cook the wings for 3 to 4 minutes on each side or until they are crispy and golden brown. Do not turn the wings until one side is crispy. Lift the cooked wings from the pan and transfer them to a shallow baking pan. Fry the remaining chicken wings.

3. When all the wings are in the baking pan, transfer it to the oven and cook the wings for about 10 minutes or until they are cooked through.

TO FINISH THE DISH

1. Meanwhile, discard the cooking oil and wipe the pan with paper towels. Return the pan to the stove and melt 1 tablespoon of the butter over medium heat. Add the garlic and cook it for about 2 minutes, stirring, until it is soft and golden.

2. Remove the pan from the heat and swirl in the juice from 1 lemon and the Tabasco. Add the sage, rosemary, oregano, red pepper flakes, and cayenne and season to taste with salt and pepper.

3. Pour the stock into the pan, bring the sauce to a boil over medium-high heat, and cook it for 2 to 3 minutes or until it is slightly thickened. Add the remaining 3 tablespoons of butter and stir the sauce over low heat until the butter is well incorporated. The faster you stir, the thicker and more cohesive the sauce will be.

4. Taste the sauce and add the remaining lemon juice, if desired. Put the hot chicken wings in the sauce and stir them around to coat them. Adjust the seasonings to taste.

5. Cut the fennel bulb in half and slice each half between the ribs into 3-inch lengths. Serve the chicken wings and the fennel with the dipping sauce on the side.

TO MAKE THE GORGONZOLA DIPPING SAUCE

Combine all the ingredients in a medium-sized bowl and mix them well. Cover the dish with plastic wrap and refrigerate it for at least 1 hour.

COLD ROASTED FIGS WITH GORGONZOLA, PROSCIUTTO BITS, GRAPES, AND BALSAMIC GLAZE

When figs are in season in the spring and early fall, try this amazing dish. It's a wonderful marriage of sweet fruit, salty Gorgonzola, and lush, fatty prosciutto that explodes in your mouth. Mark Pelligrino, the sous chef at Carmine's in Atlantic City, makes a similar appetizer that so enchanted us, we developed this variation on Mark's invention to serve at all our restaurants. The figs can stand alone or be part of a cold antipasti platter, and either way, they're a winner. We're eating more figs in this country now than ever before, and if you haven't tried them yet, don't wait another minute.

Serves 4

COLD ROASTED FIGS, ETC.

3 TABLESPOONS HEAVY CREAM

2 TABLESPOONS MAYONNAISE

2 OUNCES GORGONZOLA CHEESE

¼ TEASPOON CHOPPED GARLIC

½ TEASPOON CHOPPED FLAT-LEAF PARSLEY

FRESHLY GROUND BLACK PEPPER

5 RIPE BLACK FIGS, STEMMED

2 TABLESPOONS OLIVE OIL

SALT

2 VERY THIN SLICES PROSCIUTTO

5 FIRM CONCORD GRAPES, HALVED

BALSAMIC GLAZE

2 CUPS GOOD-QUALITY BALSAMIC VINEGAR

1. In the bowl of a food processor fitted with a metal blade, mix together the cream, mayonnaise, cheese, garlic, and parsley. Season the mixture to taste with pepper and process it until it is very smooth. Transfer the mixture to a small bowl and refrigerate it for about 20 minutes or until it is cold but still creamy.

Continued

2. Preheat the oven to 375°F. Cut the figs in half through the stem. Arrange them, cut sides up, in a baking pan or casserole and sprinkle them evenly with 1 tablespoon of the olive oil. Season them lightly with salt and pepper and bake them for about 10 minutes or until they are tender but still hold their shape. Let the figs cool slightly and then refrigerate them for about 20 minutes or until they are cool.

3. Cut the prosciutto into a fine dice.

4. Heat the remaining tablespoon of oil in a small sauté pan set over medium heat. When the oil is hot, add the diced prosciutto and cook it slowly for about 10 minutes or until it is crispy and the fat is rendered. Stir the prosciutto as it cooks to break it up into small equal-sized pieces. Drain it on paper towels.

5. Transfer the figs, cut sides up, to a platter and carefully push a grape half into the center of each one so that the grape is flush with the fig's surface.

TO MAKE THE BALSAMIC GLAZE

1. Place the vinegar in a heavy saucepan and cook it over medium heat until steam rises from the liquid. Transfer the pan to a heat diffuser if you have one and let the vinegar cook, uncovered, very slowly over low heat for 2 to 2½ hours. Do not let it simmer; it must cook very slowly. If you don't have a diffuser, use a very heavy pan on very low heat, and watch it carefully.

2. Reduce the vinegar to a syrupy consistency. You should have about ⅓ cup of glaze. Let it cool before using it. The glaze will keep in the refrigerator for up to 1 month. To reheat, set the bowl over a pan of simmering water and let the glaze heat slowly.

TO FINISH THE FIGS

1. Spoon the glaze evenly over the figs and then spoon about 1 teaspoon of the Gorgonzola mixture on top of each fig. Sprinkle the figs with the prosciutto and serve.

ROASTED PEPPERS AND MOZZARELLA WITH ANCHOVY

For this colorful and full-flavored salad, we recommend imported Italian anchovies packed in olive oil, which tend to be smoother and less assertive than some other varieties. The small mozzarella balls, called bocconcini, make a big difference, too. Paired with the roasted peppers, they provide a sweet balance to the anchovies for a lovely antipasto.

Serves 2 to 3

3 TO 4 LARGE RED BELL PEPPERS

2 TABLESPOONS FINELY CHOPPED GARLIC

8 TO 10 FRESH BASIL LEAVES, THINLY SLICED

1 TABLESPOON CHOPPED FLAT-LEAF PARSLEY

2 TABLESPOONS OLIVE OIL

SALT AND FRESHLY GROUND BLACK PEPPER

FIVE 1-OUNCE BALLS FRESH MOZZARELLA, HALVED

6 ANCHOVY FILLETS, DRAINED

1. Lightly char the peppers over a gas flame or under a broiler until they are blackened on all sides and soft. Transfer them to a bowl and cover the bowl with plastic wrap. When the peppers are cool enough to handle, remove and discard the skins. Halve the peppers and discard the ribs, seeds, and any accumulated liquid. Lay the peppers flat in a shallow glass or ceramic dish without overlapping them.

2. Sprinkle the garlic, basil, and parsley evenly over the peppers and then drizzle them with olive oil. Season them lightly with salt and pepper. Cover the dish with plastic wrap and refrigerate the peppers for at least 6 hours and up to 24 hours. The longer you refrigerate them, the better they will taste.

3. To serve, remove the peppers from the refrigerator and allow them to come to room temperature.

4. Arrange the peppers on a platter and top them with the mozzarella and anchovies. Spoon any extra dressing left in the dish over the mozzarella.

PASTA E FAGIOLI SOUP

Every Italian cook makes this wonderful vegetable soup. It's very forgiving. Just about any sweet, flavorful vegetable can be added to the pot. Ours is traditional, with carrots, onions, and celery and great imported tomatoes (we use San Marzano). The neck bone gives the soup just a hint of smokiness and broadens the flavor so that it's wholly satisfying. You can substitute a smoked turkey leg for the neck bone, or go vegetarian by omitting the meat altogether and using vegetable stock in place of chicken stock. As if this weren't enough versatility, if you thicken the soup it can be pan-fried into fritters. (See the Variation at the end of the recipe.) Delicious!

Serves 4 to 5

- 1 CUP DRIED CANNELLINI OR KIDNEY BEANS
- 2 TABLESPOONS OLIVE OIL
- 1 TABLESPOON SLICED GARLIC
- 2 OUNCES CHOPPED PANCETTA OR THICK BACON
- 1 SMALL ONION, PEELED AND DICED
- 1 MEDIUM CARROT, PEELED AND DICED
- ¼ HEART OF CELERY OR 1 RIB CELERY, DICED
- 2 BAY LEAVES
- 2 TEASPOONS CHOPPED FRESH OREGANO
- 1 TEASPOON CHOPPED FRESH ROSEMARY
- 8 CUPS CHICKEN STOCK PAGE 306
- 1 SMALL SMOKED PORK NECK BONE OR HAM HOCK
- SALT AND FRESHLY GROUND BLACK PEPPER
- 4 TO 5 CANNED PLUM TOMATOES, DRAINED
- 2 OUNCES DITALINI PASTA
- 1 CUP GRATED PARMESAN CHEESE, PLUS EXTRA FOR SERVING
- 2 TABLESPOONS CHOPPED FLAT-LEAF PARSLEY

1. Place the beans in a large pot or bowl and cover them with 1 or 2 inches of cold water. Let the beans soak at room temperature for at least 6 hours and up to 12 hours. Change the water several times during soaking.

2. In a 2-quart saucepan, heat the olive oil over medium heat. When the oil is hot, add the garlic and cook it, stirring, for about 1 minute or until lightly browned. Add the pancetta and cook the mixture slowly so that the garlic and pancetta brown. Add the onions and cook the mixture for 2 minutes, stirring. Add the

Continued

carrots and celery and cook them for about 3 minutes. Add the bay leaves, oregano, and rosemary and sauté the mixture for about 2 minutes or until the flavors meld. Add the stock and neck bone and bring it to a boil over medium-high heat. Season the stock to taste with salt and pepper.

3. Drain the beans, add them to the stock, bring back to a boil, and boil it for about 10 minutes. Using your hands, crush the tomatoes and add them to the soup. Reduce the heat and simmer the soup briskly for about 1 hour. Adjust the heat up or down to maintain the simmer. Check the beans for tenderness; if they are not tender, continue cooking until they are tender but not mushy.

4. Increase the heat and boil the soup, stirring it occasionally, for 8 to 10 minutes to intensify its flavors and let it reduce and thicken slightly.

5. Reduce the heat to a simmer and add the pasta. Cook the soup, stirring occasionally, for about 12 minutes or until the pasta is al dente. Add the cheese and stir the soup to mix it in.

6. Taste it for seasoning, and adjust if necessary.

7. Pour the soup into a tureen and ladle the hot soup into serving bowls. Serve it with a parsley garnish and grated cheese on the side.

VARIATION:
PASTA E FAGIOLI FRITTERS

Makes 20 to 25 fritters

I EGG

½ CUP GRATED PARMESAN CHEESE, PLUS MORE FOR GARNISH

I CUP ALL-PURPOSE OR WONDRA FLOUR

½ CUP OLIVE OIL

To make fritters, let the soup cool for about 1 hour, then cover it and refrigerate it for at least 8 hours or overnight. Preheat the oven to 350°F. Remove the soup from the refrigerator and stir in 1 beaten egg and ½ cup of grated Parmesan cheese. Slowly whisk in 1 cup of all-purpose or Wondra flour until it is absorbed. Return the batter to the refrigerator for at least 10 minutes.

Heat 3 tablespoons of olive oil in a large nonstick sauté pan over medium-high heat. When the oil is hot, spoon the batter into the pan in 2- or 3-tablespoon portions. Lightly tap the tops of the fritters with the bottom of the spoon so that they spread to 2 to 3 inches in diameter. They don't have to look perfect; the more homemade looking, the better.

Cook the fritters for 3 to 4 minutes or until the bottoms are very brown and crispy when you lift the edge with a small spatula and peek. Turn the fritters over; they will be very fragile at this point. Cook them for 2 to 3 minutes longer or until they are browned. Drain the fritters on paper towels. As they cool they will firm up. Repeat the process until all the batter is cooked. Add more oil to the pan as needed. You will use about ½ cup of oil in total.

Transfer the fritters to a baking sheet and bake them for 4 to 6 minutes or until they are very hot. Serve them sprinkled with a little Parmesan cheese. These reheat well the next day, too.

RED AND WHITE ZUPPA DI CLAMS

Here are two recipes for similar clam soups, one red and one white. The red clam soup is sweetened with tomatoes, and the methods for each vary slightly. Whichever you decide to try first, you will be rewarded with a straightforward, tasty soup brimming with good, fresh clam flavor. For heartier soups that are more like stews, brown a little fennel sausage in some olive oil and add it to either recipe to elevate the zuppa to a light main course.

RED ZUPPA DI CLAMS

Serves 2 to 3

2 TABLESPOONS OLIVE OIL

I TABLESPOON COARSELY CHOPPED
   GARLIC

6 FRESH BASIL LEAVES

2 BAY LEAVES

I TEASPOON CHOPPED FRESH OREGANO

I TABLESPOON CHOPPED FLAT-LEAF
   PARSLEY

PINCH OF HOT RED PEPPER FLAKES

12 TO 14 LITTLENECK CLAMS, RINSED
   AND SCRUBBED

¼ CUP WHITE WINE

½ CUP BOTTLED CLAM JUICE

I CUP CANNED PLUM TOMATOES,
   DRAINED AND COARSELY CHOPPED

SALT AND FRESHLY GROUND BLACK
   PEPPER

1. In a large sauté pan, heat the olive oil over medium-high heat. When the oil is hot, add the garlic and cook it, stirring, for about 1 minute or until it is golden brown. Take care not to let the garlic burn. Add the basil, bay leaves, oregano, parsley, and red pepper flakes and cook the mixture, stirring, for 30 seconds or until it is fragrant.

2. Add the clams and cook them, stirring, for 1 minute. Reduce the heat to medium, cover the pan, and cook them for about 4 minutes more, stirring occasionally. Add the wine, replace the lid, and cook the soup for about 1 minute. Add the clam juice and cook the soup for about 1 minute more.

3. Add the tomatoes, replace the lid, increase the heat to high, and cook the soup for 2 to 3 minutes more. Reduce the heat to medium and cook it for 1 or 2 minutes

Continued

more or until the clams open. With a small knife, pry open any that don't open, unless they are firmly and stubbornly closed, in which case discard them.

4. Season the soup to taste with salt and pepper, transfer it to a bowl, and serve.

WHITE ZUPPA DI CLAMS

Serves 2 to 3

¼ CUP OLIVE OIL

2 TABLESPOONS COARSELY CHOPPED GARLIC

8 FRESH BASIL LEAVES

2 BAY LEAVES

I TEASPOON CHOPPED FRESH OREGANO

I TEASPOON CHOPPED FLAT-LEAF PARSLEY

PINCH OF HOT RED PEPPER FLAKES

12 TO 14 LITTLENECK CLAMS, RINSED AND SCRUBBED

¼ CUP WHITE WINE

½ CUP BOTTLED CLAM JUICE

SALT AND FRESHLY GROUND BLACK PEPPER

1. In a large sauté pan, heat the olive oil over medium-high heat. When the oil is hot, add the garlic and cook it, stirring, for about 1 minute or until it is golden brown. Take care not to let the garlic burn. Add the basil, bay leaves, oregano, parsley, and red pepper flakes and cook the mixture, stirring, for 30 seconds or until it is fragrant.

2. Add the clams and cook them, stirring, for 1 minute. Reduce the heat to medium, cover the pan, and cook them for about 4 minutes more, stirring occasionally. Add the wine, replace the lid, and cook the soup for about 1 minute. Add the clam juice, replace the lid, and cook the soup for 3 to 4 minutes more or until the clams open. With a small knife, pry open any that don't open, unless they are firmly and stubbornly closed, in which case discard them.

3. Season the soup to taste with salt and pepper, transfer it to a bowl, and serve.

HOW TO BUY FRESH CLAMS

CLAMS CONFUSE A LOT OF PEOPLE BECAUSE THERE ARE BOTH HARD- AND SOFT-SHELLED VARIETIES—YET THE SOFT-SHELLED CLAMS FEEL FIRM TO THE TOUCH. THEIR SHELLS ARE SIMPLY THINNER THAN HARD-SHELL CLAM SHELLS. THE HARD-SHELLED CLAMS WE COOK WITH ARE ATLANTIC QUAHOGS, WHICH RANGE IN SIZE FROM LITTLENECKS TO CHERRYSTONES TO LARGE CHOWDER CLAMS. ON THE PACIFIC COAST, HARD-SHELLED CLAMS ARE ALSO CALLED LITTLENECKS BUT ARE NOT RELATED TO QUAHOGS. SOFT-SHELLED CLAMS HAVE VISIBLE NECKS OR SIPHONS PROTRUDING FROM THEIR SHELLS. ON THE EAST COAST, THESE ARE CALLED STEAMERS, WHILE ON THE WEST COAST RAZOR CLAMS ARE THE MOST COMMON SOFT-SHELLED CLAMS.

CLAMS SHOULD BE ALIVE WHEN YOU BUY THEM. THIS MEANS THEIR SHELLS SHOULD BE TIGHTLY CLOSED IF THEY ARE HARD-SHELLED. IF THE SHELLS ARE SLIGHTLY OPEN, TAP THE SHELL GENTLY; IT SHOULD CLOSE IMMEDIATELY. IF NOT, DON'T BUY THE CLAM. SOFT-SHELLED CLAMS MAY BE SLIGHTLY AGAPE BUT WITH THE NECK PROTRUDING. IF YOU TAP THE NECK, IT SHOULD PULL BACK INTO THE LIVE CLAM. AS A RULE, ALL CLAMSHELLS SHOULD BE EVENLY COLORED WITH NO YELLOWING.

IF YOU BUY FRESHLY SHUCKED CLAMS (SOME FISH STORES SELL THESE), THE CLAM MEAT SHOULD LOOK PLUMP AND MOIST AND SMELL BRINY AND FRESH. THERE SHOULD BE A LITTLE CLAM LIQUOR (JUICE) IN THE CONTAINER, TOO.

WHILE WE URGE EVERYONE TO USE FRESH CLAMS, WE UNDERSTAND IT'S NOT ALWAYS POSSIBLE TO FIND THEM IN EVERY REGION OF THE COUNTRY. IF NO FRESH CLAMS ARE AVAILABLE, BUY HIGH-QUALITY, QUICK-FROZEN, UNCOOKED SHUCKED CLAMS. BOTTLED CLAM JUICE IS A GOOD SUBSTITUTE FOR FISH BROTH, TOO.

RED AND WHITE ZUPPA DI MUSSELS

Just as with the clam zuppas, we offer two different mussel soups, one with tomatoes, one without. They are very similar, and both are light, refreshing, and tasty. If you haven't tried cooking with mussels, these zuppas are good places to start. Fresh mussels are key, of course, and we suggest you buy Prince Edward Island mussels (sometimes called PEI mussels) or New Zealand mussels (also called green tip mussels), both of which tend to be less sandy than some others and taste of the clean, briny deep. Most mussels are very clean these days, but if those you buy need it, run them under cold water and scrub off any beards or barnacles.

RED ZUPPA DI MUSSELS

Serves 2 to 3

2 TABLESPOONS OLIVE OIL

1 TABLESPOON COARSELY CHOPPED GARLIC

6 FRESH BASIL LEAVES

2 BAY LEAVES

1 TEASPOON CHOPPED FRESH OREGANO

1 TABLESPOON CHOPPED FLAT-LEAF PARSLEY

PINCH HOT RED PEPPER FLAKES

16 TO 20 LARGE MUSSELS, RINSED AND SCRUBBED

¼ CUP WHITE WINE

½ CUP BOTTLED CLAM JUICE

1 CUP CANNED PLUM TOMATOES, DRAINED AND COARSELY CHOPPED

1. In a large sauté pan, heat the olive oil over medium-high heat. When the oil is hot, add the garlic and cook it, stirring, for about 1 minute or until it is golden brown. Take care not to let the garlic burn. Add the basil, bay leaves, oregano, parsley, and red pepper flakes and stir the mixture. Add the mussels and cook them, stirring, for 1 minute.

Continued

2. Cover the pan and cook the mussels for 3 minutes more, shaking the pan occasionally. Remove the lid and add the white wine. Increase the heat to high and cook the soup for 1 minute.

3. Add the clam juice and cook the soup for 1 minute more. Add the tomatoes, bring the soup to a boil, cover the pan, reduce the heat to medium, and simmer the soup for 2 to 3 minutes or until the mussels have opened. With a small knife, pry open any that don't open, unless they are firmly and stubbornly closed, in which case discard them.

4. Season the soup to taste with salt and pepper, transfer it to a bowl, and serve.

WHITE ZUPPA DI MUSSELS

Serves 2 to 3

¼ CUP OLIVE OIL

1 TABLESPOON COARSELY CHOPPED GARLIC

8 FRESH BASIL LEAVES

2 BAY LEAVES

1 TEASPOON CHOPPED FRESH OREGANO

1 TEASPOON CHOPPED FLAT-LEAF PARSLEY

PINCH HOT RED PEPPER FLAKES

16 TO 20 LARGE MUSSELS, RINSED AND SCRUBBED

¼ CUP WHITE WINE

½ CUP BOTTLED CLAM JUICE

SALT AND FRESHLY GROUND BLACK PEPPER

1. In a large sauté pan, heat the olive oil over medium-high heat. When the oil is hot, add the garlic and cook it, stirring, for about 1 minute or until it is golden brown. Take care not to let the garlic burn. Add the basil, bay leaves, oregano, parsley, and red pepper flakes and stir the mixture. Add the mussels and cook them, stirring, for 1 minute.

2. Cover the pan and cook the mussels for 3 minutes more, shaking the pan occasionally. Remove the lid, and add the white wine. Increase the heat to high and cook the soup for 1 minute.

3. Add the clam juice, cover the pan, and reduce the heat to medium. Simmer the soup for 2 to 3 minutes or until the mussels have opened. With a small knife, pry open any that don't open, unless they are firmly and stubbornly closed, in which case discard them.

4. Season the soup to taste with salt and pepper, transfer it to a bowl, and serve.

RUSTIC LENTIL SOUP

This soup turns up most often on the menu at the 91st Street restaurant, where our regulars love it during the cold, icy months when New York is gray and damp. It's a hearty and warming soup made even more so with the addition of sausage, bacon, and pancetta—all of which can be tossed aside to make this soup vegetarian, with vegetable stock standing in for chicken stock. This is a terrific Sunday night family meal with a good loaf of crusty bread.

Serves 4

2 TABLESPOONS OLIVE OIL

1 TABLESPOON UNSALTED BUTTER

2 OUNCES DICED PANCETTA

2 STRIPS BACON, DICED

1 CLOVE GARLIC, PEELED AND FINELY CHOPPED

2 CARROTS, CHOPPED

2 RIBS CELERY, CHOPPED

1 ONION, PEELED AND COARSELY CHOPPED

2 SMALL PLUM TOMATOES, PEELED, CORED, AND FINELY CHOPPED

5 TO 6 CUPS CHICKEN STOCK, PAGE 306

2 BAY LEAVES

1 TEASPOON SALT

½ TEASPOON FRESH THYME LEAVES

½ TEASPOON FRESH OREGANO LEAVES

¼ TEASPOON HOT RED PEPPER FLAKES

⅛ TEASPOON FRESHLY GROUND BLACK PEPPER

1½ CUPS GREEN LENTILS, RINSED AND DRAINED

1 RUSSET POTATO, PEELED AND DICED

1 TO 2 ITALIAN SWEET OR HOT SAUSAGE LINKS (ABOUT 5 OUNCES)

1. In a large stockpot, heat the olive oil and butter over medium heat until the butter starts to foam. Add the pancetta and bacon and cook them for about 7 minutes or until the bacon is crispy. Add the garlic and cook the mixture for about 2 minutes or until the garlic has softened. Add the carrots, celery, and onions and cook the mixture for 10 to 12 minutes or until the vegetables are tender and lightly browned.

2. Strain the chopped tomatoes through a fine-mesh sieve, pressing on the pulp to extract as much liquid as possible.

Continued

3. Add 5 cups of the chicken stock to the pot and then stir in the strained tomato pulp, bay leaves, salt, thyme, oregano, red pepper flakes, and black pepper. Add the lentils, increase the heat to medium-high, and bring the soup to a boil. Partially cover the pot and reduce the heat to a simmer. Cook the soup for about 45 minutes.

4. Add the potatoes and cook the soup for about 15 minutes, stirring occasionally, or until the lentils and potatoes are tender. Add more chicken stock if the soup becomes too thick.

5. Meanwhile, remove the casings from the sausage. In a small nonstick sauté pan over high heat, cook the sausage, breaking it up with a wooden spoon, for 4 to 5 minutes or until it is nicely browned.

6. Add the sausage and any fat remaining in the pan to the soup. Simmer for about 5 minutes. Taste the soup and add salt if necessary. Remove the bay leaves and serve.

GARLIC BREAD AND GARLIC BREAD PARMIGIANA

When you place mozzarella on a slice of bread, the bread becomes "parmigiana"—essentially "with cheese." Don't ask us why! The semantics may be a little off-kilter, but the flavor of our signature garlic bread is nothing short of spectacular! We get our bread from a local bakery, but if you do not have access to a great Italian bakery, look for rustic Italian bread that measures about four inches across and has an airy crumb that allows the butter to ooze right into it. Yum! We never skimp on the butter. What would be the point?

Serves 2 to 4

4 LARGE ½-INCH-THICK SLICES ITALIAN CAMPOBASSO OR RUSTIC COUNTRY BREAD

4 TABLESPOONS GARLIC BUTTER, PAGE 286, SOFTENED

2 TEASPOONS GRATED ROMANO CHEESE

FOUR ¼-INCH SLICES MOZZARELLA, OPTIONAL

1. Preheat the broiler.

2. Toast the bread under the broiler for 1 to 2 minutes or until it is golden brown. Turn the bread and toast the other side for about 1 minute or until it is golden brown.

3. Turn off the broiler and preheat the oven to 400°F.

4. Spread about 1 tablespoon of the butter on one side of each piece of toast, making sure to cover the entire surface. Sprinkle the grated cheese over the bread.

5. Transfer the toasts to a sheet pan. Bake them for about 12 minutes or until they are crispy and lightly browned.

6. If using mozzarella, preheat the broiler. Lay a slice of mozzarella on each piece of toast and broil the toasts just until the cheese melts.

7. To serve, cut each piece of toast into 2 to 3 pieces and then transfer them to a platter.

CAESAR SALAD DRESSING

MANY RESTAURANTS HAVE THEIR VERSION OF CREAMY CAESAR DRESSING, BUT WE THINK OURS IS THE BEST! LIKE ALL OUR FOOD, IT'S GUTSY AND EXPLODES IN THE MOUTH. WE USE LOTS OF GARLIC, A LIBERAL NUMBER OF ANCHOVIES (ONLY THOSE IMPORTED FROM ITALY), AND HANDFULS OF ROMANO CHEESE, WHICH WE FIND WORKS BETTER THAN PARMESAN FOR THE DRESSING AND SALAD. THE CHEESE HAS DEEPER FLAVOR AND IS MADE FROM SHEEP'S, NOT COW'S, MILK. ALSO, IT'S LESS EXPENSIVE. TO KEEP IT REAL, WE INSIST ON A BLENDED OLIVE OIL (FOR MORE ON THIS, SEE PAGE 60). AT HOME, YOU CAN MAKE THIS DRESSING IN THE FOOD PROCESSOR OR BLENDER AND ADD THE OLIVE OIL SLOWLY AS THE MOTOR WHIRS. IN THE END, THE DRESSING SHOULD BE THICK AND CREAMY AND TASTE PLEASANTLY BUT UNMISTAKABLY OF CHEESE AND GARLIC—WITH JUST A TRACE OF SALTY ANCHOVIES.

CARMINE'S FAMOUS CAESAR SALAD

When we opened Carmine's in 1990, great word of mouth meant tables were packed from day one. Our Caesar salad was an instant hit and to this day remains a top seller. Try it and you will understand why!

Serves 4; makes about 1½ cups dressing

SALAD DRESSING

6 ANCHOVY FILLETS

3 CLOVES GARLIC, PEELED

2 LARGE EGG YOLKS

¼ CUP RED WINE VINEGAR

JUICE OF 1 SMALL LEMON

1 CUP OLIVE OIL

8 TABLESPOONS GRATED ROMANO CHEESE

1 TABLESPOON CHOPPED FLAT-LEAF PARSLEY

¼ TEASPOON DRIED OREGANO

SALT AND FRESHLY GROUND BLACK PEPPER

CROUTONS

3 TABLESPOONS OLIVE OIL

1 TABLESPOON MINCED GARLIC

¼ TEASPOON DRIED OREGANO

FOUR ¾-INCH-THICK SLICES ITALIAN CAMPOBASSO OR RUSTIC COUNTRY BREAD

5 TABLESPOONS GRATED ROMANO CHEESE

1 TABLESPOON CHOPPED FLAT-LEAF PARSLEY

SALAD

1 LARGE HEAD ROMAINE LETTUCE (ABOUT 1 POUND)

3 ANCHOVY FILLETS, FOR GARNISH

TO MAKE THE DRESSING

1. In a blender or food processor, puree the 6 anchovy fillets. Add the garlic and blend the mixture until it is well mixed. Add the egg yolks and blend the mixture for about 2 minutes. Turn off the motor, add the vinegar and lemon juice, and pulse the mixture for 30 seconds. With the motor running, add the olive oil in a slow, steady stream until it is incorporated. Add the cheese, parsley, and oregano

Continued

and pulse the mixture for 10 seconds. Season the dressing to taste with salt and pepper. Transfer it to a glass or rigid plastic container, cover it tightly, and refrigerate it for at least 4 hours and up to 24 hours. Chilling the dressing thickens it and the thicker it gets, the better it will adhere to the lettuce.

TO MAKE THE CROUTONS

1. Preheat the oven to 350°F.

2. In a large mixing bowl, stir together the olive oil, garlic, and oregano. Whisk the mixture well.

3. Trim the crusts from the bread and cut each slice into 1-inch squares. Place the bread cubes in the bowl and toss them until they are well coated with the oil.

4. Spread the bread cubes on a baking sheet and bake them for 10 to 15 minutes, stirring occasionally, until they are crispy and browned.

5. Transfer the croutons to a bowl, add 2 tablespoons of the cheese and the parsley, and toss them together well. Set the croutons aside.

TO PREPARE THE LETTUCE

1. Tear the lettuce into bite-sized pieces, wash it thoroughly in cold water, and spin it dry or dry it with paper towels. Transfer the lettuce to a plastic bag or similar container and refrigerate it until it is cold and crispy.

TO ASSEMBLE THE SALAD

1. Place the lettuce in a bowl. Add the croutons and 2 tablespoons of the cheese. Spoon 1 cup of the dressing over the salad and mix them together well, using your hands or tongs. Reserve the remaining dressing for another use.

2. Pile the salad on a platter and top it with the remaining tablespoon of cheese. Place the 3 anchovies on top of the salad.

CARMINE'S SALAD

Whew! This salad may seem to have everything in it except the proverbial kitchen sink, but that makes it a robust and incredibly tasty dish that is well worth the effort it takes to buy and prepare the ingredients. Lots of verve; lots of full, gorgeous flavors! It's Michael Ronis's favorite and is an homage to an old-fashioned Italian American antipasti platter, with the ingredients chopped and tossed in a salad.

Serves 2 to 4

½ MEDIUM-SIZED HEAD ICEBERG LETTUCE

1 MEDIUM-SIZED HEAD RADICCHIO

2 BUNCHES WATERCRESS OR 2 TO 3 BUNCHES ARUGULA

½ CUP COARSELY CHOPPED GENOA SALAMI

½ CUP COARSELY CHOPPED MORTADELLA

½ CUP DICED PROVOLONE

½ MEDIUM-SIZED RED ONION, PEELED AND THINLY SLICED

½ SMALL CUCUMBER, PEELED AND CUT INTO SMALL CHUNKS

5 PEPPERONCINI PEPPERS

5 LARGE GREEN OLIVES, PITTED

5 BLACK OLIVES, SUCH AS KALAMATA OR GAETA, PITTED

3 RADISHES, TRIMMED AND THINLY SLICED

1 LARGE RIPE TOMATO, CORED AND CUT INTO 8 WEDGES

¼ TO ½ CUP CARMINE'S VINAIGRETTE, PAGE 287

PINCH OF DRIED OREGANO

SALT AND FRESHLY GROUND BLACK PEPPER

1. Cut the iceberg lettuce into 3 equal pieces and then cut each piece into quarters. Place the lettuce in a large bowl filled with ice-cold water.

2. Core and halve the radicchio and then cut each half into 3 pieces. Add it to the bowl.

3. Remove the stems from the watercress or arugula and add it to the bowl. Using your hands, swish the greens around, breaking up the iceberg lettuce and radicchio leaves. Spin the greens dry or dry them with paper towels. Transfer them to a plastic bag or similar container and refrigerate them until they are cold and crispy.

Continued

4. In a large bowl, mix together the salami, mortadella, provolone, onions, cucumbers, pepperoncini, olives, radishes, and tomatoes. Add the lettuce, radicchio, and watercress and gently toss the salad to combine the ingredients.

5. Spoon about ¼ cup of the vinaigrette over the salad and toss it again. Add the oregano and season the salad to taste with salt and pepper. Add more dressing, if desired. Transfer the salad to a serving bowl or platter, arranging the tomatoes on top and around the edge.

THE OLIVE OIL QUESTION

SOME OF OUR RECIPES CALL FOR "OLIVE OIL" WHILE OTHERS CALL FOR "EXTRA-VIRGIN OLIVE OIL." YOU CAN IGNORE THESE SPECIFICATIONS IF YOU WISH, BUT WE'D LIKE TO EXPLAIN THE METHOD TO OUR MADNESS. THERE IS A DIFFERENCE BETWEEN THE TWO, BOTH IN FLAVOR AND IN HOW YOU'LL USE THEM IN THE KITCHEN.

EXTRA-VIRGIN OLIVE OIL IS MADE FROM THE FIRST PRESSING OF THE OLIVES AND IS GREEN-GOLD IN COLOR AND FRUITY AND RICH IN FLAVOR. THIS IS PREFERRED FOR VINAIGRETTES, FOR DRIZZLING OVER FINISHED DISHES, AND FOR DIPPING BREAD. WHEN THE OLIVE OIL IS NOT GOING TO BE COOKED, REACH FOR THE EXTRA-VIRGIN.

PURE OLIVE OIL, ALSO CALLED MILD, LIGHT, OR SIMPLY "OLIVE OIL," IS MADE NOT FROM THE VERY FIRST PRESS OF THE OLIVES, AS IS EXTRA-VIRGIN OLIVE OIL, BUT FROM A LATER PRESS. IT'S STILL VERY GOOD BUT MIGHT BE PALER IN COLOR, MORE GOLD THAN GREEN, AND LESS FRUITY IN FLAVOR. AS A RULE, IT'S ALSO LESS EXPENSIVE.

AT CARMINE'S WE USE A CUSTOMIZED BLEND OF PURE OLIVE OIL AND EXTRA-VIRGIN FOR JUST ABOUT EVERYTHING. IT'S WORTH IT TO US; WE GO THROUGH A LOT OF OLIVE OIL EVERY DAY AND LIKE TO MAKE SURE THE OIL WE USE MAKES EVERY DISH BETTER. YOU CAN MIX YOUR OWN 50/50 BLEND OF PURE AND EXTRA-VIRGIN OLIVE OIL IF YOU WANT TO APPROXIMATE OUR OIL, BUY A BLEND YOU LIKE, OR USE EITHER PURE OR EXTRA-VIRGIN OLIVE OIL, PICKING THE ONE YOU THINK WORKS BEST IN A DISH.

TASTE DIFFERENT BRANDS AND DECIDE WHICH YOU PREFER. WE LIKE OLIVE OILS IMPORTED FROM ITALY, FINDING THEY WORK BEST WITH THE FOOD WE COOK.

BOSTON LETTUCE SALAD WITH RICOTTA SALATA AND ROASTED VEGETABLES

Serves 4 to 6

SALAD

3 MEDIUM-SIZED HEADS OF BOSTON LETTUCE

1 LARGE CARROT, PEELED AND CUT INTO LARGE MATCHSTICKS

5 TABLESPOONS OLIVE OIL

18 MEDIUM-SIZED CREMINI MUSHROOMS

SALT AND FRESHLY GROUND BLACK PEPPER

1 ROASTED RED PEPPER, PAGE 303

6 TO 8 LARGE KALAMATA OLIVES

½ RED ONION, THINLY SLICED

2 LARGE RIPE PLUM TOMATOES, CUT IN HALF

1 CUP GRATED (USE THE LARGE HOLES ON A BOX GRATER) RICOTTA SALATA

DRESSING

1 EGG YOLK

1 TEASPOON FINELY CHOPPED SHALLOTS

6 TABLESPOONS WHITE WINE VINEGAR

¼ CUP OLIVE OIL

4 TEASPOONS FRESH LEMON JUICE

PINCH BLACK PEPPER

½ TEASPOON SALT

12 LEAVES FRESH BASIL, CHOPPED

1. Three hours or more before putting this salad together do the following: Take the Boston lettuce and cut it in half through the core. Soak the cut heads in cold water for 5 minutes, take them out of the water, and slightly squeeze them without bruising. Place them onto a pan lined with several layers of paper towels to absorb the water. Pat them dry on top with more paper towels to absorb any remaining water. Remove all the paper towels on the tray and reline with still more paper towels and lay the lettuce heads on top of these new towels. Place this tray in the refrigerator until you are ready to use it.

Continued

2. Place the carrot into a bowl with 2 tablespoons of the olive oil, and salt and pepper to taste. Toss and place onto a small Pyrex baking dish and bake at 400°F. until they are tender and have a roasted appearance, approximately 15 minutes. Remove them from the pan and reserve.

3. Wash and then dry the cremini mushrooms. Place them into a bowl and mix them with 3 tablespoons of olive oil. Add a pinch of salt and pepper. Roast these in the same pan as the carrots until they are tender, the caps have slightly dried out, and all the moisture has been evaporated. Reserve

4. Chop a roasted red pepper that you've prepared according to our recipe. Reserve.

TO PREPARE THE DRESSING

Place the egg yolk, the shallots, and the vinegar in a small bowl and, using a hand whip, beat the mixture well for 2 to 3 minutes until the mixture is well blended. Add the olive oil slowly. You are basically making mayonnaise. Once all the olive oil has been added, add the lemon juice and salt and pepper and beat for another 2 minutes until everything has been well mixed. Add the basil and stir. Refrigerate until ready to use. This can be made the day before.

TO ASSEMBLE

Take a large chilled platter and put approximately 4 to 5 heaping tablespoons of the dressing on the bottom. Carefully remove the stem out of each head of lettuce. Place the Boston lettuce cut side up on the dressing until all the heads are next to each other. Sprinkle the carrots, mushrooms, olives, and sliced onions over the entire salad. Dip the tomato halves into the dressing and place them on the corners of the salad. Place about 4 to 5 tablespoons of the dressing on the salad, making sure to cover as much of the lettuce as possible. Sprinkle the ricotta over the entire surface. Sprinkle the top with the chopped roasted red pepper and serve.

MISTI SALAD WITH FALL FRUITS AND WALNUTS

Our customers are insane about this salad, which was developed by Glenn Rolnick, our corporate executive chef, and Luis Javier, the chef at the 44th Street Carmine's. As long as we can get good pears, it's on the menu, which means it's especially good in the fall and winter—and the dried cranberries and nuts just make it better. It's easy to make at home, too, because mixed baby greens are sold just about everywhere these days.

Serves 4 to 6

10 OUNCES MIXED BABY GREENS (6 TO 7 PACKED CUPS)

10 GRAPE TOMATOES

¼ CUP THINLY SLICED CARROTS

¼ CUP THINLY SLICED FENNEL

2 TABLESPOONS DRIED CRANBERRIES

2 TABLESPOONS TOASTED WALNUT HALVES

¼ RED ONION, PEELED AND THINLY SLICED

¼ GRANNY SMITH APPLE

¼ RIPE ANJOU PEAR

ABOUT 6 TABLESPOONS CRUMBLED GORGONZOLA CHEESE

½ CUP CARMINE'S VINAIGRETTE, PAGE 287

SALT AND FRESHLY GROUND BLACK PEPPER

1. Place the baby greens in a large salad bowl. Add the tomatoes, carrots, fennel, cranberries, walnuts, and onions.

2. Peel, core, and thinly slice the apple and pear and add them to the salad. Toss the salad gently and then sprinkle it with the cheese. Pour the vinaigrette over the salad and toss it to mix it well. Season the salad to taste with salt and pepper and serve.

CHOPPED GRILLED CHICKEN SALAD

This is not a salad you make at the last minute, but it's a salad sure to make everyone happy. It's a deliciously composed chicken salad that is meant to be a main course. You can make the different components in stages, which makes the salad a lot easier to assemble in the long run. We love how the roasted veggies taste with the grilled chicken, small orzo pasta, and the crisp salad greens, plus the little bursts of salty, piquant flavor supplied by the olives and cheese. Michael Ronis created this salad after numerous trips to Los Angeles, where the concept of chopped salads deserves a star on the Hollywood Walk of Fame. With this one in our repertoire, Hollywood had better watch out!

Serves 3 to 4

CHICKEN

1 TEASPOON OLIVE OIL

1 TEASPOON GARLIC POWDER

1 CLOVE GARLIC, PEELED AND FINELY CHOPPED

1 TEASPOON CHOPPED FLAT-LEAF PARSLEY

½ TEASPOON CHOPPED FRESH ROSEMARY

½ TEASPOON SALT

¼ TEASPOON DRIED OREGANO

FRESHLY GROUND BLACK PEPPER

ONE 8-OUNCE BONELESS, SKINLESS CHICKEN BREAST

ROASTED VEGETABLES

¼ CUP FRESH OR FROZEN GREEN BEANS

1 LARGE PORTOBELLO MUSHROOM

1 MEDIUM-SIZED ZUCCHINI

1 YELLOW SQUASH

1 CARROT

1 SMALL RED ONION, PEELED

½ FENNEL BULB

2 TEASPOONS OLIVE OIL

1 TEASPOON GARLIC POWDER

¼ TEASPOON DRIED OREGANO

SALT AND FRESHLY GROUND BLACK PEPPER

Continued

SALAD

ABOUT 5 OUNCES LOOSELY PACKED
MIXED GREENS (ABOUT 3 LOOSELY
PACKED CUPS), COARSELY CHOPPED

I LARGE RIPE TOMATO, COARSELY
CHOPPED

10 GAETA OLIVES, PITTED AND CHOPPED

I ROASTED RED PEPPER, CHOPPED,
PAGE 303

¼ CUP SHAVED ASIAGO CHEESE

¼ TO ⅓ CUP CARMINE'S VINAIGRETTE,
PAGE 287

SALT AND FRESHLY GROUND BLACK
PEPPER

2 SLICES GARLIC BREAD, PAGE 55

ORZO

2 OUNCES ORZO

TO MARINATE AND COOK THE CHICKEN

1. In a shallow glass or ceramic bowl, mix together the olive oil, garlic powder, chopped garlic, parsley, rosemary, salt, oregano, and black pepper to taste. Add the chicken and turn it several times to coat it. Cover the bowl with plastic wrap and refrigerate it for at least 2 hours and up to 4 hours.

2. Prepare a charcoal or gas grill. Lightly spray the grill rack with vegetable oil cooking spray. The coals or heating element should be medium-hot. If you prefer, preheat the broiler.

3. Lift the chicken from the marinade and let any excess drip off. Grill or broil the chicken for about 3 minutes on each side, or until it is cooked through and golden brown. Transfer it to a plate and set it aside.

TO PREPARE THE VEGETABLES

1. Preheat the oven to 400°F.

2. In a small saucepan, blanch the green beans in lightly salted boiling water over medium-high heat for about 1 minute or until they are bright green. Drain them and set them aside.

3. Cut the mushroom, zucchini, squash, carrot, onion, and fennel into thick slices or large pieces and transfer them to a bowl. Add the green beans to the bowl.

4. Drizzle the olive oil over the vegetables, sprinkle them with the garlic powder and oregano, and gently toss them to mix the ingredients. Season them to taste with salt and pepper.

5. Spread the vegetables on a baking sheet and bake them for 12 to 15 minutes or until they are tender and nicely browned. Transfer them to a platter and set them aside to cool.

6. Chop the cooled vegetables into 1- to 1½-inch long pieces and transfer them to a large bowl.

TO PREPARE THE ORZO

1. In a large pot filled with boiling salted water, cook the orzo over medium-high heat for 7 to 8 minutes or until it is al dente. Drain the orzo and rinse it under cold water. Add it to the chopped vegetables and toss them together.

TO ASSEMBLE THE SALAD

1. Add the mixed greens and the tomatoes to the vegetable mixture. Cut the chicken into ½-inch cubes and add them to the salad.

2. Add the olives, roasted pepper, and Asiago cheese. Gently toss the salad to combine the ingredients. Drizzle the salad with the vinaigrette and season it to taste with salt and pepper. Gently toss the salad. To serve, cut each slice of garlic bread into 3 pieces and arrange them around the salad.

GRILLED PORTOBELLO SALAD

Our customers love this warm mushroom salad, in which fresh greens are topped with meaty marinated and grilled portobellos and drizzled with an earthy dressing. It may seem fussy to bake and then grill the mushrooms, but the two-step process makes the flavor outstanding—and you can always broil the mushrooms if that is easier. This is a lovely dish to serve for a party, or to make for your family when you're in the mood for something a little dressy.

Serves 2

MARINADE AND MUSHROOMS

¼ CUP OLIVE OIL

I CLOVE GARLIC, PEELED AND FINELY CHOPPED

½ TEASPOON CHOPPED FRESH ROSEMARY

½ TEASPOON CHOPPED FRESH OREGANO

½ TEASPOON CHOPPED FLAT-LEAF PARSLEY

½ TEASPOON SALT

FRESHLY GROUND BLACK PEPPER

4 LARGE PORTOBELLO MUSHROOMS

¼ CUP BALSAMIC VINEGAR

SALAD

ABOUT 5 OUNCES ARUGULA OR BABY SPINACH, WASHED AND DRIED (ABOUT 3 LOOSELY PACKED CUPS)

TO PREPARE THE MARINADE, MUSHROOMS, AND DRESSING

1. Whisk together the olive oil, garlic, rosemary, oregano, parsley, and salt. Season the marinade to taste with black pepper.

2. Remove and discard the stems and gills from the mushrooms. Gently wipe the mushrooms clean with paper towels.

3. Transfer the mushrooms to a shallow baking dish. Pour the marinade over the mushrooms and turn them to coat all sides. Set them aside for 20 minutes, turning them occasionally.

4. Preheat the oven to 350°F.

5. Bake the mushrooms for about 15 minutes or until they are tender. Using a slotted spoon, transfer the mushrooms to a plate and set them aside.

6. Strain the pan juices through a fine-mesh sieve into a small bowl. Whisk in the balsamic vinegar and set the dressing aside.

7. Prepare a charcoal or gas grill. Lightly spray the grill rack with vegetable cooking oil spray. The coals or heating elements should be medium-hot. Or preheat the broiler.

8. Grill or broil the mushrooms for about 8 minutes on each side or until they are slightly charred and hot.

TO ASSEMBLE THE SALAD

1. Spread the arugula or spinach on a platter. Put the mushrooms on top of the greens. Drizzle the reserved dressing over the mushrooms and greens and serve.

2.
CARMINE'S HERO SANDWICHES

One of the best values in town is a Carmine's hero sandwich at the bar. It easily feeds two!

—GARY BOLOGNA, CHIEF OPERATING OFFICER AND PARTNER

COLD ITALIAN HEROES ≈ TOMATO, BASIL, AND FRESH MOZZARELLA HEROES ≈ FRESH MOZZARELLA, TOMATO, AND PROSCIUTTO HEROES ≈ SAUSAGE AND PEPPER HEROES ≈ CHICKEN PARMIGIANA HEROES ≈ HOT ITALIAN COMBO HEROES WITH HOT CHERRY PEPPERS ≈ ITALIAN CHEESESTEAK HEROES ≈ MEATBALL HEROES

COLD ITALIAN HEROES

Serves 4

4 CRISPY HERO ROLLS, 6 TO 8 INCHES LONG

½ CUP OLIVE OIL

¼ CUP RED WINE VINEGAR

2 TEASPOONS DRIED OREGANO

SALT AND FRESHLY GROUND BLACK PEPPER

20 SLICES GENOA SALAMI

12 THIN SLICES PROSCIUTTO

24 SLICES MORTADELLA

16 SLICES PROVOLONE

2 LARGE ROASTED RED PEPPERS, HALVED, PAGE 303

4 CUPS FINELY SHREDDED ICEBERG LETTUCE

12 TO 16 LARGE SLICES RIPE TOMATO (ABOUT 4 TOMATOES)

1. Slice the rolls in half lengthwise, without cutting all the way through. Press them open with your hands.

2. In a small bowl, whisk together the olive oil, vinegar, oregano, and salt and pepper to taste.

3. Spoon the vinaigrette over both halves of each roll.

4. To assemble each sandwich, layer 5 slices of salami, 3 slices of prosciutto, 6 slices of mortadella, and 4 slices of provolone on one side of the roll. Top with half a roasted pepper, 1 cup of shredded lettuce, and 3 to 4 slices of tomato. Season the tomatoes with salt and pepper to taste. Fold the other side of the roll over the sandwich ingredients and press to close. Cut the sandwich in half and serve.

TOMATO, BASIL, AND FRESH MOZZARELLA HEROES

Serves 4

4 CRISPY HERO ROLLS, 6 TO 8 INCHES LONG

½ CUP OLIVE OIL

¼ CUP RED WINE VINEGAR

SALT AND FRESHLY GROUND BLACK PEPPER

12 TO 16 SLICES FRESH MOZZARELLA

16 LARGE SLICES RIPE TOMATO (ABOUT 4 TOMATOES)

24 TO 32 BASIL LEAVES, COARSELY CHOPPED

1. Slice the rolls in half lengthwise, without cutting all the way through. Press them open with your hands.

2. In a small bowl, whisk together the olive oil, vinegar, and salt and pepper to taste.

3. Spoon the vinaigrette over both halves of each roll.

4. To assemble each sandwich, layer 3 to 4 slices of mozzarella and 4 slices of tomato on one half of the roll. Sprinkle the basil over the tomatoes and season them with salt and pepper to taste. Fold the other half of the roll over the sandwich ingredients. Cut the sandwich in half and serve immediately.

FRESH MOZZARELLA, TOMATO, AND PROSCIUTTO HEROES

Serves 4

4 CRISPY HERO ROLLS, 6 TO 8 INCHES LONG

½ CUP OLIVE OIL

½ CUP RED WINE VINEGAR

16 LARGE SLICES RIPE TOMATO (ABOUT 4 TOMATOES)

16 SLICES PROSCIUTTO (ABOUT 2 OUNCES)

FOUR SMALL BALLS (EACH ABOUT 3 OUNCES) FRESH MOZZARELLA, THINLY SLICED

SALT AND FRESHLY GROUND BLACK PEPPER

24 FRESH BASIL LEAVES, THINLY SLICED

2 TEASPOONS DRIED OREGANO

1. Slice the rolls in half lengthwise, without cutting all the way through. Press them open with your hands.

2. Spoon 1 tablespoon of olive oil over each half of each roll, and then spoon 1 tablespoon of vinegar over each half.

3. To assemble each sandwich, layer 4 slices of tomato on one half of the roll. Top them with 4 slices of prosciutto and then slices of mozzarella. Season to taste with salt and pepper. Sprinkle the basil and oregano over the mozzarella.

4. Fold the other half of the roll over the sandwich ingredients. Cut the sandwich in half and serve.

ITALY'S FAMED CURED HAM

WHEN PROSCIUTTO IS LABELED "PROSCIUTTO DI PARMA," YOU KNOW YOU ARE IN FOR A TREAT. PARMA AND THE SURROUNDING REGION ARE KNOWN FOR OUTSTANDING CURED PORK AND THEIR EQUALLY EXCEPTIONAL PARMIGIANO-REGGIANO CHEESE. THE HOGS FROM THIS MOUNTAINOUS AREA OF ITALY ARE RAISED WITH THE UTMOST CARE AND FED A CAREFUL DIET. THE HAMS ARE CURED FOR AT LEAST TEN MONTHS TO PRODUCE MOIST, PLEASANTLY SALTY, LUXURIOUSLY FATTY, RICH-TASTING MEAT.

PROSCIUTTO MUST BE SLICED SO THAT IT IS ALMOST PAPER THIN. BUY IT FROM A BUTCHER OR DELI COUNTER WITH GOOD TURNOVER AND A REPUTATION FOR HIGH-QUALITY MEATS. HANDLE THE DELICATE SLICES, PACKED TENDERLY BETWEEN SHEETS OF WAXED BUTCHER PAPER, WITH CARE. AND OF COURSE, POP ONE INTO YOUR MOUTH WHEN YOU FIRST UNWRAP THE HAM. WHO CAN RESIST?

SAUSAGE AND PEPPER HEROES

Serves 4

TWELVE 3-OUNCE SAUSAGES FOR RAGU AND HERO SANDWICHES, PAGE 301

5 CUPS CARMINE'S MARINARA SAUCE, PUREED, PAGE 288

12 THIN SLICES FRESH MOZZARELLA, OPTIONAL

4 CUPS PEPPERS AND ONIONS, PAGE 297, SEE NOTE

4 CRISPY HERO ROLLS, 6 TO 8 INCHES LONG

1. Preheat the oven to 375°F.

2. Cut the sausages almost in half lengthwise. Place them, cut sides up, in a large shallow casserole or baking pan and pour the marinara sauce over them. Bake them for 12 to 15 minutes or until the sauce is bubbling hot and the sausages are heated through.

3. If using mozzarella, place it on top of the sausages and bake them for about 5 minutes longer or until the cheese melts. Set them aside.

4. In a large sauté pan, warm up the peppers and onions over medium-high heat, stirring, for 4 to 5 minutes or until they are hot. As the peppers and onions heat cut them with a fork or lightly mash them to make them easier to eat.

5. Meanwhile, slice the rolls in half lengthwise, without cutting all the way through. Arrange the rolls, cut sides up, on a baking sheet and toast them under the broiler for 2 to 3 minutes or until they are lightly browned.

6. To assemble each sandwich, spread about 3 tablespoons of the marinara sauce on each half of the roll. Place 3 butterflied sausages on each roll. Top the sausages with 1 cup of the peppers and onions. Fold the other half of the roll over the sausages. Cut the sandwich in half and serve.

NOTE: When you cut the peppers and onions for the hero, slice the vegetables into a large dice so that they cling to the other sandwich ingredients.

CHICKEN PARMIGIANA HEROES

Serves 4

FOUR 6-OUNCE SKINLESS CHICKEN
CUTLETS, SLIGHTLY FLATTENED

SALT AND FRESHLY GROUND BLACK
PEPPER

½ CUP ALL-PURPOSE FLOUR

2 LARGE EGGS

4 CUPS CARMINE'S BREAD CRUMBS,
PAGE 283

¾ CUP OLIVE OIL

8 TO 12 SLICES FRESH MOZZARELLA,
OPTIONAL

5 CUPS CARMINE'S MARINARA SAUCE,
PUREED, PAGE 288

4 CRISPY HERO ROLLS, 6 TO 8 INCHES
LONG

4 TABLESPOONS GRATED ROMANO
CHEESE

1. Season the cutlets with salt and pepper to taste.

2. Spread the flour on a large plate. In a large shallow bowl, lightly beat the eggs. Spread the bread crumbs on a baking sheet.

3. Coat the cutlets on both sides with the flour, shaking off any excess. Dip the cutlets in the egg mixture and let any excess drip off. Press the cutlets into the bread crumbs, making sure both sides are covered.

4. Heat the olive oil in a large sauté pan over medium heat. When the oil is hot, add the cutlets. Cook the cutlets for 3 to 4 minutes or until they are golden brown. Turn them over and cook the other side for 3 to 4 minutes or until it is golden brown. Drain them on paper towels.

5. If using cheese, preheat the broiler. Transfer the cutlets to a baking sheet and top with sliced mozzarella. Broil for 2 to 3 minutes or until the cheese is melted.

6. Heat the marinara sauce in a medium-sized saucepan over medium-high heat for about 5 minutes or until it is heated through.

7. Meanwhile, slice the rolls in half lengthwise, without cutting all the way through. Press them open with your hands. Arrange the rolls, cut sides up, on a baking sheet and toast them under the broiler for 2 to 3 minutes or until they are lightly browned.

Continued

8. To assemble each sandwich, spread about 3 tablespoons of the sauce over each half of the roll. Put a cutlet on one half of the roll and sprinkle it with the grated cheese. Fold the other half of the roll over the cutlet. Cut the sandwich in half and serve.

NOTE: This sandwich can be made with veal cutlets instead of chicken.

AN AUTHENTIC HERO IS ESSENTIAL TO THE NEW YORK LUNCH EXPERIENCE. UNTIL YOU'VE TASTED THE REAL THING, YOU WON'T KNOW WHAT YOU'RE MISSING, AND AS SOON AS YOU DO, YOU'LL NEVER BE SATISFIED WITH IMITATORS. ALL OUR LUNCH CUSTOMERS, FROM COPS AND FIREFIGHTERS TO BUSINESSMEN DRIVING MERCEDESES, LOVE THESE SANDWICHES. ON FRIDAYS, WHICH IS PROBABLY PAYDAY—OR MAYBE JUST BECAUSE IT'S THE END OF THE WORKWEEK—WE'LL GET FORTY OR FIFTY CONSTRUCTION WORKERS IN THE 44TH STREET RESTAURANT AND WE'LL SELL 120 SANDWICHES.

A NUMBER OF THINGS GO INTO MAKING OUR HEROES SO SPECTACULAR. FIRST—AND THIS IS CRUCIAL—THEY ARE MADE JUST BEFORE THEY ARE SERVED. A HERO THAT IS MADE HOURS AHEAD OF TIME AND WRAPPED IN PLASTIC JUST DOESN'T CUT IT. SECOND, THE BREAD HAS TO BE FIRST RATE. WE BUY OUR BREAD FROM NEW YORK'S GREAT WHOLESALE BAKERIES, WHERE THE LOAVES ARE BAKED IN BRICK OVENS FOR CRISP CRUSTS AND SOFT INTERIOR CRUMBS. THIS WAY, THE SANDWICH STAYS FIRM IN THE HAND, BUT THE TENDER CRUMB DELICIOUSLY SOAKS UP THE OIL AND VINEGAR OR TOMATO SAUCE. THIRD, WE USE THE SAME TOMATO SAUCE WE USE FOR PASTA, A SAUCE THAT IS RICH AND FRAGRANT WITH GARLIC, HERBS, AND IMPORTED ITALIAN TOMATOES. THE OIL AND VINEGAR FOR THE COLD HEROES ARE NEVER BLAND BUT INSTEAD MAGICALLY PERK UP THE FILLINGS. NEVER BUY THE CHEAP STUFF; YOU CAN FIND EXCELLENT PRODUCTS THAT WON'T BREAK THE BANK.

THE FOURTH AND MOST IMPORTANT POINT IS THAT HEROES ARE ONLY AS GOOD AS THEIR FILLINGS. WE NEVER OVERLOAD OUR SANDWICHES, ALTHOUGH THEY SURELY ARE BIGHEARTED. IF THEY OVERFLOW, THEY CAN BE HARD TO EAT, AND THAT'S NO FUN. WE SLICE THE PROSCIUTTO AND OTHER HAMS PAPER THIN. SALAMIS ARE CUT A LITTLE THICKER. WHEN YOU MAKE HEROES AT HOME, BUY MEAT AND CHEESE FROM A MARKET OR DELI THAT WILL SLICE IT FOR YOU, AND ASK THEM TO KEEP IT THIN, THIN, THIN. THIS IS FAR SUPERIOR TO BUYING PRESLICED, PACKAGED PRODUCTS.

HOT ITALIAN COMBO HEROES WITH HOT CHERRY PEPPERS

Serves 4

4 CRISPY HERO ROLLS, 6 TO 8 INCHES LONG

4 TABLESPOONS GARLIC BUTTER, PAGE 286

24 SLICES MORTADELLA

20 SLICES SWEET OR SPICY SOPPRESSATA

20 SLICES PROVOLONE

4 ROASTED RED PEPPERS, COARSELY CHOPPED, PAGE 303

I CUP COARSELY CHOPPED HOT CHERRY PEPPERS

1. Preheat the broiler.

2. Slice the rolls in half lengthwise without cutting all the way through. Press them open with your hands. Arrange the rolls, cut sides up, on a baking sheet and toast them under the broiler for 2 to 3 minutes or until they are lightly browned.

3. Spread ½ tablespoon of the garlic butter on both sides of each roll.

4. To prepare each sandwich, place 6 slices of mortadella, slightly overlapping, on a baking sheet and top them with 5 slices of soppressata. Transfer the pan to the oven and broil the meat for 3 to 4 minutes or until it is hot and lightly browned. Place 5 slices of provolone on top of the meat and broil it for 1 to 2 minutes or until the cheese has melted.

5. Remove the pan from the oven and top the sandwich filling with one-fourth of the roasted peppers. Using a spatula, slide the filling onto one half of the roll. Top it with ¼ cup of the hot cherry peppers. Fold the other half of the roll over the sandwich ingredients. Cut the sandwich in half and serve.

ITALIAN CHEESESTEAK HEROES

Serves 4

1½ TO 1¾ POUNDS BEEF, RIB EYE OR TOP ROUND STEAK, THINLY SLICED

¼ CUP OLIVE OIL

SALT AND FRESHLY GROUND BLACK PEPPER

1 TEASPOON DRIED OREGANO

1 CUP CHOPPED ONIONS

1 CUP CHOPPED RED AND YELLOW BELL PEPPERS

4 CRISPY HERO ROLLS, 6 TO 8 INCHES LONG

4 TABLESPOONS GARLIC BUTTER, PAGE 286

16 TO 20 SLICES PROVOLONE

¼ CUP GRATED ROMANO

1. Preheat the broiler.

2. Coarsely chop the steak and set it aside.

3. In a large sauté pan, heat the olive oil over medium heat. When the oil is hot but not smoking, cook the steak with salt and pepper to taste and the oregano, stirring, until it browns. Add the onions and peppers and cook the mixture for about 3 minutes or until they are slightly softened and heated through. Adjust the heat so the pan doesn't get too hot and dry out the steak.

4. Meanwhile, slice the rolls in half lengthwise, without cutting all the way through. Press them open with your hands. Arrange the rolls, cut sides up, on a baking sheet and toast them under the broiler for 2 to 3 minutes or until they are lightly browned.

5. To assemble each sandwich, spread ½ tablespoon of the garlic butter on each half of the roll. Layer 4 to 5 slices of provolone on one half of the roll. Transfer the sandwich to a baking sheet and broil it for 2 to 3 minutes or until the cheese has melted. Top the cheese with one-fourth of the steak mixture. Sprinkle it with 1 tablespoon of the grated cheese. Fold the other half of the roll over the steak. Cut the sandwich in half and serve.

MEATBALL HEROES

Serves 4

3 CUPS CARMINE'S MARINARA SAUCE, PAGE 288

12 CARMINE'S MEATBALLS, PAGE 298

16 SLICES FRESH MOZZARELLA, OPTIONAL

4 CRISPY HERO ROLLS, 6 TO 8 INCHES LONG

1. Preheat the oven to 375°F.

2. In the bowl of a food processor fitted with a metal blade, puree the marinara sauce for about 1 minute or until it is smooth.

3. Cut the meatballs in half and place them in a baking dish or casserole. Pour the sauce over the meatballs, cover the dish, and bake the meatballs for 12 to 15 minutes or until they are very hot.

4. If using mozzarella, place it on top of the meatballs. Cover the dish and bake the meatballs for 3 to 4 minutes or until the cheese is melted.

5. Preheat the broiler.

6. Meanwhile, slice the rolls in half lengthwise without cutting all the way through. Press them open with your hands. Arrange the rolls, cut sides up, on a baking sheet and toast them under the broiler for 2 to 3 minutes or until they are lightly browned.

7. To assemble each sandwich, spread 3 tablespoons of sauce on each half of the roll. Put 3 meatballs on one half of the roll. Fold the other side of the roll over the meatballs. Cut the sandwich in half and serve.

3.
PASTA

We call it the "wow" factor, whenever our pasta dishes are served in the restaurant, the size of the platter, which holds enough food for four to six people, causes jaws to drop and a quiet "Wow!" can be heard.

PASTA WITH RED CLAM SAUCE ≈ PASTA WITH WHITE CLAM SAUCE ≈ PASTA WITH WHITE CALAMARI SAUCE ≈ LINGUINE WITH WHITE SHRIMP SAUCE ≈ LINGUINE WITH RED SHRIMP SAUCE ≈ PASTA WITH GARLIC AND OIL ≈ COUNTRY-STYLE RIGATONI ≈ PASTA GIARDINIERA ≈ PASTA WITH BROCCOLI, SAUSAGE, AND TOMATOES ≈ PASTA WITH BROCCOLI, SAUSAGE, GARLIC, AND OIL ≈ PASTA MARINARA ≈ PASTA POMODORO ≈ PASTA WITH CARMINE'S MEATBALLS ≈ PENNE ALLA VODKA ≈ MANICOTTI ≈ BENSONHURST-STYLE CAPELLINI PIE ≈ CARMINE'S LASAGNE ≈ RAGU PASTA ≈ FRESH FETTUCCINE WITH WILD MUSHROOM SAUCE ≈ BAKED STUFFED SHELLS

PASTA WITH RED AND WHITE CLAM SAUCE

Pasta with white clam sauce is one of our customers' first choices. We sell plate after plate, and no one ever seems to tire of it. Pasta with red clam sauce is not quite as popular, although it's mighty good. We make both with chopped fresh clam meat taken directly from the clamshells—no canned clam meat at Carmine's. This means we have the shells and scraps to flavor our own clam broth, but, of course, it is not likely that the home cook would go to the trouble of making his own clam broth. Bottled clam juice is fine, but if you are lucky enough to have a fishmonger who sells freshly made clam juice, use it to cut the bottled juice by half. Buy small littleneck clams if you possibly can; they will flavor the sauce as they cook. The slightly larger fresh clams are flavorful, but they won't be as tender or as easy to eat.

PASTA WITH RED CLAM SAUCE

Serves 2 to 4

¼ CUP OLIVE OIL

2 TABLESPOONS COARSELY CHOPPED GARLIC

24 LITTLENECK CLAMS, RINSED AND SCRUBBED

12 FRESH OREGANO LEAVES, COARSELY CHOPPED

8 FRESH BASIL LEAVES

2 TABLESPOONS CHOPPED FLAT-LEAF PARSLEY

PINCH OF HOT RED PEPPER FLAKES

¼ CUP DRY WHITE WINE

1½ CUPS CLAM JUICE

10 OUNCES CANNED PLUM TOMATOES, DRAINED AND COARSELY CHOPPED

12 OUNCES DRIED LINGUINE, SPAGHETTI, OR FETTUCCINE

1. In a large sauté pan, heat the olive oil over medium-high heat. When the oil is hot, add the garlic and cook it, stirring, for about 1 minute or until it is golden brown. Take care not to let the garlic burn.

2. Add the clams, oregano, basil, parsley, and red pepper flakes. Cook the mixture, stirring, for 30 seconds. Cover the pan and cook it for 3 to 4 minutes more. Add the wine and cook it uncovered for 2 to 3 minutes more, or until the wine is nearly evaporated.

3. Add the clam juice, cover the pan, and raise the heat to high. Cook the sauce for 2 to 3 minutes, remove the cover, and cook it for 2 to 3 minutes more or until the sauce tastes strongly of the sea. Add the tomatoes and cook the sauce for about 3 minutes, removing the clams to a bowl as they open, until the sauce thickens. With a small knife, pry open any clams that don't open, unless they are firmly and stubbornly closed, in which case discard them. Return the clams to the sauce.

4. Meanwhile, in a large pot filled with boiling salted water, cook the pasta for 7 to 8 minutes or until it is al dente. The cooking time will vary depending on the type of pasta.

5. Drain the pasta well and transfer it to a platter. Immediately ladle the clams and sauce over the pasta. Mix them well and serve.

PASTA WITH WHITE CLAM SAUCE

Serves 2 to 4

¼ CUP OLIVE OIL

2 TABLESPOONS COARSELY CHOPPED GARLIC

24 LITTLENECK CLAMS, RINSED AND SCRUBBED

8 FRESH BASIL LEAVES

2 TABLESPOONS CHOPPED FLAT-LEAF PARSLEY

PINCH HOT RED PEPPER FLAKES

¼ CUP DRY WHITE WINE

2¼ CUPS CLAM JUICE

12 OUNCES DRIED SPAGHETTI, LINGUINE, PENNE, OR RIGATONI

SALT AND FRESHLY GROUND BLACK PEPPER

1. In a large sauté pan, heat the olive oil over medium-high heat. When the oil is hot, add the garlic and cook it, stirring, for about 1 minute or until it is golden brown. Take care not to let the garlic burn.

2. Add the clams, basil, parsley, and red pepper flakes. Raise the heat to high and cook the mixture, stirring, for about 1 minute or until the ingredients are well combined.

3. Reduce the heat to medium and cover the pan. Cook the sauce, shaking the pan occasionally, for 3 to 4 minutes.

4. Remove the cover and add the wine. Cook the sauce uncovered for 1 minute. Add the clam juice and simmer the sauce, covered, for 2 to 3 minutes or until all the clams have opened. With a small knife, pry open any that don't open, unless they are firmly and stubbornly closed, in which case discard them.

5. Meanwhile, in a large pot filled with boiling salted water, cook the pasta for 7 to 8 minutes or until it is al dente. The cooking time will vary depending on the type of pasta. Reserve 1 cup of the pasta cooking water.

6. Drain the pasta well and transfer it to a shallow bowl or platter. Bring the sauce to a boil and season it to taste with salt and pepper. Immediately ladle it over the pasta and mix in ¼ cup of the reserved water. Add more water, if desired, and serve.

CHOOSING THE RIGHT PASTA

FOR NEARLY ALL OUR PASTA RECIPES, WE SUGGEST DRIED PASTA. FRESH PASTA IS GREAT, AND IF YOU LIKE TO MAKE IT YOURSELF OR HAVE A FAVORITE SUPPLIER, BY ALL MEANS USE IT—BUT REMEMBER THAT IT TAKES LESS TIME TO COOK. MOST OF US, HOWEVER, COOK WITH DRIED PASTA AT HOME. IT'S READILY AVAILABLE IN EVERY SUPERMARKET IN THE COUNTRY AND KEEPS FOR MONTHS IN THE CUPBOARD.

WHEN YOU BUY IT, TRY TO STAY WITH ITALIAN BRANDS MADE FROM 100 PERCENT DURUM SEMOLINA FLOUR—ALTHOUGH IF YOU HAVE A FAVORITE DOMESTIC BRAND, USE IT. WHAT YOU WANT IS PASTA THAT COOKS WITHOUT STICKING TOGETHER AND THAT TASTES SILKEN, WITH JUST A LITTLE BITE. TRY A FEW BRANDS; DON'T ASSUME THAT ALL DRIED PASTAS ARE ALIKE, BECAUSE THEY ARE NOT. WHEN YOU FIND A BRAND YOU LIKE, STAY WITH IT.

DRIED PASTA WILL KEEP FOR AT LEAST TWO MONTHS IN ITS PACKAGING AND WHEN TRANSFERRED TO AN AIRTIGHT CONTAINER WILL KEEP FOR UP TO A YEAR. ONCE THE PACKAGE IS OPENED, IT'S A GOOD IDEA TO COOK IT WITHIN A FEW WEEKS UNLESS YOU STORE IT VERY CAREFULLY.

WE SUGGEST VARIOUS SHAPES FOR DIFFERENT DISHES. WHILE THIS CAN BE A MATTER OF PERSONAL TASTE, THERE ARE REASONS FOR THE SHAPES. AS A RULE, VERY THIN, DELICATE PASTAS SUCH AS VERMICELLI AND ANGEL HAIR ARE RECOMMENDED FOR LIGHT, DELICATE CREAM SAUCES; THICKER-STRAND PASTAS, SUCH AS FETTUCCINE AND SPAGHETTI, DO WELL WITH MARGINALLY HEAVIER, LIGHTLY TEXTURED SAUCES MADE FROM SEAFOOD, VEGETABLES, AND CREAM; CHUNKIER SHAPES ARE GOOD FOR MEATY SAUCES WITH INGREDIENTS THAT NESTLE IN THEIR NOOKS AND CRANNIES. LARGE TUBULAR PASTAS AND SHEETS OF PASTA ARE BEST FOR BAKED DISHES. IN ITALY, DEDICATED COOKS USE A SPECIFIC TYPE OF PASTA WITH A SPECIFIC SAUCE: NO EXCEPTIONS! WE ARE A LITTLE MORE FORGIVING BUT IT MAKES SENSE TO MATCH A SAUCE WITH A SHAPE THAT ACCOMMODATES IT.

PASTA WITH WHITE CALAMARI SAUCE

Another top seller at Carmine's, this dish appeals to anyone who likes white clam sauce (and who doesn't?) because calamari, too, are light and refreshing. The calamari cook quickly in the sauce and are as tender as can be prepared this way. You can buy calamari precut, but if you have to purchase whole, cleaned calamari, they are easy to cut into ⅛- to ¼-inch-thick slices. If they are much thicker, the rings could be a little chewy.

Serves 2 to 4

¼ CUP OLIVE OIL

2 TABLESPOONS COARSELY CHOPPED GARLIC

8 FRESH BASIL LEAVES

2 TABLESPOONS CHOPPED FLAT-LEAF PARSLEY

1 TEASPOON CHOPPED FRESH OREGANO

PINCH OF HOT RED PEPPER FLAKES

¼ CUP DRY WHITE WINE

1 POUND VERY THINLY SLICED CALAMARI RINGS, DRAINED (ABOUT 2 CUPS)

SALT AND FRESHLY GROUND BLACK PEPPER

2¼ CUPS CLAM JUICE

12 OUNCES DRIED SPAGHETTI, LINGUINE, PENNE, OR RIGATONI

1. In a large sauté pan, heat the olive oil over medium-high heat. When the oil is hot, add the garlic and cook it, stirring, for about 1 minute or until it is golden brown. Take care not to let the garlic burn.

2. Add the basil, parsley, oregano, and red pepper flakes. Cook the mixture, stirring, for 30 seconds.

3. Add the wine and cook the sauce uncovered for about 3 minutes or until most of the wine has evaporated. Add the calamari and season the sauce to taste with salt and pepper.

4. Raise the heat to high and bring the sauce to a boil. Cook it for 2 to 3 minutes or until the small amount of liquid released by the calamari has evaporated.

5. Add the clam juice, cover the pan, and simmer the sauce for 2 to 3 minutes. Remove the cover and simmer the sauce briskly for 4 minutes. Season it to taste with salt and pepper.

6. Meanwhile, in a large pot filled with boiling salted water, cook the pasta for 7 to 8 minutes or until it is al dente. The cooking time will vary depending on the type of pasta.

7. Drain the pasta well and transfer it to a platter. Immediately ladle the sauce over the pasta. Mix them well and serve.

LINGUINE WITH WHITE AND RED SHRIMP SAUCE

Linguine with shrimp is one of the jewels of the Carmine's crown. Our guests love it, and for good reason. We use plump white shrimp from Mexico, which are tasty with perfect texture, and we add just enough seasonings to make these dishes standouts. Buy large shrimp that look great and peel them yourself. To add even more flavor, steep the shrimp shells in the clam juice for about 10 minutes over very low heat, strain it, and use the clam juice as the recipes instruct. Brilliant!

LINGUINE WITH WHITE SHRIMP SAUCE

Serves 2 to 4

¼ CUP OLIVE OIL

2 TABLESPOONS COARSELY CHOPPED GARLIC

8 FRESH BASIL LEAVES, SLICED

2 TABLESPOONS CHOPPED FLAT-LEAF PARSLEY

¼ CUP DRY WHITE WINE

2¼ CUPS CLAM JUICE

20 LARGE SHRIMP, PEELED AND DEVEINED

SALT AND FRESHLY GROUND BLACK PEPPER

12 OUNCES DRIED LINGUINE

1. In a large sauté pan, heat the olive oil over medium-high heat. When the oil is hot, add the garlic and cook it, stirring, for about 1 minute or until it is golden brown. Take care not to let the garlic burn.

2. Add the basil and parsley and cook the mixture, stirring, for 30 seconds. Add the wine and cook it for 2 to 3 minutes uncovered or until most of the wine has evaporated. Add the clam juice and boil the sauce for 4 to 5 minutes or until the liquid has reduced by half.

3. Add the shrimp, lower the heat, and cook the sauce for 1 minute. Remove the shrimp and set aside. Season the sauce to taste with salt and pepper. Just before serving, reheat the sauce so that it bubbles. Return the shrimp to the pan and cook in the bubbling sauce for about 1 minute or until cooked through.

4. Meanwhile, in a large pot of boiling salted water, cook the pasta for 7 to 8 minutes or until it is al dente.

5. Drain the pasta well and transfer it to a platter. Immediately ladle the sauce over the pasta. Mix them well and serve.

LINGUINE WITH RED SHRIMP SAUCE

Serves 2 to 4

¼ CUP OLIVE OIL

2 TABLESPOONS COARSELY CHOPPED GARLIC

12 FRESH OREGANO LEAVES, CHOPPED

8 FRESH BASIL LEAVES, SLICED

2 TABLESPOONS CHOPPED FLAT-LEAF PARSLEY

10 OUNCES CANNED ITALIAN PLUM TOMATOES, DRAINED AND COARSELY CHOPPED

¼ CUP DRY WHITE WINE

2¼ CUPS CLAM JUICE

20 LARGE SHRIMP, PEELED AND DEVEINED

SALT AND FRESHLY GROUND BLACK PEPPER

12 OUNCES DRIED LINGUINE

1. In a large sauté pan, heat the olive oil over medium-high heat. When the oil is hot, add the garlic and cook it, stirring, for about 1 minute or until it is golden brown. Take care not to let the garlic burn.

2. Add the oregano, basil, and parsley. Cook the mixture, stirring, for 30 seconds.

3. Add the tomatoes, raise the heat to high, and cook the mixture for 3 minutes. Add the wine and cook it for about 2 minutes or until most of the wine has evaporated. Add the clam juice, reduce the heat to medium, and simmer the sauce for 3 to 4 minutes or until the liquid is reduced by half.

4. Add the shrimp, lower the heat, and cook the sauce for 1 minute. Remove the shrimp and set it aside. Season the sauce to taste with salt and pepper. Just before serving, reheat the sauce so that it bubbles. Return the shrimp to the pan and cook in the bubbling sauce for about 1 minute or until cooked through.

5. Meanwhile, in a large pot of boiling salted water, cook the linguine for 7 to 8 minutes or until it is al dente.

6. Drain the pasta well and transfer it to a platter. Immediately ladle the sauce over the pasta. Mix them well and serve.

PASTA WITH GARLIC AND OIL

A number of years ago, Michael Ronis traveled to Italy with his friend and tennis teacher, who was on a visit to his family in their village about an hour from Bologna. While they ate at some good restaurants, Michael was most impressed by the food prepared by his friend's mother and sisters. Salt-of-the-earth cooking, he called it; its genius was in its simplicity. This is how we cook at Carmine's: simply.

This is about as simple as a pasta dish gets, but that doesn't mean it is always easy to execute well. One of the secrets is the chicken broth, which adds deep, true flavor; the toasted bread crumbs also make a big difference. This recipe proves that if all you have on hand are a few simple ingredients, you can still make a sublime meal.

Serves 2 to 4

¾ CUP OLIVE OIL

2 TABLESPOONS COARSELY CHOPPED GARLIC

8 FRESH BASIL LEAVES, SLICED

2 TABLESPOONS CHOPPED FLAT-LEAF PARSLEY

I CUP CHICKEN STOCK, PAGE 306

SALT AND FRESHLY GROUND BLACK PEPPER

¾ CUP GRATED ROMANO CHEESE

12 OUNCES DRIED ANGEL HAIR PASTA

2 TABLESPOONS TOASTED BREAD CRUMBS, PAGE 284

1. In a large sauté pan, heat the olive oil over medium-high heat. When the oil is hot, add the garlic and cook it, stirring, for about 1 minute or until it is golden brown. Take care not to let the garlic burn.

2. Add the basil and parsley and cook the mixture, stirring, for 30 seconds.

3. Raise the heat to high and add the chicken stock. Bring it to a boil and cook it for 3 to 4 minutes or until the stock is reduced by a quarter. Season the sauce with salt and pepper to taste.

4. Remove the sauce from the heat and stir in ¼ cup of the cheese until it is well blended.

5. Meanwhile, in a large pot of boiling salted water, cook the pasta for 7 to 8 minutes or until it is al dente. Reserve 2 cups of the pasta cooking water.

6. Drain the pasta well. Bring the sauce to a boil and add the pasta to the sauce. Add ½ to 1 cup of the reserved cooking water and stir it well. Season it to taste with salt and pepper. Transfer it to a shallow bowl or platter. Sprinkle with the bread crumbs and serve it with the remaining ½ cup of grated cheese on the side.

COUNTRY-STYLE RIGATONI

This rigatoni is one of our signature dishes and sells like crazy when it's cold and blustery outside. It's a hearty dish made with beans, sausage, and broccoli, as well as plenty of rigatoni. Paired with a glass of good red wine, it can't be beat. You will find that the addition of chicken broth, onions, and prosciutto make this full-flavored and magnificent. Of course, you can always substitute blanched broccoli rabe for the broccoli, if your family prefers it. (Turn to page 236 for blanching instructions.)

Serves 2 to 4

¼ CUP OLIVE OIL

2 TABLESPOONS COARSELY CHOPPED GARLIC

¼ CUP THINLY SLICED ONIONS

8 OUNCES FENNEL SAUSAGE, CASING REMOVED

8 FRESH BASIL LEAVES, CHOPPED

2 TABLESPOONS CHOPPED FLAT-LEAF PARSLEY

ONE 18-OUNCE CAN CANNELLINI BEANS, DRAINED AND RINSED

2 CUPS CHICKEN STOCK

¼ CUP UNSALTED BUTTER

1¼ CUPS GRATED ROMANO CHEESE

SALT AND FRESHLY GROUND BLACK PEPPER

2 TABLESPOONS THINLY SLICED PROSCIUTTO

12 OUNCES DRIED RIGATONI

8 TO 10 SPEARS BROCCOLI, EACH ABOUT 3 INCHES LONG

1. In a large sauté pan, heat the olive oil over medium-high heat. When the oil is hot, add the garlic and cook it, stirring, for about 1 minute or until it is golden brown. Take care not to let the garlic burn. Add the onions and cook the mixture for about 3 minutes, stirring occasionally, or until the onions are golden brown.

2. Add the sausage, basil, and parsley. Break up the sausage, using a wooden spoon or long-handled fork, and cook the mixture for 2 to 3 minutes or until the sausage

Continued

is browned. Add the beans, chicken stock, and butter, raise the heat to high, and bring the sauce to a boil. Reduce the heat slightly and simmer it briskly for 5 to 8 minutes or until it starts to thicken. Stir in ¼ cup of the grated cheese and cook the sauce for about 3 minutes or until it thickens. Season it to taste with salt and pepper. Stir in the prosciutto and ½ cup of the cheese. Let the mixture simmer for 2 minutes before removing it from the heat.

3. Meanwhile, in a large pot filled with boiling salted water, cook the pasta for 4 minutes. Add the broccoli and cook it for another 3 to 4 minutes or until the pasta is al dente.

4. Drain the pasta well. Bring the sauce to a boil. Add the pasta and broccoli to the sauce and mix them well. Stir in ¼ cup of grated cheese, if desired. Serve the pasta with the remaining ¼ cup of grated cheese passed on the side.

PASTA GIARDINIERA

"Giardiniera" roughly means "with vegetables." This pasta is our answer to pasta primavera. The vegetables are cooked in the sauce long enough to flavor it with their green, earthy goodness. To make this dish vegetarian, substitute vegetable stock for the chicken stock. For the best flavor, let the sauce sit for at least 10 to 15 minutes before tossing it with the pasta. That's the secret to this dish.

Serves 2 to 4

¼ CUP OLIVE OIL

½ SMALL ONION, THINLY SLICED

2 TABLESPOONS CHOPPED FRESH GARLIC

1½ CUPS SLICED CREMINI MUSHROOMS (4½ TO 5 OUNCES)

1 CUP FINELY DICED ZUCCHINI (ABOUT 1 ZUCCHINI)

2 TABLESPOONS THINLY SLICED PROSCIUTTO

8 FRESH BASIL LEAVES, SLICED

2 TABLESPOONS CHOPPED FLAT-LEAF PARSLEY

2 CUPS CARMINE'S MARINARA SAUCE, PAGE 288

1 CUP CHICKEN STOCK, PAGE 306

½ CUP HEAVY CREAM

1 CUP GRATED ROMANO CHEESE

½ CUP FRESH OR FROZEN AND THAWED GREEN PEAS

SALT AND FRESHLY GROUND BLACK PEPPER

¼ HEAD BROCCOLI, CUT INTO 3-INCH SPEARS WITH FLORETS

12 OUNCES DRIED PENNE, LINGUINE, FUSILLI, OR RIGATONI

1. In a large sauté pan, heat the olive oil over medium-high heat. When the oil is hot, add the onions and garlic and cook them, stirring, for about 2 to 3 minutes or until the onions turn golden brown.

Continued

2. Add the mushrooms, zucchini, prosciutto, basil, and parsley. Raise the heat to high and cook the mixture for 3 to 4 minutes or until the vegetables start to soften.

3. Add the marinara sauce, chicken stock, and heavy cream. Bring the sauce to a boil over medium-high heat and boil it for 3 to 4 minutes or until it starts to thicken. Stir in ½ cup of the cheese and the peas. Season the sauce to taste with salt and pepper.

4. Meanwhile, in a large pot of boiling salted water, cook the broccoli for 3 to 4 minutes or until it is al dente. Lift it from the water with a slotted spoon and add it to the sauce. Reserve the water in the pot to cook the pasta. Let the sauce sit, off the heat, for 10 to 15 minutes to flavor it with the vegetables.

5. Bring the water to a boil, add the pasta, and cook it for 7 to 8 minutes. The cooking time will vary depending on the type of pasta.

6. Drain the pasta well and transfer it to a shallow bowl or platter. Bring the sauce to a simmer. Immediately ladle it over the pasta and serve it with the remaining ½ cup of grated cheese on the side.

PASTA WITH BROCCOLI, SAUSAGE, AND TOMATOES AND PASTA WITH BROCCOLI, SAUSAGE, GARLIC, AND OIL

These pasta dishes, both chock-full of broccoli and sausage, are slightly different from each other, but both exemplify the kind of "grandmother's cooking" we strive for at Carmine's, anchored in the Italian American cooking traditions of the northeastern United States. Nothing is better than familiarity paired with flawless implementation, and you'll get that in both of these pastas. Always use the best sausage you can find. Buy it from an Italian market, if possible, and don't be tempted to substitute lean sausage for regular. The ratio of fat to meat in the sausage makes these pasta dishes shout with flavor. When it comes to the second recipe, with garlic and oil, our homemade bread crumbs make a tremendous difference. Don't substitute store-bought bread crumbs; ours are very easy to make yourself (see page 283).

PASTA WITH BROCCOLI, SAUSAGE, AND TOMATOES

Serves 2 to 4

¼ CUP OLIVE OIL

8 OUNCES FENNEL SAUSAGE, CASING REMOVED

2 TABLESPOONS COARSELY CHOPPED GARLIC

8 FRESH BASIL LEAVES, SLICED

2 TABLESPOONS CHOPPED FLAT-LEAF PARSLEY

½ CUP CHICKEN STOCK, PAGE 306

3 CUPS CARMINE'S MARINARA SAUCE, PAGE 288

12 OUNCES DRIED PENNE, RIGATONI, FUSILLI, OR SMALL SHELLS

½ HEAD BROCCOLI, CUT INTO 3-INCH SPEARS

1 CUP GRATED ROMANO CHEESE

SALT AND FRESHLY GROUND BLACK PEPPER

1. In a large sauté pan, heat the olive oil over medium-high heat. When the oil is hot, add the sausage and cook it, using a long-handled fork or wooden spoon to break it up, for 3 to 4 minutes or until it starts to brown. Add the garlic and cook the mixture for 4 to 5 minutes or until the sausage and garlic are nicely browned. Add the basil and parsley and cook the mixture, stirring, for 30 seconds.

2. Add the chicken stock, bring the mixture to a boil, and cook it for 1 minute, stirring any browned bits from the bottom of the pan with a wooden spoon to deglaze it. Add the marinara sauce, bring the sauce to a simmer, and cook it for 5 to 7 minutes or until it thickens.

3. Meanwhile, in a large pot of boiling salted water, cook the pasta and broccoli for 7 to 8 minutes or until the pasta is al dente. The cooking time will vary depending on the type of pasta.

4. Drain the pasta and broccoli well and add them to the sauce. Add ½ cup of the cheese. Mix it well to combine the ingredients. Season it to taste with salt and pepper.

5. Transfer it to a shallow bowl or platter and serve it with the remaining ½ cup of cheese on the side.

PASTA WITH BROCCOLI, SAUSAGE, GARLIC, AND OIL

Serves 2 to 4

¾ CUP OLIVE OIL

8 OUNCES FENNEL SAUSAGE, CASING REMOVED

2 TABLESPOONS COARSELY CHOPPED GARLIC

8 FRESH BASIL LEAVES, SLICED

2 TABLESPOONS CHOPPED FLAT-LEAF PARSLEY

1 CUP CHICKEN STOCK, PAGE 306

12 OUNCES DRIED PENNE, RIGATONI, SMALL SHELLS, OR FUSILLI

½ HEAD BROCCOLI, CUT INTO 3-INCH SPEARS

1 CUP GRATED ROMANO CHEESE

SALT AND FRESHLY GROUND BLACK PEPPER

2 TABLESPOONS TOASTED BREAD CRUMBS, PAGE 284

Continued

1. In a large sauté pan, heat the olive oil over medium-high heat. When the oil is hot, add the sausage and cook it, using a long-handled fork or wooden spoon to break it up, for 3 to 4 minutes or until it begins to brown. Add the garlic and cook the mixture for 3 to 4 minutes or until the sausage and garlic are nicely browned. Add the basil and parsley and cook it, stirring, for 30 seconds.

2. Add the chicken stock and bring the mixture to a boil. Boil it for 1 minute, stirring any browned bits from the bottom of the pan with a wooden spoon to deglaze it, or until the liquid reduces by a quarter.

3. Meanwhile, in a large pot of boiling salted water, cook the pasta for 4 minutes. Add the broccoli and cook it for another 3 to 4 minutes or until the pasta is al dente. The cooking time will vary depending on the type of pasta. Reserve 2 cups of the pasta cooking water.

4. Drain the pasta and broccoli well in a colander. Bring the sauce to a boil. Stir the pasta and broccoli into the sauce. Add ¼ cup of the cheese and ½ cup of the reserved cooking liquid. Mix it well to combine the ingredients. Season it to taste with salt and pepper and add more cheese and reserved cooking water, if desired.

5. Transfer it to a shallow bowl or platter, garnishing it with the bread crumbs. Serve it with any remaining cheese on the side.

PASTA MARINARA

If you agree with us that a good way to judge an Italian restaurant is by its marinara sauce—just as many people think a good roast chicken is the hallmark of a superior French kitchen—then we win high marks with this pasta. There is nothing grand about this straightforward dish. It's just simple, down-to-earth, and delicious!

¼ CUP OLIVE OIL

2 TABLESPOONS COARSELY CHOPPED GARLIC

8 FRESH BASIL LEAVES, SLICED

2 TABLESPOONS CHOPPED FLAT-LEAF PARSLEY

3 CUPS CARMINE'S MARINARA SAUCE, PAGE 288

12 OUNCES DRIED SPAGHETTI, RIGATONI, OR PENNE

SALT AND FRESHLY GROUND BLACK PEPPER

1 CUP GRATED ROMANO CHEESE

1. In a large sauté pan, heat the olive oil over medium-high heat. When the oil is hot, add the garlic and cook it, stirring, for about 1 minute or until it is golden brown. Take care not to let the garlic burn.

2. Add the basil and parsley and cook the mixture, stirring, for about 30 seconds. Add the marinara sauce, reduce the heat to medium, and bring the sauce to a simmer.

3. Meanwhile, in a large pot of boiling salted water, cook the pasta for 7 to 8 minutes or until it is al dente. The cooking time will vary depending on the type of pasta. Reserve 1 cup of the pasta cooking water.

4. Drain the pasta well in a colander. Bring the sauce to a boil and add the pasta to the sauce. Season it to taste with salt and pepper. If the sauce is too thick, add some of the reserved cooking water. Add the pasta and ½ cup of the grated cheese.

5. Transfer it to a shallow bowl or platter and serve it with the remaining cheese on the side.

PASTA POMODORO

Even after we opened Carmine's, Michael Ronis and the other partners kept up the habit of eating at Italian restaurants in the Bronx, Brooklyn, and the other boroughs of the city where the pasta pomodoro was, we had to admit, a little better than ours. Why? We served a glorious simple dish at the restaurant, using the best Italian tomatoes, lots of garlic, parsley, basil, and olive oil, and our pasta was top-notch! But something kept it from going over the top. Finally, we realized it was the oil slick. To be really, really, really good, pomodoro demands lots of oil. We use a quarter cup of olive oil for four servings, which puts our pomodoro right over the top. Try it!

Serves 2 to 4

¼ CUP OLIVE OIL

8 CLOVES GARLIC, SLICED

1 OUNCE PROSCIUTTO, THINLY SLICED

7 FRESH BASIL LEAVES, SLICED

1 BAY LEAF

2 TABLESPOONS FINELY CHOPPED FLAT-LEAF PARSLEY

¼ CUP DRY WHITE WINE

ONE 20-OUNCE CAN ITALIAN PLUM TOMATOES, DRAINED

SALT AND FRESHLY GROUND BLACK PEPPER

12 OUNCES DRIED RIGATONI, SPAGHETTI, OR PENNE

1. In a large sauté pan, heat the olive oil over medium-high heat. When the oil is hot, reduce the heat, add the garlic, and cook it, stirring, for about 1 minute or until it is golden brown. Take care not to let the garlic burn. Add the prosciutto, the basil, the bay leaf, and 1 tablespoon of the parsley. Cook the mixture, stirring, for 30 seconds. Raise the heat to high, add the wine, and cook it for about 10 seconds or until the wine is well mixed.

2. Add the tomatoes and, using a wooden spoon or long-handled fork, break them up as they cook. Bring the sauce to a boil, reduce the heat slightly, and simmer it

Continued

briskly for 2 to 3 minutes or until the liquid reduces by half. Season the sauce to taste with salt and pepper.

3. Meanwhile, in a large pot filled with boiling salted water, cook the pasta for 7 to 8 minutes or until it is al dente. The cooking time will vary depending on the type of pasta.

4. Drain the pasta well and transfer it to a shallow bowl or platter. Bring the sauce to a boil and immediately ladle it over the pasta and serve the dish, garnished with the remaining tablespoon of parsley.

PASTA AND PASTA WATER

AT CARMINE'S WE ALWAYS COOK THE PASTA JUST BEFORE SERVING IT. THIS IS TRUE TO OUR "GRANDMOTHER'S COOKING" PHILOSOPHY, AND LET'S FACE IT, GRANDMA COOKED HER PASTA JUST BEFORE SERVING IT BECAUSE THAT'S HOW IT TASTES BEST! WE INVENTED A PASTA-COOKING DEVICE THAT ALLOWS US TO DO THIS AT ALL OUR RESTAURANTS, EVEN WITH OUR TREMENDOUS VOLUME. IN EVERY KITCHEN THERE ARE ONE OR TWO COOKS WHO DO NOTHING BUT COOK PASTA TO ORDER. MOST HOME COOKS DO THIS NATURALLY, SO YOU HAVE AN EDGE ON MOST RESTAURANTS IN YOUR OWN KITCHEN. IT'S ALSO CRITICAL TO COOK THE PASTA ONLY UNTIL IT IS AL DENTE, OR "TO THE BITE," SO THAT THERE IS A LITTLE CHEW IN THE CENTER OF THE NOODLE. OVERCOOKED PASTA IS MUSHY AND UNAPPEALING; UNDERCOOKED, CHEWY PASTA IS EQUALLY UNAPPETIZING.

COOK THE PASTA IN LIGHTLY SALTED WATER AND STIR IT ONCE OR TWICE TO DISCOURAGE STICKING. DON'T ADD OIL TO THE WATER—IT DOES NO GOOD AND ONLY INTERFERES WITH THE PASTA'S FLAVOR AND TEXTURE. WHEN YOU DRAIN THE PASTA, HOLD BACK SOME OF THE COOKING WATER. THIS LIQUID, WITH ITS HINTS OF STARCH AND SALT, IS JUST THE THING TO LOOSEN AND THIN SAUCES. YOU MAY WANT TO USE CHICKEN OR VEGETABLE BROTH INSTEAD, DEPENDING ON THE RECIPE, BUT YOU WILL NEVER GO WRONG WITH A LITTLE PASTA WATER.

PASTA WITH CARMINE'S MEATBALLS

If you like spaghetti with meatballs, we have just the recipe for you and your family. When parents order it at the restaurant for the kids, Mom and Dad end up serving themselves from the platter as well. It's that good! The meatballs make all the difference. We're extremely proud of our meatballs, and once you taste them you'll understand why.

Serves 2 to 4

4 TO 6 CARMINE'S MEATBALLS WITH 3 CUPS SAUCE, PAGE 298

SALT AND FRESHLY GROUND BLACK PEPPER

12 OUNCES SPAGHETTI, RIGATONI, PENNE, SMALL SHELLS, OR MEZZI RIGATONI

½ CUP GRATED ROMANO CHEESE

1. In a large saucepan, heat the meatballs and their sauce over low heat, covered, for about 15 minutes or until they are heated through. Add salt and pepper to taste.

2. Meanwhile, in a large pot filled with boiling salted water, cook the pasta for 7 to 8 minutes or until it is al dente. The cooking time will vary depending on the type of pasta.

3. Drain the pasta and transfer it to a platter. Top it with the meatballs and spoon the sauce over the pasta. Serve it with the grated cheese on the side.

PENNE ALLA VODKA

Our president, Alice, who has "seen it all" since the days when Carmine's was nothing more than an idea, smiles when she thinks of this dish. Americans have taken to penne alla vodka in a big way, she says. As the story goes, the recipe was developed when vodka was a relatively new spirit here and marketing professionals were looking for ways to promote it. This is one promotion that worked! On the other hand, some people claim the dish was invented in Italy and called Penne alla Russia, for obvious reasons. However it originated, people like the pink, creamy sauce. When we make it, we add the vodka just before serving, never ahead of time. And guess what? It's our number-one-selling pasta of all time, a fact that leaves us flabbergasted—but uncomplaining! Our version is smooth, creamy, and just super.

Serves 2 to 4

¼ CUP OLIVE OIL

½ SMALL ONION, THINLY SLICED

2 TABLESPOONS COARSELY CHOPPED GARLIC

8 FRESH BASIL LEAVES, CHOPPED

3 TABLESPOONS CHOPPED FLAT-LEAF PARSLEY

¼ TO ½ TEASPOON HOT RED PEPPER FLAKES

¼ CUP VODKA

3 CUPS CARMINE'S MARINARA SAUCE, PAGE 288

½ CUP HEAVY CREAM

12 OUNCES DRIED PENNE

1 CUP GRATED ROMANO CHEESE

SALT AND FRESHLY GROUND BLACK PEPPER

1. In a large sauté pan, heat the olive oil over medium-high heat. When the oil is hot, add the onions and reduce the heat to medium. Cook the onions, stirring, for 1 to 2 minutes or until they begin to soften. Add the garlic and cook the mixture for 1 to 2 minutes or until the onions are golden brown. Do not let the garlic brown.

Continued

2. Add the basil, parsley, and red pepper flakes to taste. Cook the mixture, stirring, for 30 seconds.

3. Remove the pan from the heat and add the vodka. Take care to stand back when adding the vodka, as the alcohol could flame. (If you prefer, you do not have to flame the vodka, although we think it improves the sauce.) Return the pan to the heat and cook the sauce for about 1 minute or until any flames die out.

4. Add the marinara sauce and simmer it for 3 minutes. Add the cream and bring the sauce to a boil. Boil it for 3 minutes or until it thickens, stirring occasionally. Cover it and keep it warm while cooking the pasta.

5. Meanwhile, in a large pot of boiling salted water, cook the penne for 7 to 8 minutes or until it is al dente.

6. Drain the penne well and transfer it to a shallow bowl or platter. Bring the sauce to a boil, stir in ½ cup of the grated cheese, and season it to taste with salt and pepper. Ladle the sauce over the pasta and serve it with the remaining grated cheese on the side.

MANICOTTI

We use crepes instead of pasta dough to make our manicotti, so they're lighter and in many ways easier to make at home. The tomato and cheese filling oozes rapturously into the crepes for one delicious mouthful after another. This manicotti is wonderful for a casual dinner party as well as a family meal. Just be sure you make extra for a crowd!

Serves 2

MANICOTTI FILLING

I CUP FRESH RICOTTA

I CUP COARSELY GRATED MOZZARELLA

½ CUP COARSELY GRATED SMOKED MOZZARELLA

¾ CUP GRATED ROMANO CHEESE

SALT AND FRESHLY GROUND BLACK PEPPER

2 TABLESPOONS CHOPPED FRESH BASIL

I TABLESPOON CHOPPED FLAT-LEAF PARSLEY

I LARGE EGG, LIGHTLY BEATEN

SAVORY CREPES

2 LARGE EGGS, LIGHTLY BEATEN

½ CUP ALL-PURPOSE FLOUR

¼ CUP COLD MILK

I TABLESPOON SNIPPED FRESH CHIVES

⅛ TEASPOON SALT

I TABLESPOON OLIVE OIL

FINISHING THE MANICOTTI

2 CUPS CARMINE'S MARINARA SAUCE, PAGE 288

2 TABLESPOONS UNSALTED BUTTER, AT ROOM TEMPERATURE

TO MAKE THE FILLING

1. In a large bowl, combine the ricotta and mozzarella, 3 tablespoons of the Romano cheese, ½ teaspoon salt, and pepper to taste. Blend the mixture gently with a wooden spoon.

2. Add the basil and parsley and stir the mixture to blend it. Fold the egg into the cheese mixture, cover it with plastic wrap, and refrigerate it for 30 minutes.

Continued

TO MAKE THE CREPES

1. In a mixing bowl, whisk together the eggs, flour, milk, chives, and salt until the mixture is smooth. Cover it and refrigerate it for at least 30 minutes and up to 24 hours, so that the liquid has time to absorb the flour. This will yield 8-9 crepes.

2. Heat a few drops of olive oil in a nonstick 10-inch skillet or crepe pan over medium-high heat. Ladle about ¼ cup of batter into the pan and tilt the pan in all directions to evenly coat the bottom. Cook the crepe for about 30 seconds or until the center is dry but not colored. Loosen the edge with a spatula and flip the crepe over with the spatula or your fingers. Cook the other side for about 10 seconds or until it is set and dry. Slide the crepe onto a flat plate and cover it with wax paper.

3. Repeat with the remaining batter, drizzling a few drops of oil in the pan as needed and stacking the crepes between sheets of wax paper. Use them when they have cooled, or cover them with plastic wrap and refrigerate them for up to 1 week, or wrap them well in plastic and freeze them in a freezer-safe plastic bag for up to 1 month.

TO FINISH THE MANICOTTI

1. Spread the crepes on a work surface. Spoon about 3 tablespoons of the filling onto the lower third of each crepe, roll the crepe to form a cigar-shaped cylinder, and transfer it to a plate. Repeat with the remaining crepes. Cover the crepes with plastic wrap and refrigerate them for 20 minutes so that they cool completely.

2. Preheat the oven to 375°F.

3. In a small saucepan, heat the marinara sauce over medium heat for about 5 minutes or until it is hot.

4. Spoon 1 cup of the sauce over the bottom of a baking dish large enough to hold the manicotti in a single layer. Reserve the rest of the sauce for serving. Place the manicotti on the sauce and spread the butter evenly over them. Sprinkle 1 tablespoon of the grated cheese over the manicotti. Bake them for 10 to 12 minutes or until the sauce is bubbling hot and the cheese is browned and melted.

5. Remove the manicotti from the oven and let them rest for 10 minutes before serving. Warm the remaining marinara sauce in a saucepan and serve it with the manicotti, along with the remaining ½ cup of Romano cheese.

BENSONHURST-STYLE CAPELLINI PIE

Brooklyn and spaghetti pie go hand in hand. This one, named in honor of Bensonhurst, a Brooklyn neighborhood with its fair share of great Italian delis and Italian American home cooks, uses slender capellini, but the spirit is the same. The roots of this dish lie in the frugality of Italian American cooks, who use up leftover pasta by binding it with eggs, tossing it with whatever else is in the larder, and cooking the mixture into pies that could be eaten warm or at room temperature. Don't wait until you have leftovers to make this!

Makes 12 patties

2 SMALL RUSSET POTATOES (ABOUT 8 OUNCES TOTAL)

6 LARGE EGGS

8 OUNCES FRESH MOZZARELLA, DICED

6 OUNCES MORTADELLA, VERY THINLY SLICED

6 OUNCES SALAMI OR SOPRESSATA, VERY THINLY SLICED

I CUP PLUS 2 TABLESPOONS GRATED ROMANO CHEESE

I SMALL ROASTED RED PEPPER, THINLY SLICED, PAGE 303

I TABLESPOON FINELY CHOPPED FLAT-LEAF PARSLEY

6½ OUNCES DRIED CAPELLINI OR ANGEL HAIR PASTA

¾ CUP FRESH OR FROZEN GREEN PEAS

SALT AND FRESHLY GROUND BLACK PEPPER

I CUP OLIVE OIL

3 CUPS CARMINE'S MARINARA SAUCE, PUREED, PAGE 288

I CUP FRESH RICOTTA WHISKED WITH I TABLESPOON WARM WATER

1. In a saucepan filled with enough lightly salted water to cover the potatoes by a few inches, bring the potatoes to a boil over high heat and cook them for 10 to 12 minutes or until they are tender. Drain the potatoes and immediately submerge them in a bowl of cold water and let them cool. Drain them again, peel them, transfer them to a small bowl, cover the bowl with plastic wrap, and refrigerate the potatoes until they are needed.

2. In a large bowl, whisk the eggs until they are well blended. Stir in the

mozzarella, the mortadella, the salami or soppressata, 1 cup of the grated cheese, the red peppers, and the parsley. Dice the potatoes and stir them into the egg mixture.

3. Meanwhile, in a large pot filled with boiling salted water, cook the pasta for 7 minutes or until it is al dente. Add the peas and cook them for about 1½ minutes. Drain the pasta and peas and add them to the egg mixture. Season the mixture to taste with salt and pepper. Stir it well.

4. Preheat the oven to 350°F.

5. In a large nonstick sauté pan, heat the olive oil over medium heat until it is hot. Ladle about ¼ cup of the pasta mixture into the pan. Using a spatula, shape it into a round patty, about 3 inches in diameter and 1 inch thick in the center. Add as many patties to the pan as it will hold with a little space between them and cook them for 3 to 4 minutes or until the bottoms are golden brown. Carefully turn the patties over and cook them for 3 to 4 minutes or until they are golden brown on both sides. Transfer them to paper towels to drain. Repeat with any remaining pasta.

6. Transfer the patties to a baking sheet and bake them for about 5 minutes or until they are heated through.

7. Meanwhile, in a saucepan, heat the marinara sauce for about 5 minutes or until it is heated through. Spread half the sauce over a large platter and place the patties on top. Spoon some ricotta on top of each patty. Serve the patties with the remaining sauce on the side.

CARMINE'S LASAGNE

How could we write a book about great Italian American food and not include lasagne? Ours is a big seller, especially with kids. During the winter holidays and school breaks when our dining rooms are packed with families, there seems to be a big lasagne on every table. This one uses our classic marinara sauce as well as a luscious meat sauce. It's about as good as it gets, but if you want to make it a little more interesting, replace half the mozzarella with smoked mozzarella. You also could put some sliced fennel sausage or meatballs on top of the meat sauce in the casserole. If you prefer a vegetarian lasagne, replace the beef and pork with tender, precooked vegetables and the beef broth with vegetable broth or more tomatoes. At the restaurant, the lasagne is three times as high as this one, but for the home kitchen we make it in an 8-by-11-inch dish and with fewer layers. It's easier to tackle, but just as tasty! Any way you make it, this lasagne will be a hit with your family.

Serves 6 to 8

LASAGNE NOODLES

I POUND LASAGNE NOODLES

I TABLESPOON OLIVE OIL

MEAT SAUCE

2 TABLESPOONS OLIVE OIL

½ ONION, FINELY DICED

3 CLOVES GARLIC, MINCED

I CARROT, PEELED AND FINELY CHOPPED

I RIB CELERY, FINELY CHOPPED

8 OUNCES GROUND CHUCK BEEF

8 OUNCES GROUND PORK

½ CUP RED WINE

I¼ TEASPOONS SALT

FRESHLY GROUND BLACK PEPPER

ONE 28-OUNCE CAN CHOPPED PLUM TOMATOES, AND JUICE

I TEASPOON CHOPPED FRESH ROSEMARY

I TEASPOON CHOPPED FRESH OREGANO

I TEASPOON CHOPPED FLAT-LEAF PARSLEY

8 TO 10 FRESH BASIL LEAVES, SLICED

2 BAY LEAVES

I CUP BEEF STOCK, PAGE 308

RICOTTA FILLING

2 POUNDS RICOTTA (SUCH AS POLLY-O)

2 LARGE EGGS, LIGHTLY BEATEN

2 TEASPOONS CHOPPED FLAT-LEAF
  PARSLEY

1 TEASPOON SALT

¼ TEASPOON FRESHLY GROUND PEPPER

ASSEMBLY

5 CUPS CARMINE'S MARINARA SAUCE,
  PAGE 288

6 TABLESPOONS GRATED ROMANO
  CHEESE

1½ CUPS SHREDDED MOZZARELLA
  (SHREDDED ON THE LARGE HOLES OF
  A GRATER)

TO COOK THE NOODLES

1. In a large pot of lightly salted boiling water set over high heat, cook the lasagne noodles for 10 to 12 minutes or until they are tender. Stir the noodles once or twice during cooking to prevent sticking. Taste the noodles to make sure that they are done; they should not be hard in the center. Drain and rinse the noodles under cool running water. While they are still in the colander, gently toss the noodles with 1 tablespoon of the olive oil. Place the noodles on a platter. The olive oil will keep them from sticking together.

TO MAKE THE MEAT SAUCE

1. Heat a large saucepan on medium heat for about 2 minutes. Place 2 tablespoons of olive oil in the pan for about 1 minute, then add the onions and garlic. Cook them over low heat for about 4 minutes or until the onions soften. Take care not to let the garlic burn. Add the carrots and celery and cook, stirring, for about 4 minutes longer.

2. Raise the heat to high, add the beef and pork, and cook for about 10 minutes, stirring to break up the meat and encourage even cooking, until the meat is browned without a trace of pink.

3. Add the wine, a ¼ teaspoon of the salt, and a sprinkling of pepper. Reduce the heat to medium and cook the sauce for about 5 minutes or until the wine nearly evaporates.

4. Add the tomatoes, rosemary, oregano, parsley, basil, and bay leaves, reduce the heat to medium-low, and stir for about 30 seconds. Add the broth and the remaining teaspoon of salt, raise the heat again to high, and bring the sauce to a

Continued

boil. Reduce the heat to medium-high so that the tomatoes and broth simmer and cook for about 30 minutes, adjusting the heat up or down to maintain the simmer, until the sauce reduces slightly and thickens a little. Set it aside to cool, remove and discard the bay leaves, and then refrigerate the sauce for at least 2 hours. The meat sauce cannot be hot when you assemble the lasagne. This can be done up to 3 days in advance, with the meat sauce cooled and refrigerated.

TO MAKE THE RICOTTA FILLING

1. In a bowl, mix together the ricotta, eggs, parsley, salt and pepper. Set the filling aside or refrigerate it until you are ready to use it.

TO ASSEMBLE THE LASAGNE

1. Preheat the oven to 400°F.

2. Spread about 1 cup of marinara sauce in the bottom of an 8-by-11-inch baking pan. Place 4 lasagne noodles over the sauce across the width of the pan so that they overlap the sides of the pan. Top the noodles with 2½ to 3 cups of the meat sauce and with the back of a spoon, spread the sauce over the noodles. Sprinkle it with 1 tablespoon of grated cheese.

3. Place 3 noodles down the length of the pan so that they overlap each other slightly. Spread about 2 cups of the ricotta filling over the noodles, making sure the filling reaches the corners of the pan. Sprinkle about ¾ cup of the shredded mozzarella over the cheese filling and top it with another tablespoon of grated cheese.

4. Place 4 more noodles across the width of the pan, but cut the ends so that the noodles fit snugly in the pan. Top the noodles with 2½ to 3 cups of the meat sauce and, with the back of a spoon, spread the sauce over the noodles. Sprinkle it with 1 tablespoon of grated cheese.

5. Place 3 more noodles down the length of the pan so that they overlap each other slightly. Spread about 2 cups of the ricotta filling over the noodles, making sure the filling reaches the corners of the pan. Sprinkle about ¾ cup of the shredded mozzarella over the cheese filling and top it with another tablespoon of grated cheese.

6. Fold the noodles overlapping the sides of the pan up and over the top of the lasagne. Place 2 to 3 more noodles on top of these and then cover the entire

lasagne with 2 cups of marinara sauce, spreading it evenly over the top of the casserole. Sprinkle with the remaining grated cheese.

7. Bake the lasagne, uncovered, for about 1 hour or until heated through and the sauce is bubbling. The interior temperature should be 150°F, if you want to check it with an instant-read thermometer. Let the lasagne rest at room temperature for 1 to 1½ hours to give it time to settle and make it easy to slice. Serve the lasagne with the remaining marinara sauce at the table.

RAGU PASTA

From the five boroughs of New York to the North End of Boston and the hills of San Francisco, Italian Americans hold this dish dear. It's Michael Ronis's number-one favorite because he feels it captures the true essence of Carmine's, with its bold flavors and gutsy attitude. It's the three meats and their individual sauces that infuse this ragu with such special goodness. While this is not a pasta to make in a flash, it is easy to assemble once you have the sauces prepared.

Serves 4 to 6

3 TO 4 CARMINE'S MEATBALLS WITH 2 CUPS SAUCE, PAGE 298

3 TO 4 LINKS CARMINE'S SAUSAGE FOR RAGU WITH 1 CUP SAUCE, PAGE 301

2 BRACIOLE WITH 1 CUP SAUCE, PAGE 292, CUT INTO 1-INCH-THICK SLICES

12 OUNCES DRIED MEZZI RIGATONI OR PASTA SHELLS

¾ CUP GRATED ROMANO CHEESE

1. In a large saucepan, mix together the meatballs, sausages, and braciole and their sauces. If there is not enough sauce to cover the meat, add more until there is. Cover the pan, bring the sauce to a simmer over medium heat, and cook the meats for about 30 minutes or until they are heated through. Adjust the heat up or down to maintain a simmer.

2. Meanwhile, in a large pot filled with boiling salted water, cook the pasta for 7 to 8 minutes or until it is al dente. The cooking time will vary depending on the type of pasta.

3. Drain the pasta and transfer it to a shallow bowl or platter.

4. Increase the heat and bring the sauce to a boil. Using a slotted spoon, remove the meats from the sauce and place them on top of the pasta. Keeping a high heat under the sauce, stir in ¼ cup of the grated cheese. Ladle the sauce over the pasta and meat. Serve the dish with the remaining grated cheese on the side.

FRESH FETTUCCINE WITH WILD MUSHROOM SAUCE

When James Yacyshyn, our beverage director, was the chef at the 91st Street Carmine's, he developed this ethereal fettuccine with a heady mixture of forest mushrooms. It's probably the most sophisticated dish we serve, and our customers can't get enough of it. Pasta and mushrooms are a beloved flavor combination, and this dish exploits it to the fullest. We use the same sauce over roast loin of veal and have served it spooned over roast chicken, too. It's always on our menu.

Serves 2 to 4

¼ OUNCE DRIED PORCINI MUSHROOMS

1½ CUPS WATER

1 POUND MIXED FRESH MUSHROOMS, SUCH AS CREMINI, SHIITAKE, PORTOBELLO, AND OYSTER MUSHROOMS

2½ CUPS CHICKEN STOCK, PAGE 306

1 BAY LEAF

2 SPRIGS FRESH THYME

½ CUP OLIVE OIL

1 CLOVE GARLIC, PEELED AND SLICED

8 FRESH BASIL LEAVES, SLICED

2 TABLESPOONS CHOPPED FLAT-LEAF PARSLEY

1 TEASPOON CHOPPED FRESH OREGANO

SALT AND FRESHLY GROUND BLACK PEPPER

1 CUP DRAINED AND CHOPPED CANNED PLUM TOMATOES

8 OUNCES FRESH SPINACH FETTUCCINE OR A SIMILAR PASTA

2 TABLESPOONS UNSALTED BUTTER, CUT INTO SMALL PIECES

¾ CUP GRATED ROMANO CHEESE

2 TABLESPOONS WHITE TRUFFLE OIL, OPTIONAL

1. In a small bowl, cover the dried porcini mushrooms with about 1 cup of cool water and set them aside to soak for at least 20 minutes.

2. Wipe the fresh mushrooms clean and remove and reserve the stems. Slice the mushrooms about ⅛-inch-thick and set them aside.

3. Using a slotted spoon, carefully lift the porcinis from the water, making sure any grit stays in the bowl. Empty the water and clean the bowl. If there is any grit on the porcinis, wipe them clean with a soft cloth. Return the mushrooms to the

bowl and cover them with about ½ cup of water. Let them soak for about 10 minutes.

4. Lift the porcinis from the water and gently squeeze them dry over the bowl. Chop them coarsely and set them aside. Strain the soaking water and reserve it. You should have a little less than ½ cup of soaking water.

5. In a saucepan, bring the chicken broth, reserved mushroom stems, bay leaf, and thyme to a simmer over medium heat. Measure half of the chopped porcinis and add them to the pan. Reserve the rest of the porcinis. Simmer the chicken broth for about 15 minutes, adjusting the heat to maintain a simmer.

6. Increase the heat to high and cook the broth briskly for about 5 minutes or until it reduces to about 2 cups. Strain the broth and discard the solids. Set the strained broth aside.

7. Heat a small sauté pan over high heat for about 1 minute and then pour the olive oil into the pan. Let the oil heat for 1 minute and add the sliced garlic. Cook it for 30 to 60 seconds or until it is golden brown. Add the basil, parsley, oregano, reserved porcinis, and fresh mushrooms. Season with salt and pepper to taste. Toss the mushrooms a few times and then cook them, without stirring, for 2 minutes. Move the mushrooms gently in the pan so that they brown. Let them sit for 1 minute without stirring before taking them off the heat.

8. Pour the reserved chicken stock and reserved mushroom liquid into the pan, add the tomatoes, bring the sauce to a boil over high heat, and cook it for 3 minutes. Stir in the mushrooms. Remove the sauce from the heat and set it aside, covered, to keep it warm.

9. Meanwhile, in a large pot of boiling salted water, cook the pasta for 4 to 5 minutes or until it is al dente. The cooking time will vary depending on the type of pasta. Drain the pasta and transfer it to a platter.

10. Add the butter and ¼ cup of the cheese to the pasta and toss it well. Pour half of the mushroom sauce over the pasta and toss them to mix them. Pour the remaining sauce on top of the pasta and drizzle it with truffle oil, if desired. Serve the dish with the remaining ½ cup of cheese on the side.

BAKED STUFFED SHELLS

Just the words "baked stuffed shells" conjure up feelings of cozy well-being. Our version will not let you down. The luscious cheese stuffing, fortified with chicken sausage and fresh herbs, is cradled by the jumbo shells for a perfect union of soft textures and warm flavors. The ultimate comfort food.

Serves 2 to 4; makes 10 to 12 stuffed shells

16 JUMBO SHELLS FOR STUFFING, SEE NOTE, PAGE 136

5 TABLESPOONS OLIVE OIL

½ TEASPOON CHOPPED GARLIC

⅓ CUP CHOPPED CELERY

11 OUNCES CHICKEN SAUSAGE, CASING REMOVED

1 SMALL GREEN BELL PEPPER, SEEDED AND CHOPPED

1 TABLESPOON CHOPPED FLAT-LEAF PARSLEY

1 TABLESPOON CHOPPED FRESH BASIL

SALT AND FRESHLY GROUND BLACK PEPPER

5½ OUNCES FRESH RICOTTA

1 LARGE EGG

1 CUP PLUS 2 TABLESPOONS GRATED ROMANO CHEESE

2½ OUNCES SMOKED MOZZARELLA, CUT INTO SMALL DICE

2½ OUNCES FRESH MOZZARELLA, CUT INTO SMALL DICE

3 CUPS CARMINE'S MARINARA SAUCE, PAGE 288

2 TABLESPOONS UNSALTED BUTTER

1. In a pot of boiling lightly salted water set over high heat, cook the pasta shells for 10 to 12 minutes or until they are tender. Drain them and rinse them under cool running water. (Do not run the water too hard—you could damage a shell.) Let the shells drain in the colander.

2. Transfer the drained shells to a bowl, toss them with a teaspoon of olive oil, and refrigerate them until they are needed.

Continued

3. In a large sauté pan, heat the remaining olive oil over medium-high heat. When the oil is hot, add the garlic and cook it, stirring, for about 20 seconds or until it begins to soften. Add the celery, reduce the heat to medium, and cook the mixture for about 5 minutes or until the celery is tender.

4. Add the chicken sausage and the green peppers and cook them, stirring, for about 10 minutes or until the sausage browns and the peppers become tender. Add the parsley and basil and season the mixture to taste with salt and pepper. Transfer it to a bowl and set it aside for about 15 minutes or until it cools almost to room temperature.

5. In another bowl, mix the ricotta with the egg until it is smooth. Add ½ cup of the grated Romano cheese, the mozzarella, and salt and pepper. Taste the mixture for seasonings. If needed, add more salt and pepper. Refrigerate it for 30 minutes.

6. Preheat the oven to 400°F.

7. Spread about 2 cups of the marinara sauce in the bottom of a shallow casserole.

8. Take the shells and stuffing out of the refrigerator. Using a teaspoon, fill the shells with as much stuffing as you can. Take care not to tear the shells. Place the shells, stuffed side up, on the sauce. Ladle the remaining cup of sauce over the shells. Sprinkle the shells with about 2 tablespoons of the grated Romano cheese and dot them with butter.

9. Cover the casserole with aluminum foil and bake the shells for about 12 minutes. Remove the foil and bake them for 8 to 10 minutes longer or until the sauce is bubbling and the tops of the shells are slightly browned. Serve the shells with the remaining ½ cup of grated cheese on the side.

NOTE: We suggest that you begin with at least 16 jumbo shells as some will inevitably break during stuffing. The amount of stuffing will generously fill 10 shells and very nicely fill 12.

LEFTOVER MAGIC

OUR PORTIONS ARE GENEROUS, WHICH MEANS YOU MIGHT HAVE SOME SURPLUS. FOR EXAMPLE IF YOU HAVE SOME EXTRA MEATBALLS (PAGE 298), WARM A LITTLE OLIVE OIL IN A LARGE SAUCEPAN OVER MEDIUM HEAT AND SAUTÉ A CLOVE OF SLICED GARLIC FOR ABOUT 2 MINUTES OR UNTIL LIGHTLY BROWNED. ADD THE MEATBALLS AND SMASH THEM IN THE OIL. RAISE THE HEAT TO HIGH AND LET THE MEAT BROWN JUST A LITTLE. A LITTLE MARINARA SAUCE (PAGE 288) SPOONED OVER THE MEAT MOISTENS IT AND MAKES THE MEATBALLS THE IDEAL PAIRING FOR SOME COOKED SHELLS. LINGUINI, OR ANY OTHER COOKED—PERHAPS LEFTOVER—PASTA, AS LONG AS THE PASTA IS AL DENTE. STIR THE CONTENTS OF THE PAN TOGETHER AND ALLOW THE MIXTURE TO COOK OVER LOW HEAT, TOSSING TO COAT, BEFORE ADDING A FEW SPOONFULS OF FRESH RICOTTA OR DICED MOZZARELLA TO THE PAN. ONCE THE CHEESE MELTS AND THE DISH IS WARM ALL THE WAY THROUGH, SERVE IT TO YOUR WAITING FAMILY. WHAT A GREAT WAY TO USE LEFTOVERS. OF COURSE, WE DON'T THINK OF THIS AS "REHEATING LEFTOVERS." TO US, IT'S COOKING GREAT FOOD IN A WAY THAT MAKES GOOD SENSE!

4.
FISH AND SEAFOOD
MAIN COURSES

Before Carmine's, I had never seen such a large kitchen, much less one that served over a thousand customers a day.

—CHRIS O'NEIL, CORPORATE SOUS CHEF, CARMINE'S

HALIBUT WITH SEAFOOD RISOTTO ≈ CARMINE'S SOLE FRANCESE ≈ HERB-CRUSTED SALMON ARRABBIATA ≈ BAKED CHILEAN SEA BASS MARICHARA ≈ SALMON PUTTANESCA ≈ HALIBUT CASINO-STYLE ≈ SHRIMP SCAMPI ≈ SHRIMP PARMIGIANA ≈ SHRIMP MARINARA ≈ SHRIMP FRA DIAVOLO ≈ LOBSTER FRA DIAVOLO ≈ MIXED SEAFOOD WITH PASTA

HALIBUT WITH SEAFOOD RISOTTO

Credit goes to Joe Delgado, our chef at 91st Street, for this lovely halibut recipe. We serve a different fish daily, and when this shows up on the menu, we tend to sell out. The risotto is key—as, of course, is fresh halibut—and like all risotto, this one demands time and attention to achieve its creamy texture. There's just no other way to make it, and the final dish is superb.

Serves 2 to 4

RISOTTO

3½ CUPS CHICKEN STOCK, PAGE 306

2 TABLESPOONS UNSALTED BUTTER

2 TABLESPOONS FINELY CHOPPED SHALLOTS

1 CUP MEDIUM-GRAIN ITALIAN RICE, SUCH AS ARBORIO, CARNAROLI, OR VIALONE NANO

¼ CUP DRY WHITE WINE

½ TEASPOON CHOPPED FRESH OREGANO

½ TEASPOON CHOPPED FRESH ROSEMARY

SALT AND FRESHLY GROUND BLACK PEPPER

HALIBUT

¼ CUP ALL-PURPOSE FLOUR

ONE 10-OUNCE SKINLESS HALIBUT FILLET

5 TO 6 JUMBO SCALLOPS

12 LARGE SHRIMP, PEELED AND DEVEINED

SALT AND FRESHLY GROUND BLACK PEPPER

½ CUP VEGETABLE OIL

8 TABLESPOONS UNSALTED BUTTER

3 TABLESPOONS FINELY CHOPPED SHALLOTS

¼ CUP WHITE WINE

2 CUPS BOTTLED CLAM JUICE

¼ CUP CHOPPED FRESH PLUM TOMATOES

8 FRESH BASIL LEAVES, SLICED

2 TABLESPOONS CHOPPED FLAT-LEAF PARSLEY

JUICE OF 2 LEMONS

SALT AND FRESHLY GROUND BLACK PEPPER

1 BUNCH CHOPPED CHIVES, FOR GARNISH

TO MAKE THE RISOTTO

1. In a saucepan, bring 2½ cups of the chicken stock to a simmer over medium heat. Reduce the heat and keep it at a low simmer.

2. Set a large saucepan over medium heat. When it is very hot, melt 2 tablespoons of the butter in the pan. Add the shallots and cook them, stirring, for 3 to 4 minutes or until they are lightly browned and tender. Add the rice and stir it to coat it with the butter.

3. Add the wine and, stirring constantly, cook the rice for another 1 to 2 minutes or until most of the wine has evaporated.

4. Add the stock, ½ cup at a time, stirring the rice before and after each addition and letting it absorb the stock. Stir in the oregano and rosemary. Season to taste with salt and pepper. When all the stock has been added and absorbed by the rice, remove the pan from the heat. This will take 12 to 15 minutes.

TO PREPARE THE HALIBUT

1. Preheat the oven to 350°F.

2. Spread the flour on a plate. Lightly season the halibut, scallops, and shrimp with salt and pepper. Coat both sides of the halibut and the scallops and shrimp with the flour and shake off any excess.

3. In a large sauté pan, heat the oil over medium heat. When the oil is hot, put the halibut, scallops, and shrimp in the pan and cook them for 2 to 4 minutes until they are lightly browned on one side. Turn them and cook them for 2 to 4 minutes longer or until they are lightly browned on all sides. Transfer the scallops and shrimp to an ovenproof platter and set them aside.

4. Place the halibut in a small baking dish and bake it for about 4 minutes or until it is cooked through. Add the halibut to the platter with the scallops and shrimp.

5. Pour out any oil from the pan and return the pan to the stove. Add 4 tablespoons of the butter to the pan. When it melts, add the shallots and cook them, stirring, for 2 to 3 minutes or until they are lightly browned.

6. Add the wine and cook the mixture for about 1 minute, stirring the bottom of the pan with a wooden spoon to scrape up any browned bits. Add the clam juice,

Continued

tomatoes, basil, and parsley. Raise the heat to high and bring the sauce to a boil. Boil it for about 5 minutes or until the liquid is reduced by half.

7. Reduce the heat to low. Whisk in the remaining 2 tablespoons of butter and the lemon juice and season the sauce to taste with salt and pepper. Remove the sauce from the heat and set it aside.

TO FINISH THE DISH

1. Heat the remaining 1 cup of chicken broth in a medium-sized saucepan over medium heat until it comes to a boil. Add the reserved rice and bring it to a boil over medium-high heat. Reduce the heat and simmer the risotto, stirring occasionally, for about 5 minutes or until the rice is tender. Stir in the remaining 2 tablespoons of butter and season it to taste with salt and pepper.

2. Transfer the halibut, scallops, and shrimp to the oven and heat them for 2 to 3 minutes or until they are heated through.

3. Heat the sauce over medium heat for 3 to 4 minutes or until it is heated through. Do not let the sauce boil or it will separate.

4. Spoon the risotto down the center of a platter. Put the halibut in the center of the platter and surround it with the scallops and shrimp. Pour the sauce over the fish. Sprinkle it with the chopped chives and serve.

CARMINE'S SOLE FRANCESE

Our Sole Francese is a little different from the traditional because we add shrimp, fingerling potatoes, and mushrooms. Plus, our trick of stirring grated cheese into the egg-and-parsley wash coats the fish with just enough extra flavor and texture to make the difference between very good and "Wow!"

Serves 2 to 4

4 TO 5 LARGE FINGERLING POTATOES

8 TO 9 OUNCES MEDIUM-SIZED CREMINI OR OYSTER MUSHROOMS, STEMS TRIMMED BUT LEFT IN PLACE

2 TABLESPOONS OLIVE OIL

SALT AND FRESHLY GROUND BLACK PEPPER

TWO 8- TO 9-OUNCE FILLETS OF SOLE

1 CUP ALL-PURPOSE FLOUR

3 LARGE EGGS

3 TABLESPOONS GRATED ROMANO CHEESE

2 TABLESPOONS FINELY CHOPPED FLAT-LEAF PARSLEY

½ CUP VEGETABLE OIL

½ CUP UNSALTED BUTTER

2 TABLESPOONS FINELY CHOPPED SHALLOTS

¼ CUP DRY WHITE WINE

1½ CUPS CHICKEN STOCK, PAGE 306

JUICE OF 2 LEMONS

¼ CUP SMALL SHRIMP, PEELED, DEVEINED, AND HALVED

1. Preheat the oven to 400°F.

2. In a saucepan, cover the potatoes with enough lightly salted cold water to cover them by about 1 inch. Bring them to a boil over medium-high heat. Reduce the heat and simmer them, partially covered, for about 20 minutes or until they are tender. Drain them, submerge them in cold water, and drain them again. Cut them in half lengthwise. Lay the potato halves, cut side up, in a single layer on a baking sheet and set them aside.

3. In a bowl, toss the mushrooms with the olive oil and season them to taste with salt and pepper. Transfer them to a baking sheet and arrange them in a single layer, leaving space between the mushrooms. Roast them for 15 to 20 minutes or until they are slightly dried and tender. Remove them from the oven and set them aside.

Continued

4. Season the sole with salt and pepper to taste.

5. Spread the flour on a plate. In a shallow bowl, whisk together the eggs, the grated cheese, and 1 tablespoon of the parsley.

6. Coat the sole with flour and shake off any excess. Dip the sole in the egg mixture and let any excess drip off.

7. Meanwhile, in a large sauté pan, heat the oil over medium heat. When the oil is hot, carefully place the fish in the pan, increase the heat to medium-high, and cook it for about 3 minutes or until it is golden brown, gently shaking the pan from time to time. Turn the fish over and cook the other side for about 3 minutes or until the fish is golden brown on both sides and cooked through. Drain the fish on paper towels and then transfer it to an ovenproof platter.

8. Reduce the oven temperature to 250°F.

9. Discard any oil from the sauté pan and wipe it clean with paper towels. Melt 1 teaspoon of the butter in the sauté pan over medium heat. Add the shallots and cook them, stirring occasionally, for 2 to 3 minutes or until they are lightly browned.

10. Add the wine and cook the shallots for 30 seconds. Add the chicken stock, raise the heat to high, and bring it to a boil. Boil it for 3 to 4 minutes or until it is reduced by half. Reduce the heat to low and whisk in the remaining butter, about 1 tablespoon at a time, until it is incorporated. Adjust the heat up or down to maintain a low simmer.

11. Add the lemon juice and shrimp to the sauce and season it to taste with salt and pepper. Simmer it for 2 minutes or until the shrimp are pink and cooked through. Stir in the remaining 1 tablespoon of the parsley.

12. Meanwhile, heat the potatoes, mushrooms, and fish in the oven for about 5 minutes or until they are heated through.

13. Place the fish in the center of a platter. Arrange the potatoes and mushrooms around the fish. Spoon the sauce over the sole and serve.

HERB-CRUSTED SALMON ARRABBIATA

Our executive chef and partner, Glenn Rolnick, came up with this for a springtime private party, and it was a keeper. Arrabbiata means "Arab-style," which translates to "spicy." If you don't like heat, leave out the hot pepper. The sauce also tastes good with veal or chicken, replacing the clam juice with chicken stock. Because it's thinly sliced, the salmon cooks quickly.

Serves 2 to 4

SAUCE

¼ CUP OLIVE OIL

I TEASPOON CHOPPED GARLIC

2 SMALL CUBANO PEPPERS SEEDED, CORED, AND CHOPPED

I SMALL HOT ITALIAN GREEN PEPPER, SEEDED, CORED, AND CHOPPED OR ANOTHER SMALL, HOT PEPPER SUCH AS A JALEPEÑO

½ RED BELL PEPPER, SEEDED, CORED, AND THINLY SLICED

½ YELLOW BELL PEPPER, SEEDED, CORED, AND THINLY SLICED

½ ONION, SLICED

SAUCE (CONT'D)

¼ CUP DRY WHITE WINE

3 SWEET VINEGAR CHERRY PEPPERS, THINLY SLICED

4 CANNED PLUM TOMATOES, DRAINED

1¾ CUPS BOTTLED CLAM JUICE

6 FRESH BASIL LEAVES, SLICED

I TABLESPOON CHOPPED FLAT-LEAF PARSLEY

SALT AND FRESHLY GROUND BLACK PEPPER

½ CUP CARMINE'S MARINARA SAUCE, PAGE 288

HERBED BREAD CRUMBS

I CUP CARMINE'S BREAD CRUMBS, PAGE 283

I SPRIG FRESH THYME LEAVES, CHOPPED

I SPRIG FRESH OREGANO LEAVES, CHOPPED

½ TEASPOON CHOPPED FRESH BASIL

FINELY GRATED ZEST OF ½ LEMON

SALMON

ONE I-POUND 6-OUNCE PIECE CENTER CUT SALMON FILLET, CUT HORIZONTALLY INTO 3 EQUAL PIECES, SKIN REMOVED

SALT AND FRESHLY GROUND BLACK PEPPER

2 TEASPOONS GARLIC BUTTER, SOFTENED, PAGE 286

I TABLESPOON OLIVE OIL

TO MAKE THE SAUCE

1. In a large sauté pan, heat the olive oil over high heat. When the oil is hot, add the garlic and cook it for 10 seconds. Add the cubano peppers, Italian green peppers, red and yellow bell peppers, and onions. Cook them, stirring occasionally, for about 5 minutes or until the peppers start to soften.

2. Add the wine, cook the peppers and onions for 3 minutes, and then add the sweet cherry peppers and any accumulated juice from the cutting board.

3. Add the tomatoes, breaking them up with a wooden spoon. Add the clam juice, basil, and parsley and season the sauce to taste with salt and pepper. Cover the pan, reduce the heat to medium, and cook the sauce for about 15 minutes or until the peppers are tender.

4. Add the marinara sauce, reduce the heat to low, and cook the sauce, uncovered, for about 10 minutes or until the peppers are very tender. The sauce may be prepared up to this point 2 to 3 hours in advance.

TO MAKE THE BREAD CRUMBS

1. In a mixing bowl, stir together all of the ingredients for the bread crumbs. Set aside.

TO MAKE THE SALMON

1. Lightly season both sides of the fish with salt and pepper and spread the garlic butter over the top.

2. Spread the bread crumbs on a shallow plate. Press the buttered side of the salmon into the bread crumbs and use a little pressure to make sure the crumbs adhere.

3. In a large nonstick sauté pan, heat the olive oil over medium-high heat. When the oil is hot, place the salmon, crumbed side down, in the pan and cook it for about 3 minutes or until it is golden brown. Turn the salmon over and cook the other side for about 1 minute.

Continued

TO ASSEMBLE THE DISH

1. Meanwhile, reheat the sauce over medium heat for about 5 minutes or until it is hot.

2. Ladle the sauce onto a platter. Place the salmon crumbed side up on top of the sauce and serve.

HOW TO BUY AND STORE FRESH FISH

FISH HAS TO BE FRESH TO BE GOOD, SO IT IS IMPORTANT TO BUY IT FROM A FISH COUNTER YOU CAN TRUST. THIS PROBABLY WILL BE AT THE LOCAL SUPERMARKET, AND YOU CAN TELL A LOT JUST BY LOOKING. THE FISH SHOULD BE DISPLAYED ON CHOPPED ICE. FILLETS SHOULD LOOK MOIST AND PLUMP, NEVER SLIMY. WHOLE FISH SHOULD HAVE RED HEALTHY-LOOKING GILLS, BRIGHT SCALES, AND CLEAR EYES. THE AREA SURROUND-ING THE FISH COUNTER SHOULD BE CLEAN AND SMELL FRESH—AND THE FISH ITSELF SHOULD NEVER, EVER SMELL "FISHY." IF IT HAS ANY ODOR AT ALL, IT SHOULD SMELL OF THE OCEAN. OTHERWISE, DON'T BUY IT.

BUY THE FISH NEAR THE END OF YOUR SHOPPING TRIP AND REFRIGERATE IT, STILL IN ITS WRAPPER, AS SOON AS YOU GET HOME. IF IT'S AVAILABLE, ASK THE FISH MONGER TO PACK THE FISH ON ICE FOR THE TRIP HOME. PUT IT IN THE COOLEST PART OF THE FRIDGE, WHICH MIGHT BE THE BACK OF THE LOWEST SHELF (PARTICULARLY IF THE FREEZER IS BELOW IT) OR IN A CHILL DRAWER. THE VERY BEST WAY TO REFRIGERATE IT IS TO PUT THE WRAPPED FISH ON A RACK SUSPENDED OVER A SHALLOW BOWL FILLED WITH CRACKED ICE. NEVER STORE THE FISH FOR LONGER THAN 24 HOURS—IF YOU CAN'T EAT IT IN THAT TIME PERIOD, YOU'RE BETTER OFF FREEZING IT FOR ANOTHER DAY.

BAKED CHILEAN SEA BASS MARICHARA

This is a stunning dish, made extra special by the addition of Israeli couscous, which gives the sauce a texture you might not expect. Israeli couscous is larger than other couscous and is quite easy to find in most supermarkets. Chef Luis Javier, the head chef at the 44th Street restaurant, developed this recipe. He likes the heat provided by the hot pepper, but if you want to tame it, scrape out and discard the seeds. Chef Luis makes his recipe with Chilean sea bass, but it works well with halibut or cod, too.

Serves 4

FOUR 5-OUNCE PIECES SKINLESS CHILEAN SEA BASS

SALT AND FRESHLY GROUND BLACK PEPPER

2 TABLESPOONS UNSALTED BUTTER, SOFTENED

¼ CUP ISRAELI COUSCOUS

¼ CUP OLIVE OIL

2 CLOVES GARLIC, PEELED AND SLICED

6 OUNCES SCALLOPS (5 TO 6 SCALLOPS)

6 MUSSELS, RINSED AND SCRUBBED

4 LITTLENECK CLAMS, RINSED AND SCRUBBED

10 TO 12 FRESH BASIL LEAVES, SLICED

2 TABLESPOONS CHOPPED FLAT-LEAF PARSLEY

1 LONG HOT GREEN ITALIAN PEPPER, SEEDED AND CHOPPED

PINCH HOT RED PEPPER FLAKES

¼ CUP DRY WHITE WINE

2 CUPS BOTTLED CLAM JUICE

1 CUP CANNED PLUM TOMATOES, DRAINED AND CRUSHED

Continued

1. Preheat the oven to 400°F.

2. Season the sea bass on both sides with salt and pepper to taste. Transfer it to a broiler-safe baking dish. Spread 1 tablespoon of the butter over the top of the fish. Transfer it to the oven and bake it for about 8 minutes or until it is browned on top and tender and flaky inside. Set the fish aside.

3. In a pot of boiling water, cook the couscous for about 3 minutes or until it is tender. Drain it in a colander. Transfer it to a bowl and set it aside.

4. In a large sauté pan, heat the olive oil over medium-high heat. When the oil is hot, add the garlic and cook it for about 1 minute or until it is golden brown. Take care not to let the garlic burn. Add the scallops, mussels, clams, basil, parsley, hot green peppers, and red pepper flakes. Sauté the mixture, stirring occasionally, for about 4 to 5 minutes. Remove the scallops from the pan and set them aside to prevent overcooking.

5. Add the wine and cook the sauce for 2 minutes or until most of the wine has evaporated. Add the clam juice and tomatoes. Reduce the heat to medium and cover the pan. Cook the sauce for 3 to 4 minutes or until the mussels and clams have opened. With a small knife pry open any that don't open, unless they are firmly and stubbornly closed, in which case, discard them. Season it to taste with salt and pepper.

6. Meanwhile, preheat the broiler.

7. Transfer the fish to the broiler and broil the bottom for about 3 minutes or until it is browned.

8. Add the remaining butter, the reserved scallops, and the couscous to the pan with the clams and mussels and bring it to a simmer over medium-high heat. Stir it and remove it from the heat.

9. Ladle the sauce onto a platter. Place the sea bass on top of the sauce. Scatter the scallops, mussels, and clams around the sea bass and serve.

SALMON PUTTANESCA

You may not think of puttanesca sauce over salmon, but it's a great combination. Puttanesca goes well with pasta, to be sure, and it's also good over halibut, snapper, or bass, but we love it with salmon. The sauce can be made in advance. In fact, it just gets better if it sits for at least 20 minutes before serving to give the olives, capers, and anchovies time to mingle so that their flavors bloom.

Serves 2 to 4

3 TABLESPOONS OLIVE OIL

2 CLOVES GARLIC, PEELED AND SLICED

3 ANCHOVY FILLETS

I TABLESPOON CHOPPED FLAT-LEAF PARSLEY

I TABLESPOON CHOPPED FRESH BASIL

PINCH OF HOT RED PEPPER FLAKES

2 TABLESPOONS DRY WHITE WINE

2 CUPS CANNED PLUM TOMATOES, COARSELY CHOPPED

I CUP BOTTLED CLAM JUICE

IO GAETA OLIVES, PITTED AND HALVED

6 KALAMATA OLIVES, PITTED AND QUARTERED

2 TABLESPOONS CAPERS, RINSED AND DRAINED

TWO IO-OUNCE SKINLESS SALMON FILLETS

SALT AND FRESHLY GROUND BLACK PEPPER

1. In a medium-sized saucepan, heat 2 tablespoons of the olive oil over medium-high heat. When the oil is hot, add the garlic and sauté it for 30 to 60 seconds or until it is golden brown. Add the anchovies, parsley, basil, and red pepper flakes. Sauté the mixture, stirring occasionally, for about 3 minutes or until the anchovies have dissolved.

2. Add the wine, increase the heat to high, and bring it to a boil. Boil it for 2 to 3 minutes or until the wine has evaporated. Add the tomatoes, clam juice, olives,

Continued

and capers and return it to a boil. Reduce the heat and simmer it for 3 minutes, or until the sauce is slightly reduced. Remove it from the heat and set it aside for at least 10 or 15 minutes.

3. Season the salmon with salt and pepper to taste.

4. In a large sauté pan over medium-high heat, heat the remaining tablespoon of olive oil. When the oil is hot, add the salmon and cook it for 3 minutes. Carefully turn the salmon over, reduce the heat to medium, and cook the other side for 3 minutes or until the salmon is slightly pink in the center.

5. Bring the sauce to a boil. Transfer the salmon to a large platter. Spoon the sauce over the salmon and serve.

WHY WE LOVE ANCHOVIES

THESE TINY FISH ARE ABUNDANT IN THE MEDITERRANEAN AND ALONG SOUTHERN EUROPE'S ATLANTIC COASTLINES, WHICH EXPLAINS THEIR UBIQUITOUS PRESENCE IN THE COOKING OF SPAIN, PORTUGAL, SOUTHERN FRANCE, GREECE, AND, OF COURSE, ITALY. YOU CAN EVEN FIND THEM GRILLED AND SERVED WHOLE IN SOME PARTS OF EUROPE. RARELY ARE THEY SOLD FRESH IN THE UNITED STATES. HERE, ANCHOVIES ARE MOST READILY AVAILABLE AS FILLETS PACKED IN TWO-OUNCE TINS OR SMALL GLASS JARS AND COVERED WITH OLIVE OIL. IN EUROPE AND INCREASINGLY IN THIS COUNTRY, YOU CAN BUY THEM SALTED, WITHOUT OIL.

NOT SURPRISINGLY, WE PREFER ANCHOVIES IMPORTED FROM ITALY AND PACKED IN SMALL JARS. THEY TEND TO BE MEATIER, AND WE LIKE THE QUALITY OF THE OLIVE OIL USED TO MARINATE THEM. WHEN YOU COOK THEM WITH OTHER FOOD, THEY PRETTY MUCH DISSOLVE AND LEAVE BEHIND A LOVELY SALTY FLAVOR THAT CAN TEASE AND DELIGHT THE TASTE BUDS OF THE MOST AVOWED ANCHOVY "HATER."

HALIBUT CASINO-STYLE

Clams Casino may be a great favorite, but Halibut Casino elevates the concept to a new level. The meaty fish works beautifully with the clams and bacon for a main course that will seduce even the most hesitant fish eater, and the seasoned butter just makes everything taste rich, smooth, and oh-so-good. This preparation is also superb with salmon.

Serves 2 to 4

6 SLICES OF BACON

FOUR 5-OUNCE PIECES HALIBUT FILLET

SALT AND FRESHLY GROUND BLACK PEPPER

2 TABLESPOONS OLIVE OIL

5 TABLESPOONS CASINO BUTTER, PAGE 285

6 LITTLENECK CLAMS

¾ CUP BOTTLED CLAM JUICE

½ CUP CARMINE'S BREAD CRUMBS, PAGE 283

1½ TEASPOONS CHOPPED FLAT-LEAF PARSLEY

1. Preheat the broiler.

2. Place the bacon in a broiling pan and broil it for 3 to 4 minutes, turning the bacon once, or until it is just crispy. (Cooking the bacon under a broiler makes it easier to keep the bacon from curling.) Drain it on paper towels and set it aside.

3. Preheat the oven to 450°F.

4. Season the halibut on both sides with salt and pepper.

5. Heat a large ovenproof sauté pan over low heat for 1 minute. Add the olive oil, and when the oil is hot, add the halibut and cook it for 3 minutes. Turn it and cook it for about 2 minutes longer. Top the halibut with 2 tablespoons of the casino butter. Add the clams and the clam juice. Transfer the pan to the oven and cook the halibut for about 3 minutes. With a spatula, transfer the halibut to a platter and set it aside, leaving the clams and juices in the pan.

Continued

6. Return the clams to the oven and roast them for 5 to 7 minutes or until they open. Transfer the clams to the platter with the halibut. Pry the clams wide open and sprinkle a teaspoon of the bread crumbs into each one. Place a teaspoon of the casino butter on top of each halibut fillet, spread it over the fish, and top it with a sprinkling of the bread crumbs, pressing so that they adhere to the fish. The goal is to coat the fish completely but not too heavily.

7. If there are any remaining bread crumbs, place them in the sauté pan that the fish was cooked in. Add the parsley to the sauté pan and bring the liquid remaining in it to a boil. Cook the sauce for 2 to 3 minutes until blended with the parsley and then set it aside.

8. Put the halibut and clams in a shallow ovenproof dish and roast them for about 2 minutes, just until they are hot and the halibut is cooked all the way through. Remove them from the oven and put the bacon in the oven for 2 to 3 minutes to get hot and crispy. Allow it to cool slightly and break it into small pieces.

9. Turn on the broiler and broil the halibut and clams for 1 minute or less, just until they are browned.

10. Ladle the sauce onto a large platter and arrange the halibut in the center. Place the clams around the halibut, scatter the bacon over both, and serve immediately.

SHRIMP SCAMPI

Our scampi is a surefire hit with our guests, who order it all year long when they come to the restaurant or plan private parties. This time-honored preparation can be served as it is here, or double the sauce ingredients and spoon it over pasta. When scampi is made with our garlic butter and bread crumbs, it's fresh and rich and perfect.

Serves 2

1 TEASPOON CHOPPED GARLIC

16 LARGE SHRIMP, PEELED AND DEVEINED

4 TEASPOONS GARLIC BUTTER, SOFTENED, PAGE 286

¾ CUP BOTTLED CLAM JUICE

½ CUP CARMINE'S BREAD CRUMBS, PAGE 283

2 TABLESPOONS OLIVE OIL

1 LEMON, HALVED, FOR GARNISH

1. Preheat the oven to 425°F.

2. Scatter the garlic over the bottom of an ovenproof baking dish. Place the shrimp on top of the garlic and spread ½ teaspoon of the garlic butter over each shrimp. Pour the clam juice over the shrimp. Coat each one with 1 tablespoon of the bread crumbs, pressing the bread crumbs into the shrimp. Drizzle the shrimp with the olive oil.

3. Bake the shrimp for 12 to 15 minutes or until they are golden brown and crispy. Serve them right from the baking dish or transfer them to a platter. Serve the shrimp garnished with the lemon halves.

SHRIMP PARMIGIANA

It's long been considered a no-no to pair seafood with cheese, but this is the exception that might just prove the rule. It is one of our best-loved dishes, and even food critics who turn their noses up at shrimp and cheese revel in the preparation. Spoon it over a crusty hero roll for a sandwich to die for! You can also double the recipe to serve 4.

Serves 2

½ CUP ALL-PURPOSE FLOUR

2 LARGE EGGS

2½ CUPS CARMINE'S BREAD CRUMBS, PAGE 283

16 LARGE SHRIMP, PEELED AND DEVEINED

½ CUP VEGETABLE OIL

FOUR ⅛-INCH-THICK SLICES FRESH MOZZARELLA

2 TABLESPOONS GRATED ROMANO CHEESE

2 CUPS CARMINE'S MARINARA SAUCE, PAGE 288

1. Preheat the broiler.

2. Spread the flour on a large plate. Whisk the eggs in a shallow bowl. Spread the bread crumbs out on a flat pan.

3. Coat the shrimp with flour and shake off any excess. Dip the shrimp, one at a time, in the egg mixture and let any excess drip off. Coat the shrimp with bread crumbs, pressing the crumbs onto the shrimp.

4. In a large sauté pan, heat the oil over medium heat. When the oil is hot, add the shrimp and cook them for about 3 minutes or until they are lightly browned. Turn them over and cook the other side for about 3 minutes or until the shrimp are golden brown. Drain them on paper towels.

5. Transfer the shrimp to a small ovenproof dish.

6. Cut the mozzarella slices in half. Top each shrimp with a slice of mozzarella and sprinkle it with the grated cheese. Broil the shrimp for 2 to 3 minutes or until the cheese is melted.

7. Meanwhile, in a saucepan, heat the marinara sauce over medium-high heat for about 5 minutes or until it is very hot. Spoon the sauce onto a platter, top it with the shrimp, and serve.

SHRIMP MARINARA

Our marinara sauce makes this perennial favorite so good. The white wine provides subtle flavor to underscore the bold flavor of the clam juice. We use white Mexican shrimp, and you should start with the best shrimp you can find, taking care not to overcook them.

Serves 2

6 TABLESPOONS OLIVE OIL

6 CLOVES GARLIC, PEELED AND SLICED

16 LARGE SHRIMP, PEELED AND DEVEINED

10 FRESH OREGANO LEAVES

5 BASIL LEAVES, SLICED

1 BAY LEAF

1 TEASPOON CHOPPED FLAT-LEAF PARSLEY

¼ CUP DRY WHITE WINE

1 GENEROUS CUP DRAINED, CANNED PLUM TOMATOES

½ CUP BOTTLED CLAM JUICE

½ CUP CARMINE'S MARINARA SAUCE, PAGE 288

SALT AND FRESHLY GROUND BLACK PEPPER

1. In a large sauté pan, heat the olive oil over medium heat. When the oil is hot, add the garlic and cook it, stirring, for about 30 seconds. Reduce the heat and slowly cook the garlic for about 2 minutes or until it is browned. Take care not to let the garlic burn. Remove it from the heat.

2. In a shallow bowl or on a plate, mix together the shrimp, oregano, basil, bay leaf, and parsley. Transfer the shrimp to the pan with the garlic mixture and stir-fry them over medium-high heat for 2 to 3 minutes. With a slotted spoon, lift the shrimp from the pan and set them aside.

3. Add the wine and swirl it in the pan for about 30 seconds. Add the tomatoes, clam juice, and marinara sauce and cook the sauce for about 3 minutes, crushing the tomatoes lightly with the back of a spoon, or until some of the liquid evaporates. Season it to taste with salt and pepper.

4. Return the shrimp to the sauce and cook them on medium heat for 2 to 3 minutes or until the shrimp turn pink and are just cooked through.

5. Spoon the shrimp and sauce into bowls or serve them over pasta.

SHRIMP FRA DIAVOLO

If you like your marinara sauce and seafood with a little bite, you will love Fra Diavolos. We use a good half teaspoon of pepper flakes—actually, in the restaurant we use an espresso spoonful—but you can cut the amount a little if you like less heat. The best advice we can give you is to cook the seafood only until it is done. The moment the shrimp is pink and opaque throughout, remove them from the heat so they stop cooking. Overcooked shrimp can be tough and rubbery. Double this recipe to serve 4, if you want.

Serves 2

¼ CUP OLIVE OIL

16 LARGE SHRIMP, PEELED AND DEVEINED

SALT AND FRESHLY GROUND BLACK PEPPER

1 TABLESPOON COARSELY CHOPPED GARLIC

5 BASIL LEAVES, SLICED

1 TABLESPOON CHOPPED FRESH OREGANO

1 TEASPOON CHOPPED FLAT-LEAF PARSLEY

¼ CUP DRY WHITE WINE

½ CUP BOTTLED CLAM JUICE

½ TEASPOON HOT RED PEPPER FLAKES, OR MORE TO TASTE

2 CUPS CARMINE'S MARINARA SAUCE, PAGE 288

1. In a large sauté pan, heat the olive oil over medium-high heat. When the oil is hot, add the shrimp and salt and pepper to taste. Sauté the shrimp for about 2 minutes or until they turn pink. Turn them over and cook them for about 2 minutes or until they are just cooked through. With a slotted spoon, lift the shrimp from the pan and set them aside.

2. Add the garlic to the pan and cook it, stirring, for about 30 seconds. Reduce the heat and cook it for about 2 minutes or until it is browned. Take care not to let the garlic burn.

3. Add the basil, oregano, and parsley and cook the mixture, stirring, for 30 seconds. Add the wine and raise the heat to high. Cook the sauce for 1 to 2 minutes or until most of the wine has evaporated.

4. Add the clam juice and the red pepper flakes and cook the sauce for 1 minute. Stir in the marinara sauce and season it with salt, pepper, and more red pepper flakes, if desired, to taste.

5. Return the shrimp to the pan and cook them for about 3 minutes or until they are just heated through. Be careful not to overcook the shrimp. Transfer them to a platter and serve.

LOBSTER FRA DIAVOLO

When you want to splurge, try our spectacular Fra Diavolo made with lobster, clams, shrimp, and mussels. As Michael Honea, our assistant director of operations, says, it's a veritable feast of seafood and a luxurious dish. If you are lucky the lobsters will come from Maine, where the best in the country are caught in the deep, cold waters off the rocky coast.

Serves 4

2 LIVE 2-POUND LOBSTERS

½ CUP OLIVE OIL

¼ CUP COARSELY CHOPPED GARLIC

10 FRESH BASIL LEAVES, SLICED

3 TABLESPOONS CHOPPED FRESH OREGANO

2 TABLESPOONS CHOPPED FLAT-LEAF PARSLEY

2 BAY LEAVES

ABOUT 1 TEASPOON HOT RED PEPPER FLAKES, OR LESS TO TASTE

SALT AND FRESHLY GROUND BLACK PEPPER

6 LITTLENECK CLAMS, RINSED AND SCRUBBED

½ CUP BOTTLED CLAM JUICE

3 CUPS CARMINE'S MARINARA SAUCE, PAGE 288

16 OUNCES CANNED PLUM TOMATOES, DRAINED AND COARSELY CHOPPED

16 LARGE SHRIMP, PEELED AND DEVEINED

6 MUSSELS, RINSED AND SCRUBBED

18 OUNCES DRIED RIGATONI, SPAGHETTI, OR PENNE

1. Bring a large pot half filled with water to a boil over high heat. Drop the lobsters, head first, into the pot, cover the pot, and cook the lobsters for about 5 minutes or until they are bright red. (The lobsters will not be fully cooked at this point but will finish cooking in step 5.) Remove the pot from the heat and submerge the lobsters in a bowl of ice water for about 10 minutes to cool.

Continued

2. Cut the tail off each lobster and cut it crosswise into 3 pieces. Remove the claws and crack them slightly, using the back of a large knife or a claw cracker. Cut the body of the lobster in half lengthwise and then cut the halves into 2 pieces so that you have 4 pieces of the body. Put all the lobster pieces in a large bowl.

3. In a large pot, heat the olive oil over medium-high heat. When the oil is hot, add the garlic, reduce the heat, and sauté it, stirring occasionally, for about 1 minute or until it is golden brown. Take care not to let the garlic burn. Add the basil, the oregano, the parsley, the bay leaves, and the red pepper flakes and cook the mixture for about 2 minutes, stirring occasionally.

4. Add the lobster pieces and season the mixture to taste with salt and pepper. Increase the heat to high and stir it, using a long-handled spoon, until all the lobster pieces are coated with oil. Stir in the clams.

5. Cover the pot and cook the mixture for 3 to 4 minutes. Stir it and continue to cook it, covered, for 2 to 3 minutes. Add the clam juice, bring it to a boil, and boil it, uncovered, for 2 to 3 minutes.

6. Stir in the marinara sauce and tomatoes. Cook the sauce for 3 minutes. Reduce the heat and simmer it, uncovered, for 6 minutes. Add the shrimp and mussels. Raise the heat to high, stir the sauce well, and cook it for 3 minutes or until the clams and mussels have opened. With a small knife pry open any that don't open, unless they are firmly and stubbornly closed, in which case discard them.

7. Meanwhile, in a large pot filled with boiling salted water, cook the pasta for 7 to 8 minutes or until it is al dente. The cooking time will vary depending on the type of pasta.

8. Drain the pasta and transfer it to a large bowl. Spoon the sauce over the pasta and mix them. Serve the dish immediately. Provide lobster crackers to crack the shells and small forks for the meat, if desired.

MIXED SEAFOOD WITH PASTA

The Carmine's way is to go for the most full-bodied, robust food we can cook—our rendering of frutti di mare relies on the flavors of clams, mussels, and lobster to boost it into the stratosphere. Cooking them in their shells in the oil pulls the flavor from them and infuses the dish with an amazing richness. The taste is a little hard to pin down, but the flavors make this a thrilling dish. One more thing: Don't neglect to season this with a little salt. It pulls the flavors together at the end.

Serves 4

8 OUNCES CALAMARI

4 LITTLENECK CLAMS, RINSED AND SCRUBBED

4 MUSSELS, RINSED AND SCRUBBED

I LIVE 1½-POUND LOBSTER

¾ CUP OLIVE OIL

6 CLOVES GARLIC, PEELED AND SLICED

12 TO 14 FRESH BASIL LEAVES, SLICED

4 TEASPOONS CHOPPED FLAT-LEAF PARSLEY

12 OUNCES DRIED RIGATONI, SPAGHETTI, OR PENNE

16 OUNCES CANNED PLUM TOMATOES, DRAINED

¾ CUP BOTTLED CLAM JUICE

½ CUP CARMINE'S MARINARA SAUCE, PAGE 288

SALT AND FRESHLY GROUND PEPPER

16 LARGE SHRIMP, PEELED AND DEVEINED

1. Clean the calamari by rinsing them well under cool running water. Break off and discard any extralong tentacles. Set the calamari aside.

2. In a large pot of lightly salted boiling water, cook the lobster for about 5 minutes or until the lobster shell is bright red. (The lobster will not be completely cooked at this point but will finish cooking in step 4.) Lift the lobster from the water with tongs and put it in a bowl of ice water for about 10 minutes to cool.

Continued

When it is cool enough to handle, remove the claws and crack them slightly, using the back of a large knife or claw cracker. Cut the body of the lobster in half lengthwise, and cut the tail into 3 pieces crosswise. Leave the lobster in the shells.

3. In a large sauté pan, heat the olive oil over medium-high heat. When the oil is hot, add the garlic, reduce the heat, and sauté it for about 1 minute or until it is golden brown. Take care not to let the garlic burn. Cook the mixture, stirring, for 2 to 3 minutes until it is aromatic and the garlic has softened.

4. Add a little more than half of the basil and 2 teaspoons of the parsley. Stir the seasonings to mix them well and add the lobster, calamari, clams, and mussels. Increase the heat to high, stir the seafood well, and cook it for about 3 minutes.

5. Meanwhile, in a large pot filled with boiling salted water, cook the pasta for 7 to 8 minutes or until it is al dente. The cooking time will vary depending on the type of pasta.

6. Add the tomatoes, clam juice, and marinara sauce to the sauté pan with the seafood and bring it to a simmer. Season it to taste with salt and pepper. Reduce the heat to medium and simmer it, stirring, for about 4 minutes, when the clams and mussels will be open and cooked. With a small knife, pry open any that don't open unless they are firmly and stubbornly closed, in which case discard them. The lobster will be bright red and cooked through. The calamari will be tender.

7. Add the shrimp and simmer the mixture for about 3 minutes or until they are cooked through and pink. Add a little more clam juice or tomato juice to thin the sauce, if needed. Stir in the remaining basil and parsley and season the sauce to taste with salt and pepper.

8. Drain the pasta and transfer it to a large bowl. Spoon the sauce and seafood over the pasta and serve immediately.

5.
MEAT AND POULTRY
MAIN COURSES

The huge portions and family-style dining bring me back to my youth when I went to my grandmother's house in Greenpoint, Brooklyn, on Sunday afternoons. We'd get there right after Mass, and the food would start flowing: meatballs, pasta, chicken, sausage. It never seemed to end!

—CARL DELPONTE, GENERAL MANAGER AND ASSOCIATE PARTNER

PORTERHOUSE STEAK CONTADINA ∾ PORTERHOUSE STEAK WITH PEPPERS AND ONIONS OR PIZZAIOLA ∾ BEEF CUTLET MILANESE WITH CAPER, ROASTED PEPPER, AND TOMATO BUTTER SAUCE ∾ SHORT RIBS WITH CABBAGE AND POTATOES ∾ STUFFED PORK FILLET WITH BROCCOLI RABE FONTINA AND PINE NUTS WITH CREAMY POLENTA ∾ PORK CHOPS WITH SWEET AND HOT VINEGAR PEPPERS ∾ GRILLED SAUSAGE RING WITH PARSLEY AND PROVOLONE OVER PEPPERONATA ∾ SAUSAGE, CLAMS, AND POTATOES ∾ SLOW-ROASTED LAMB SHOULDER CHOPS WITH VEGETABLE ORZO RISOTTO ∾ CHICKEN OR VEAL MARSALA ∾ CHICKEN OR VEAL PARMIGIANA ∾ CHICKEN OR VEAL SALTIMBOCCA ∾ CHICKEN ALLA ROMANA ∾ CHICKEN SCARPARIELLO ∾ CHICKEN CONTADINA ∾ CHICKEN WITH LEMON BUTTER ∾ STUFFED BRAISED CHICKEN LEGS AND FONTINA POTATO CROQUETTES ∾ CRISPY ROMANO-CRUSTED CHICKEN BREAST WITH ARUGULA, RICOTTA SALATA, AND SMOKED MOZZARELLA SALAD

PORTERHOUSE STEAK CONTADINA

Before we rave about how impressive this big, over-the-top steak and sausage dish is, we must confess to our "secret" ingredient: garlic powder. The garlic powder caramelizes on the meat as it cooks and is responsible for the "Wow!" factor of our Contadina. It was our founder, Artie, who suggested serving a Steak Contadina, guessing it would be even more impressive than the Chicken Contadina already on the menu. As usual, he was right.

Serves 4

4 SWEET ITALIAN SAUSAGE LINKS (ABOUT I POUND TOTAL)

3 TABLESPOONS PLUS I TEASPOON OLIVE OIL

2 LARGE RUSSET POTATOES, PEELED AND CUT INTO ¼-INCH-THICK SLICES, PATTED DRY

SALT AND FRESHLY GROUND BLACK PEPPER

15 CLOVES GARLIC (ABOUT 2 HEADS), PEELED AND LEFT WHOLE

2 LARGE SPANISH ONIONS, EACH PEELED AND CUT INTO 8 THICK SLICES

2 RED BELL PEPPERS, SEEDED, CORED, AND CUT INTO 6 EQUAL PIECES

2 GREEN BELL PEPPERS, SEEDED, CORED, AND CUT INTO 6 EQUAL PIECES

36- TO 38-OUNCE PORTERHOUSE STEAK, ABOUT 2 INCHES THICK, AT ROOM TEMPERATURE

2 TEASPOONS GARLIC POWDER

I TEASPOON DRIED OREGANO

¼ CUP SWEET PEPPER VINEGAR (FROM A JAR OF SWEET VINEGAR RED PEPPERS) OR WHITE WINE VINEGAR

8 FRESH BASIL LEAVES, SLICED

2 TABLESPOONS CHOPPED FLAT-LEAF PARSLEY

1. Preheat the oven to 400°F.

2. Separate the sausage links if they are tied together. Rub 1 teaspoon of the olive oil over the links and place them in a small roasting pan. Roast them for 12 to 15 minutes or until they are cooked through. Remove them from the oven and set them aside. Leave the oven on.

3. Place the dried potato slices in a shallow roasting pan. Drizzle them with 1 tablespoon of the olive oil and sprinkle them with about ½ teaspoon of salt and ½

Continued

teaspoon of pepper. Rub the oil over the potatoes and turn them to coat them. Bake them for 30 to 35 minutes until they are tender and browned. Set them aside.

4. In a medium sauté pan, heat 2 tablespoons of the olive oil over medium heat. Add the garlic cloves and slowly brown them for 5 to 6 minutes. Make sure the oil does not get too hot; the garlic should cook slowly.

5. Add the onion slices and peppers and season them to taste with salt and pepper. Cook them over medium heat for 15 to 20 minutes, stirring often, until they are lightly browned and tender. Transfer them to a colander and let them drain for about 5 minutes.

6. Prepare a charcoal or gas grill so that the coals or heating elements are medium-hot; first, lightly spray the grilling rack with vegetable oil spray to prevent sticking. Or preheat the broiler.

7. Season both sides of the steak with the garlic powder and salt and pepper to taste, gently rubbing the seasonings into the meat.

8. Use the oven at 400°F. unless you are using the broiler in the oven. In that case, the oven will be hot enough from the broiler.

9. Spread the sausages, peppers, and potatoes in a shallow baking pan and sprinkle them with the oregano. Roast them for about 15 minutes or until they are heated through. Stir them once or twice to encourage even heating, making sure the food doesn't bunch up in the pan. (If you are using the broiler, you will have to keep the vegetables warm while you cook the steak.)

10. While the sausage and peppers cook, grill the steak, covered, or broil it uncovered, for 10 to 12 minutes. Turn it and grill it for about 10 minutes longer for medium-rare. Let the cooked meat rest for about 5 minutes so the juices will distribute evenly.

11. Using the bone in the porterhouse as a guide, slice the fillet and the sirloin from the bone. Slice the fillet into 6 to 7 slices and the sirloin into 8 to 10 slices.

12. Spread the peppers, onions, and potatoes on a large platter. Place the porter-house bone in the center of the platter for presentation. Add the sliced steak. Slowly sprinkle the vinegar over the meat and the vegetables. Sprinkle the top with basil and parsley and serve.

PORTERHOUSE STEAK WITH PEPPERS AND ONIONS

This is a natural spin-off from the Steak Contadina and a little easier to prepare. That doesn't mean it's any less impressive as a main course, with the sweetness of the peppers and onions playing off the juicy steak. The vegetables have to be cooked until they are soft and tender—not al dente—for this dish to be great. If you add marinara sauce to the peppers and onions, you can turn this dish into Steak Pizzaiola!

Serves 2 to 4

½ CUP OLIVE OIL

6 CLOVES GARLIC, PEELED AND LEFT WHOLE

2 LARGE SPANISH ONIONS, PEELED AND CUT INTO 6 WEDGES EACH

2 RED BELL PEPPERS, SEEDED, CORED, AND CUT INTO 6 EQUAL PIECES

2 GREEN BELL PEPPERS, SEEDED, CORED, AND CUT INTO 6 EQUAL PIECES

SALT AND FRESHLY GROUND BLACK PEPPER

8 BASIL LEAVES, SLICED

1 TABLESPOON CHOPPED FRESH FLAT-LEAF PARSLEY

36- TO 38-OUNCE PORTERHOUSE STEAK, AT ROOM TEMPERATURE

2 TEASPOONS GARLIC POWDER

2 TABLESPOONS FINELY CHOPPED GARLIC

⅛ TEASPOON DRIED OREGANO

1. In a large sauté pan, heat ¼ cup of the olive oil over medium heat. When the oil is hot, add the garlic cloves and cook them for 3 to 4 minutes or until they are browned. Using a slotted spoon, remove the garlic and set it aside on paper towels to drain.

2. Add the onions and peppers. Season them to taste with salt and pepper. Sauté them, stirring occasionally, for 4 to 5 minutes or until they start to brown. Return the garlic to the pan and add the basil and parsley. Reduce the heat to medium and cook the mixture, stirring occasionally, for about 15 minutes or until the peppers have softened and both the peppers and onions are caramelized. *Continued*

3. Prepare a charcoal or gas grill so that the coals or heating elements are medium hot; first, lightly spray the grilling rack with vegetable oil spray to prevent sticking. Or preheat the broiler.

4. Meanwhile, generously season both sides of the steak with garlic powder and salt and pepper, rubbing the seasonings into the meat.

5. Preheat the oven to 500°F. unless you are using the broiler in the oven. In that case, the oven will be hot enough from the broiler.

6. Grill the steak, covered, or broil it uncovered, for 10 to 12 minutes. Turn it and grill it for about 10 minutes longer for medium-rare. Let the cooked meat rest for 7 to 8 minutes.

7. Spread the onions and peppers in a shallow baking pan. Transfer them to the bottom shelf of the oven and cook them for 5 to 10 minutes or until they are very hot.

8. In a small bowl, whisk together the remaining ¼ cup of olive oil, the chopped garlic, and the oregano. Season it to taste with salt and pepper.

9. Using the bone in the porterhouse as a guide, slice the fillet and the sirloin steak from the bone. Slice the fillet into 5 to 6 slices and the sirloin steak into 12 to 15 slices.

10. Lay the porterhouse bone in the center of a large platter for presentation. Add the sliced steak. Pour the oil and garlic mixture over the meat. Spread the onions and peppers over the meat and serve.

VARIATION
STEAK PIZZAIOLA

Add 2 cups of Carmine's Marinara Sauce, page 288, to the peppers and onions in step 7. Heat the sauce in the oven until it is hot and proceed with the recipe.

BEEF CUTLET MILANESE WITH CAPER, ROASTED PEPPER, AND TOMATO BUTTER SAUCE

Because beef can stand up to strong flavors, this may appeal to beef lovers more than the more familiar Chicken Milanese. To butterfly, the steaks are cut crosswise, (through their sides,) but remain attached. The attached sides are spread open like a book and pounded thin, like a chicken cutlet. This may seem strange, but take our word for it, the dish is out of this world.

Serves 2 to 4

TWO 8-OUNCE, THICK, BONELESS SIRLOIN STEAKS, BUTTERFLIED

½ CUP ALL-PURPOSE FLOUR

3 LARGE EGGS

2 CUPS CARMINE'S BREAD CRUMBS, PAGE 283

GRATED ZEST OF 1 LEMON

SALT AND FRESHLY GROUND BLACK PEPPER

½ CUP VEGETABLE OIL

6 TABLESPOONS PLUS 1 TEASPOON UNSALTED BUTTER

1 TABLESPOON MINCED SHALLOTS

¼ CUP DRY WHITE WINE

1 CUP CHICKEN STOCK, PAGE 306

5 TABLESPOONS CARMINE'S MARINARA SAUCE, PAGE 288

2 TABLESPOONS CHOPPED ROASTED RED PEPPERS, PAGE 303

2 TABLESPOONS THINLY SLICED FRESH BASIL

2 TEASPOONS CAPERS, RINSED AND DRAINED

PINCH HOT RED PEPPER FLAKES

1. Using the flat side of a cleaver, a mallet, or a small heavy frying pan, flatten each piece of steak until it is ¼ inch thick. To make at easier, cover the steak with plastic wrap before flattening it. *Continued*

2. Spread the flour on a plate. Whisk the eggs together in a shallow bowl. Combine the bread crumbs and lemon zest in a small bowl and mix them well. Spread the bread crumbs out on a shallow plate.

3. Lightly season the steaks with salt and pepper.

4. Coat the steaks on both sides with flour and shake off any excess. Dip the steaks in the egg and let the excess drip off. Coat the steaks completely with the bread crumbs and press them into the meat to adhere. Set them aside on a tray or large plate.

5. In a large nonstick sauté pan, heat the oil over medium-high heat. When the oil is hot, add the steaks and cook them for about 2 to 3 minutes or until the bottoms are golden brown. Turn the steaks over and cook the other side for about 2 to 3 minutes or until it is golden brown. Transfer the steaks to paper towels to drain. Transfer them to a baking sheet and set them aside.

6. Preheat the oven to 400°F.

7. In a small saucepan over medium heat, melt 1 teaspoon of the butter, add the shallots, and sauté them for 1 to 2 minutes or until they are lightly browned. Add the wine and cook the sauce for about 30 seconds. Add the chicken stock, bring it to a boil, and cook it for 1 minute.

8. Reduce the heat to low. When the sauce is simmering slowly, use a small whisk to whip the remaining 6 tablespoons of butter into the sauce and cook it for about 2 minutes. Add the marinara sauce, roasted peppers, basil, capers, and red pepper flakes. Season the sauce to taste with salt and pepper. Remove it from the heat and set it aside.

9. Transfer the steaks to the oven and bake them for 3 to 4 minutes or until they are hot. Ladle the sauce onto a large platter, place the steaks on top of the sauce, and serve.

SHORT RIBS WITH CABBAGE AND POTATOES

This is one of those dishes in which the sum equals more than the parts. Sure, short ribs are tasty, and cabbage can be cooked in a number of different ways, but when you put the two together, the flavors mingle and the result is unexpectedly delicious. The addition of the soffritto, the classic Italian vegetable base cooked with rendered pork fat (from the pancetta) and "fried gently," takes this to even loftier heights.

Serves 3 to 4

SHORT RIBS

2 TABLESPOONS PLUS ¼ CUP OLIVE OIL

2 TABLESPOONS GARLIC POWDER

2 CLOVES GARLIC, PEELED AND MINCED

2 TEASPOONS CHOPPED FRESH THYME LEAVES

PINCH FRESHLY GROUND BLACK PEPPER

3½ POUNDS SHORT RIBS, INCLUDING BONES, SEPARATED INTO INDIVIDUAL RIBS

¾ HEAD GREEN CABBAGE, CORED, AND TOUGH OUTER LEAVES DISCARDED

½ CUP ALL-PURPOSE FLOUR

4 RIBS CELERY, CHOPPED

2 CARROTS, PEELED AND CHOPPED

I LARGE ONION, PEELED AND CHOPPED

½ CUP DRY WHITE WINE

2 BAY LEAVES

4 CUPS CHICKEN STOCK, PAGE 306

3 CUPS WATER

7 CANNED PLUM TOMATOES, CRUSHED

ONE 6-OUNCE SMOKED PORK NECK BONE OR HAM HOCK

2 TEASPOONS FRESH OREGANO LEAVES

I TEASPOON SALT

½ TEASPOON FRESHLY GROUND BLACK PEPPER

Continued

SOFFRITTO

I TABLESPOON OLIVE OIL

I SERRANO PEPPER

2 OUNCES PANCETTA, FINELY CHOPPED

I ONION, PEELED AND FINELY CHOPPED

I LARGE CUBANO OR ITALIAN PEPPER,
SEEDED, CORED, AND FINELY
CHOPPED

½ RED BELL PEPPER, CORED, SEEDED,
AND FINELY CHOPPED

½ SMALL FENNEL BULB, TRIMMED AND
FINELY CHOPPED

ROUX

2 TABLESPOONS ALL-PURPOSE FLOUR

I TABLESPOON UNSALTED BUTTER,
MELTED

SALT AND FRESHLY GROUND BLACK
PEPPER

POTATOES

12 CLASSIC BOILED POTATOES, PAGE
246

TO MAKE THE SHORT RIBS

1. Combine 2 tablespoons of the olive oil, the garlic powder, the garlic, the thyme, and the black pepper in a small bowl. Mix them well.

2. Coat the short ribs on all sides with the marinade. Transfer them to a large bowl, cover the bowl with plastic wrap, and refrigerate them for at least 8 hours or overnight.

3. Cut the cabbage into ⅛-inch-thick slices, transfer it to a bowl, and set it aside.

4. Spread the flour on a plate. Coat all sides of the short ribs with flour and shake off any excess.

5. In a large round or oval saucepan, heat the remaining ¼ cup of olive oil over medium heat. When the oil is hot, add the short ribs and cook them for 6 to 8 minutes total, turning them several times, or until they are dark golden brown on all sides. Using tongs, remove the ribs to a platter and set them aside.

6. Add the celery, carrots, and onions to the same saucepan and sauté them for 10 to 15 minutes or until they are tender and golden brown. Add the cabbage and cook it for about 15 minutes or until it is wilted and lightly browned.

7. Add the wine and bay leaves. Cook the mixture for about 2 to 3 minutes or until most of the wine has evaporated. Add the chicken stock, water, tomatoes, and pork neck bone or ham hock. Return the ribs to the saucepan. Increase the

heat to medium-high and bring the liquid to a boil. Add the oregano, salt, and pepper.

8. Partially cover the pot, reduce the heat to a simmer, and cook the ribs for 2 to 2½ hours or until the meat is very tender and nearly falling from the bone. You can also accomplish this is a moderate (350°F.) oven, in which case keep the pot fully covered. Transfer the ribs to a platter and set them aside.

9. Strain the sauce from the ribs through a fine-mesh sieve into a bowl, gently moving the vegetables around with a wooden spoon to prevent crushing them. Set the sauce aside and reserve the vegetables separately. Keep them warm

TO MAKE THE SOFFRITTO

1. In a medium-sized sauté pan, heat the olive oil over medium heat. When the oil is hot, add the serrano pepper. Cook it for 1 to 2 minutes, turning the pepper, or until the skin is blistered and the pepper is tender. Transfer it to a paper towel and rub the skin off. When the pepper is cool enough to handle, remove the seeds and finely chop it. Set it aside.

2. Add the pancetta to the same sauté pan and cook it for about 3 to 4 minutes or until it is browned and crispy. Add the onions, cubano peppers, red peppers, and fennel. Sauté them for 10 to 12 minutes or until they are tender. Add the serrano pepper and mix the soffritto well. Transfer it to a small bowl and set it aside.

TO ASSEMBLE THE DISH

1. Cut the meat off the bone and cut it into large chunks, removing and discarding any fat, bone, or cartilage. Transfer the meat to a bowl and set it aside.

2. Transfer the sauce to a medium-sized saucepan. Set it on medium-high heat and bring it to a boil. Boil it for about 5 minutes or until it is slightly thickened.

3. Meanwhile, mix the flour and melted butter together in a small bowl to make a roux. Add 1 tablespoon of the roux to the sauce and whisk it until it starts to thicken. Whisk in the remaining roux. Reduce the heat to a simmer and cook the sauce, stirring it occasionally with a wooden spoon, for about 10 minutes or until it is smooth and thick.

Continued

4. Add the soffritto to the meat. Mix them and season the meat to taste with salt and pepper. Transfer the meat into the pan with the sauce.

5. Transfer the beef and sauce into a large bowl. Transfer the cabbage into another large bowl. Serve them with the potatoes on the side.

THAT'S A LOT OF GARLIC!

PEOPLE JOKE ABOUT HOW MUCH GARLIC WE USE AT CARMINE'S. WE LAUGH ALONG BECAUSE THEY'RE RIGHT, BUT ON THE OTHER HAND, WE TAKE OUR GARLIC SERIOUSLY. IT ADDS PUNGENT FLAVOR AND AROMA TO ALMOST ANY SAVORY DISH, AND WE NEVER SKIMP ON IT. WE USE FRESH GARLIC UNLESS A RECIPE CALLS FOR GARLIC POWDER, WHICH WE HAVE FOUND OCCASIONALLY WORKS WONDERS, AS IN THE PORTERHOUSE STEAK CONTADINA RECIPE ON PAGE 177. OTHERWISE, IT'S FRESH GARLIC ALL THE WAY.

DON'T BE AFRAID OF GARLIC. AS IT COOKS, IT MELLOWS, WHICH MEANS IT'S SHARPEST WHEN RAW, AS IN A SALAD DRESSING. WHEN YOU SAUTÉ GARLIC IN HOT OIL, TAKE CARE NOT TO SCORCH IT, WHICH MAKES IT BITTER AND INEDIBLE. SAUTÉ IT OVER LOW TO MEDIUM-HIGH HEAT JUST UNTIL IT'S GOLDEN, AND IF IT LOOKS LIKE IT'S COOKING TOO QUICKLY, REMOVE THE PAN FROM THE HEAT AND LET THE OIL COOL DOWN BEFORE RETURNING IT TO COOK OVER A LOWER FLAME. WHEN A RECIPE CALLS FOR SAUTÉING ONIONS AND GARLIC, WE OFTEN PUT THE GARLIC IN THE PAN FIRST AND THEN ADD THE ONIONS. THIS PREVENTS THE GARLIC FROM BURNING.

A HEAD OF GARLIC CONTAINS 12 TO 16 INDIVIDUAL CLOVES, EACH WRAPPED IN A PAPERY SKIN THAT NEEDS TO BE REMOVED. DO THIS BY GENTLY CRUSHING THE CLOVE WITH THE FLAT SIDE OF A LARGE KNIFE. THE SKIN WILL SEPARATE FROM THE CLOVE AND CAN EASILY BE PEELED AWAY. YOU CAN ALSO USE A ROLLED RUBBER MAT TO LOOSEN THE SKINS, OR IF YOU ARE WORKING WITH DOZENS OF CLOVES, SEPARATE THEM, BLANCH THEM IN BOILING WATER FOR 50 OR 60 SECONDS, THEN DRAIN AND PEEL THEM.

DON'T STORE FRESH GARLIC IN THE REFRIGERATOR—IT WILL SPROUT IF YOU DO—BUT INSTEAD KEEP IT AT ROOM TEMPERATURE IN A WELL-VENTILATED CONTAINER OR AN OPEN DISH. BUT WE GUARANTEE THAT ONCE YOU START COOKING OUR RECIPES, YOUR GARLIC WILL DISAPPEAR RAPIDLY.

STUFFED PORK FILLET WITH BROCCOLI RABE FONTINA AND PINE NUTS WITH CREAMY POLENTA

You will want to serve this elegant dream of a main course over and over again. Our Atlantic City chef, Jeff Gotta, came up with this combination of classic Italian ingredients such as broccoli rabe, sun-dried tomatoes, fontina, prosciutto, pine nuts, and plum tomatoes, and the result is a luxurious stuffed pork fillet. The creamy polenta mixes gorgeously with the gravy—but mashed potatoes would also be delicious!

Serves 4

3 TO 4 OUNCES BROCCOLI RABE, TRIMMED

¼ CUP OLIVE OIL

1 CLOVE GARLIC, PEELED AND MINCED

½ TEASPOON HOT RED PEPPER FLAKES

SALT AND FRESHLY GROUND BLACK PEPPER

2 TABLESPOONS FINELY SLICED SUN-DRIED TOMATOES

1 TO 1¼ POUNDS FRESH PORK TENDERLOIN,

4 THIN SLICES PROSCIUTTO (ABOUT 3 OUNCES)

4 SLICES FONTINA

2 TABLESPOONS TOASTED PINE NUTS, SEE NOTE, PAGE 275

½ TABLESPOON CHOPPED FRESH ROSEMARY

6 FRESH BASIL LEAVES, SLICED

2 TABLESPOONS CHOPPED FRESH FLAT-LEAF PARSLEY

1 TABLESPOON CHOPPED SHALLOTS

¼ CUP DRY WHITE WINE

6 CANNED PLUM TOMATOES, DRAINED

½ CUP CHICKEN STOCK, PAGE 306

½ CUP BROWN SAUCE, PAGE 307

3 CUPS CREAMY POLENTA, PAGE 247

1. In a large pot of lightly salted boiling water, blanch the broccoli rabe for 4 minutes or until it is soft and tender. Drain it and immediately submerge it in ice-cold water. Drain it again. Gently squeeze the broccoli rabe to remove any excess water.

2. In a medium-sized sauté pan, heat 2 tablespoons of the olive oil over medium-high heat. When the oil is hot, add the broccoli rabe, garlic, and red pepper flakes.

Continued

Season it to taste with salt and pepper. Cook it, stirring, for about 2 minutes and then add the sun-dried tomatoes. Cook the mixture, stirring, for about 1 minute or until it is hot. Transfer it to a bowl and set it aside.

3. Preheat the oven to 375°F.

4. Butterfly the pork tenderloin by cutting it down the center lengthwise without cutting all the way through. Open the tenderloin like a book. Using the flat side of a cleaver, a mallet, or the bottom of a small heavy frying pan, flatten the fillet so that it is a little less than ¼ inch thick, 6 to 8 inches wide, and 10 to 12 inches long. To make it easier, lay a sheet of plastic wrap over the meat before flattening it.

5. Place the meat lengthwise on a work surface and season it with salt and pepper. Lay the prosciutto slices on the pork without overlapping. Spread the broccoli rabe mixture over the prosciutto, leaving a 1-inch border around the fillet. Put the fontina on top of the broccoli rabe mixture, making sure it covers the prosciutto. Sprinkle the pine nuts over the fontina.

6. Fold the left and right ends of the tenderloin 2 inches toward the center and then roll the meat into a tight roll. Tie it with kitchen string or secure it with sturdy toothpicks or short metal skewers.

7. Rub the rosemary into the pork. Season the pork to taste with salt and pepper.

8. In a large sauté pan, heat the remaining 2 tablespoons of oil over medium-high heat. When the oil is hot, add the rolled fillet. Cook it, occasionally turning, for about 10 minutes or until it is dark golden brown on all sides.

9. Transfer the meat to an ovenproof casserole and roast it in the oven for about 12 minutes or until the meat is cooked through and registers 155°F. on an instant-read thermometer. Remove it from the pan and set it aside, covered to keep it warm, to rest for about 10 minutes.

10. Pour off all but 1 tablespoon of fat from the sauté pan. Set the pan over medium-high heat. Add the basil, parsley, and shallots to the pan. Cook them, stirring occasionally, for about 1 minute. Add the wine, increase the heat to high, and cook the mixture for 10 seconds. Add the tomatoes, breaking them up with a wooden spoon or your hands. Add the chicken stock and brown sauce and then season the sauce to taste with salt and pepper. Bring it to a boil and cook it for 2 to 3 minutes.

11. Remove the string from the pork roll and cut the roll into ½-inch-thick slices. Spoon the polenta onto a platter. Place the sliced pork on top of the polenta and ladle some of the sauce over and around the pork. Serve any remaining sauce on the side.

PORK CHOPS WITH SWEET AND HOT VINEGAR PEPPERS

These pork chops are the exact opposite of a dish such as pasta with shaved white truffles. Both are earthy and splendid in their own way, but, the former is hometown, blue-collar food, while the latter is upscale and elegant. When Michael and Artie visited the old-time Italian restaurants in the Bronx, Brooklyn, and Queens while researching their menu for Carmine's, both of them fell in love with this dish. A little heat and extra-juicy brined pork conspire to make this a robust, satisfying dish without equal.

Serves 2 to 4

BRINE

3 TABLESPOONS DARK BROWN SUGAR

3 TABLESPOONS KOSHER SALT

I CUP HOT WATER

2 CUPS COLD WATER

5 BLACK PEPPERCORNS

I ONION, PEELED AND SLICED

I CLOVE GARLIC, PEELED AND CRUSHED

I WHOLE CLOVE

I BAY LEAF

I TABLESPOON VEGETABLE OIL

½ STICK CINNAMON

PORK CHOPS

4 LOIN PORK CHOPS, EACH I INCH THICK

2 TABLESPOONS OLIVE OIL

I TABLESPOON COARSELY CHOPPED GARLIC

I CUP CHICKEN STOCK, PAGE 306

IO SMALL WHOLE SWEET VINEGAR PEPPERS, QUARTERED AND SEEDED

IO SMALL WHOLE HOT VINEGAR PEPPERS, QUARTERED AND SEEDED

7 TABLESPOONS SWEET VINEGAR PEPPER JUICE FROM JAR

7 TABLESPOONS HOT VINEGAR PEPPER JUICE FROM JAR

4 TABLESPOONS UNSALTED BUTTER

2 TABLESPOONS CHOPPED FRESH BASIL

2 TABLESPOONS CHOPPED FLAT-LEAF PARSLEY

Continued

TO PREPARE THE BRINE AND BRINE THE PORK CHOPS

1. Dissolve the sugar and kosher salt in the hot water. Add the cold water and the rest of the brine ingredients. Mix the brine well and transfer it to a large resealable plastic bag.

2. Place the pork chops in the bag, seal it, and gently shake the bag to make sure the chops are covered by the brine. Put the bag in a bowl. Refrigerate them for 2 days, turning the bag from time to time.

TO COOK THE PORK CHOPS

1. Preheat the oven to 400°F. Remove the pork chops from the brine, pat them dry with paper towels, and set them aside. Discard the brine.

2. In a large ovenproof sauté pan, heat the olive oil over high heat. When the oil is hot, cook the pork chops for 3 to 4 minutes or until they are golden brown on one side. Reduce the heat to medium-high and brown the other side of the pork chops for 2 to 3 minutes. Transfer the pan to the oven and cook the pork chops for 3 minutes or until they are pale pink in the center and the internal temperature is 150°F. Transfer the chops to a platter, cover them, and keep them warm. (You can keep them warm in a 200°F. oven for up to 10 minutes.)

3. Add the garlic to the sauté pan and cook it over low heat for about 1 minute or until it is lightly browned. Add the chicken stock, sweet and hot peppers, and pepper juice, a little at a time. Taste the sauce and add only as much hot or sweet pepper juice as you like to make it pleasantly tart. Add the butter, basil, and parsley, increase the heat to medium-high, and boil the sauce for about 2 minutes.

4. Return the chops to the pan and turn them to coat them with the sauce. Put the chops on a platter, spoon the sauce over them, and serve.

GRILLED SAUSAGE RING WITH PARSLEY AND PROVOLONE OVER PEPPERONATA

When the air turns crisp and cool and you are lucky enough to find yourself going to a college football game, bring this in a large heatproof container as the ideal tailgating dish to spoon over crispy rolls. Closer to home, serve it on its own or in a sandwich. It's a superb take on sausage and peppers, especially if you can find sausage rings from a good Italian market. We also like it chopped into pieces and tossed into scrambled eggs. Talk about a show-stopping breakfast, brunch, or light supper!

Serves 4

3 CUBANELLE PEPPERS OR OTHER MILD PEPPERS

2 HOT ITALIAN PEPPERS OR OTHER HOT PEPPERS

2 MEDIUM OR I LARGE GREEN PEPPER

I RED BELL PEPPER

I YELLOW BELL PEPPER

4 TABLESPOONS OLIVE OIL

I TABLESPOON CHOPPED GARLIC

2 LARGE SPANISH ONIONS, PEELED AND THINLY SLICED

20 CHERRY TOMATOES

15 LEAVES FRESH OREGANO, CHOPPED

½ TEASPOON DRIED OREGANO

I LARGE BAY LEAF

SALT AND FRESHLY GROUND BLACK PEPPER

1½- TO 2-POUND SAUSAGE RING WITH PARSLEY AND PROVOLONE OR LINK ITALIAN SAUSAGE, SEE NOTE, PAGE 199

CRUSTY BREAD, FOR SERVING

1. Core the peppers, cut them in half, and cut them into ⅛-inch-thick slices.

2. In a large sauté pan, heat 2 tablespoons of the olive oil over medium-high heat. When the oil is hot, add the peppers. Cook them for 2 minutes without stirring. Stir them well and cook them for 2 more minutes without stirring. Repeat this routine 2 to 3 times or until the peppers start to brown and wilt. Add the garlic and sauté the mixture for 2 minutes or until the garlic softens. With a slotted spoon, transfer the peppers to a large bowl. Set them aside.

Continued

3. Add the remaining 2 tablespoons of olive oil to the pan. When the oil is hot, add the onions. Sauté them for about 3 minutes or until they are lightly browned. Return the peppers to the pan. Add the tomatoes, fresh and dried oregano, and bay leaf. Season the sauce to taste with salt and pepper. Reduce the heat to medium and cook the sauce, partially covered, stirring occasionally, for 10 to 13 minutes or until the peppers have softened completely.

4. Prepare a charcoal or gas grill so that one side of the coals or heating elements is medium-hot and the other side has a low heat; first, lightly spray the grilling rack with vegetable oil spray to prevent sticking. Or preheat the broiler.

5. Lightly brush the sausage with olive oil. Grill it on high heat for 2 to 3 minutes or until it is browned. Turn it over and grill the other side for 2 to 3 minutes or until it is browned. Transfer it to the lower heat and grill it for 7 to 8 minutes. Check for doneness by cutting into the sausage. Return it to high heat and grill it for about 1 minute on each side to complete the cooking.

6. Spread the pepperonata on a large platter. Lay the sausage ring on top. Serve with crusty bread.

NOTE: Most Italian delis and markets sell sausage rings flavored with provolone and parsley. These are long ropes of sausage, not divided into links, and about half the diameter of Italian link sausages. They are called "sausage rings" or "sausage rolls" because the rope is wrapped into a tight, snail-like roll and held together with large toothpicks. If you can't find a sausage ring, buy link sausage flavored with provolone and parsley, and if neither one is sold in your local markets, buy the best Italian sausage you can find.

SAUSAGE, CLAMS, AND POTATOES

This is a classic one-bowl comfort meal, and you can eat it with a spoon—and who doesn't love eating soothing food with a spoon? It's heavenly on a rainy day or in front of the fireplace. This dish is as good on the second day as the day you made it. Mixing sausage, clams, and potatoes in a stew is a Rhode Island Italian tradition, with a nod to the significant Portuguese influence in that small state. You can serve this as a main course or a first course with crusty bread and great wine.

Serves 4

2 LARGE RUSSET POTATOS

½ CUP OLIVE OIL

5 CLOVES GARLIC, PEELED AND CRUSHED

TWO 3-OUNCE HOT ITALIAN SAUSAGE LINKS, EACH CUT INTO 6 PIECES

TWO 3-OUNCE SWEET ITALIAN SAUSAGE LINKS, EACH CUT INTO 6 PIECES

24 LITTLENECK CLAMS, RINSED AND SCRUBBED

20 FRESH BASIL LEAVES, SLICED

4 TABLESPOONS CHOPPED FLAT-LEAF PARSLEY

4 TEASPOONS CHOPPED FRESH OREGANO

1 BAY LEAF

A GENEROUS PINCH HOT RED PEPPER FLAKES

½ CUP DRY WHITE WINE

2 CUPS CANNED PLUM TOMATOES, DRAINED AND COARSELY CHOPPED

2 CUPS CHICKEN STOCK, PAGE 306

SALT AND FRESHLY GROUND BLACK PEPPER

CRUSTY BREAD, FOR SERVING

1. Place the potatoes in a small pot. Add enough lightly salted cold water to cover the potatoes by 1 inch and bring it to a boil over high heat. Reduce the heat to medium and simmer the potatoes for about 20 minutes or until they are just tender. Drain the potatoes and put them in a small bowl. Refrigerate them for 20 minutes. When they cool, peel them and cut each into 10 to 12 pieces. Set them aside.

2. In a large pot, heat the olive oil over medium-high heat. When the oil is hot, add the garlic and cook it, turning it occasionally, for 2 to 3 minutes or until it is golden brown. Remove the garlic with a slotted spoon and set it aside.

3. Add the sausages to the pot and cook them, stirring occasionally, for about 8 minutes or until they are browned. Add the garlic, clams, basil, and parsley. Stir the mixture, cover the pot, and cook it for 3 minutes.

4. Add the oregano, bay leaf, and red pepper flakes. Stir the mixture, cover the pot, and cook it for 3 minutes.

5. Add the wine, increase the heat to high, and cook the mixture, uncovered, stirring occasionally, for 2 minutes. Add the tomatoes and chicken stock, and stir the mixture. Boil it for 3 minutes, or until all the clams have opened. With a small knife pry open any unopened clams. Discard any clams that do not open. Season the dish to taste with salt and pepper.

6. Serve the dish in bowls, with the bread on the side.

SLOW-ROASTED LAMB SHOULDER CHOPS WITH VEGETABLE ORZO RISOTTO

In this recipe, the lamb shoulder chops are roasted until they are fall-off-the-bone tender, then are served with a vegetable-packed orzo pasta that is cooked like risotto. That is the secret of this dish. The orzo is soft and comforting and sops up any gravy from the lamb and vegetables. In fact, make the orzo on its own when you have leftover veggies, meat, and gravy. Grate some cheese over the impromptu dish and dig in! As we say in New York, "Fuggeddaboutit!"

Serves 6

MARINADE

¼ CUP OLIVE OIL

¼ CUP DRY WHITE WINE

I TABLESPOON FINELY CHOPPED GARLIC

2 TEASPOONS CHOPPED FRESH SAGE

2 TEASPOONS CHOPPED FRESH ROSEMARY

2 TEASPOONS CHOPPED FRESH OREGANO

I TEASPOON SALT

¼ TEASPOON FRESHLY GROUND BLACK PEPPER

ORZO

3 TO 4 CUPS CHICKEN STOCK, PAGE 306

2 TABLESPOONS UNSALTED BUTTER

I TABLESPOON OLIVE OIL

I ONION, FINELY CHOPPED

12 OUNCES DRIED ORZO

SALT AND FRESHLY GROUND BLACK PEPPER

I BUNCH SNIPPED FRESH CHIVES

½ TO I CUP GRATED ROMANO CHEESE

I TABLESPOON CHOPPED FLAT-LEAF PARSLEY

LAMB CHOPS AND VEGETABLES

3 TO 4 LAMB SHOULDER BLADE CHOPS, EACH I- TO I½-INCHES THICK (ABOUT 3 TO 4 POUNDS)

5 RIBS CELERY WITH LEAVES, EACH CUT INTO 4 TO 5 PIECES

3 CARROTS, PEELED AND CUT IN HALF LENGTHWISE, AND THEN CUT INTO 3 TO 4 PIECES

Continued

2 LARGE ONIONS, PEELED, CUT IN HALF, AND THEN QUARTERED

6 CLOVES GARLIC, PEELED AND CRUSHED

3 BAY LEAVES

6 CUPS CHICKEN STOCK, PAGE 306

2 TABLESPOONS OLIVE OIL

4 FRESH PLUM TOMATOES, CUT IN HALF

I TEASPOON CHOPPED FRESH THYME

SALT AND FRESHLY GROUND BLACK PEPPER

6 TABLESPOONS ALL-PURPOSE RED SAUCE, PAGE 304

TO MAKE THE MARINADE AND MARINATE THE LAMB CHOPS

1. Combine all the ingredients in a small bowl and mix them well.

2. Put the lamb chops in a large glass, ceramic, or other nonreactive bowl. Pour the marinade over them and toss them to coat them. Cover the bowl with plastic wrap and refrigerate the lamb chops for at least 8 hours or overnight.

TO MAKE THE LAMB CHOPS

1. Preheat the oven to 375°F.

2. Spread the celery, carrots, onions, garlic, and bay leaves in a large roasting pan. Add the chicken stock to the roasting pan.

3. In a small sauté pan, heat the olive oil over medium heat. When the oil is hot, add the tomatoes, cut side down. Cook them for 2 to 3 minutes or until the bottoms are lightly browned. With a slotted spoon, transfer them to the roasting pan. Season the vegetables with the thyme and salt and pepper to taste.

4. Lift the lamb chops from the marinade and place them on top of the vegetables, with room between the chops. Pour the marinade over the lamb chops.

5. Cover the pan with aluminum foil and roast the lamb chops for 1½ hours, basting them occasionally with the pan juices. Remove the foil. Break up the tomatoes if they are still whole.

6. Increase the oven temperature to 425°F. Roast the lamb chops for 1 hour longer or until they are nicely browned and fork-tender.

7. Transfer the lamb chops to a plate and set them aside. Reserve 3 cups of the vegetables. When they are cool enough to handle, cut these vegetables into 1-inch pieces and set them aside. Keep the chops and vegetables warm.

8. Strain the broth through a fine-mesh sieve into a small saucepan and discard the remaining vegetables. Skim the fat from the lamb broth and season the broth with salt and pepper to taste. Set it aside.

TO MAKE THE ORZO

1. In a medium-sized saucepan, heat the chicken stock over low heat to a simmer.

2. In a large saucepan, melt 1 tablespoon of the butter and the olive oil over medium heat. Add the onions and cook them, stirring occasionally, for 2 to 3 minutes or until they are translucent. Add the orzo and cook the mixture, stirring occasionally, for 5 to 6 minutes or until the onion is golden brown. Add the chicken stock, 1 cup at a time, stirring constantly until it is absorbed before adding the next cup. Season it with a pinch of salt and pepper. Reduce the heat to low, and cook the orzo, stirring, until it is tender.

3. Remove the orzo from the heat. Stir in the remaining 1 tablespoon of the butter, the chives, 1 to 1½ cups of the reserved chopped vegetables, and ½ to ¾ cup of the cheese. Add the parsley, season the orzo to taste with salt and pepper, and transfer it to a serving bowl.

TO ASSEMBLE THE DISH

1. Meanwhile, bring the lamb broth to a simmer over medium heat, and heat the red sauce.

2. Spread the remaining reserved chopped vegetables on a platter. Place the lamb chops on the vegetables and spoon about 1 cup of the lamb broth over the lamb. Garnish each lamb chop with a dollop of red sauce. Serve the remaining lamb broth and sauce alongside the lamb chops.

CHICKEN OR VEAL MARSALA

To make this dish taste deep and delicious, you need to plan ahead and make the brown sauce at least a day or two in advance. You will be rewarded with real depth of flavor. If you decide to make it with veal, don't skimp—buy the best veal you can find. The meat should be white or pale pink and never marbled. Marbling is only desirable in beef.

Serves 2 to 4

I CUP FLOUR

SALT AND FRESHLY GROUND BLACK PEPPER

SIX TO SEVEN 1½-OUNCE CHICKEN OR VEAL CUTLETS

½ CUP VEGETABLE OIL

I TABLESPOON UNSALTED BUTTER

I LARGE SHALLOT, FINELY CHOPPED

2 CUPS SLICED CREMINI MUSHROOMS (6 TO 7 OUNCES)

½ CUP MARSALA WINE

I CUP BROWN SAUCE, PAGE 307

1. Spread the flour on a large plate and season it with salt and pepper. Coat the chicken or veal with flour and shake off any excess.

2. In a large sauté pan, heat the oil over medium-high heat. When the oil is hot, add the cutlets, one at a time, and cook them for about 2 minutes a side or until they are lightly browned all over. Set them aside on a plate to collect any juices that accumulate.

3. Discard the oil from the pan. Reduce the heat to medium and add the butter. When it is melted, add the shallots and cook them, stirring, for about 2 minutes or until they are lightly browned and softened.

4. Add the mushrooms to the pan and increase the heat to high. Cook them for 2 minutes without stirring. Stir them and then cook them for 2 minutes longer without stirring. Remove the pan from the heat and add the wine. Return the pan to the heat and cook the sauce for about 1 minute until it is bubbling. The wine may flame but will die out after a minute or so.

5. Add the brown sauce, reduce the heat to medium, and let the sauce simmer for 2 to 3 minutes. Season it to taste with salt and pepper.

6. Transfer the cutlets to a platter, ladle the sauce over them, and serve.

CHICKEN OR VEAL PARMIGIANA

The captivating combination of crispy bread crumbs and melted cheese atop a perfectly cooked chicken or veal cutlet makes this a timeless and much-loved dish. It's a great favorite with kids, but adults are equally drawn to it—in other words, it's perfect for a family-style meal. To make it the Carmine's way, start with the best ingredients you can find—which includes our bread crumbs and marinara sauce. Bellisimo!

Serves 2 to 3

I CUP FLOUR

2 LARGE EGGS

3 CUPS CARMINE'S BREAD CRUMBS, PAGE 283

TWO 5-OUNCE CHICKEN BREASTS OR VEAL CUTLETS, POUNDED TO ¼-INCH
    THICKNESS BETWEEN 2 PIECES OF WAXED PAPER

SALT AND FRESHLY GROUND BLACK PEPPER

½ CUP VEGETABLE OIL

2 CUPS CARMINE'S MARINARA SAUCE, PAGE 288

FIVE OR SIX ¼-INCH-THICK SLICES MOZZARELLA, ABOUT 7 OUNCES TOTAL

2 TABLESPOONS GRATED ROMANO CHEESE

1. Preheat the oven to 450°F. or preheat the broiler.

2. Spread the flour on a large plate. Whisk the eggs in a shallow bowl. Spread the bread crumbs on a baking sheet.

3. Season the cutlets with salt and pepper. Coat them with flour and shake off any excess. Dip them in the egg mixture and let any excess drip off. Press the cutlets into the bread crumbs, making sure they are covered with bread crumbs on both sides. Set them aside on a plate. Refrigerate for 2 to 3 hours until needed.

4. In a large sauté pan, heat the oil over medium heat. When the oil is hot, add the cutlets and cook them for about 3 minutes on each side or until they are a deep golden brown all over. Transfer them to paper towels to drain.

Continued

5. Meanwhile, in a medium-sized saucepan, heat the marinara sauce over medium-high heat for 4 to 5 minutes or until it is hot.

6. Transfer the cutlets to a shallow ovenproof casserole. Place the mozzarella on top and sprinkle it with the grated cheese.

7. Transfer the cutlets to the oven and cook them for 3 to 4 minutes or until the cheese is melted. If you are cooking under the broiler, this will take 2 to 3 minutes.

8. Ladle the sauce onto a large platter. Place the cutlets on top of the sauce and serve.

CHICKEN OR VEAL SALTIMBOCCA

We serve our saltimbocca on a bed of spinach, which instantly turns it into a full meal. This is a legendary Italian dish, characterized by the prosciutto and sage but made our own by the addition of melted mozzarella, as well as the big, exhilarating flavors that infuse nearly all our dishes.

Serves 2

FOUR 2-OUNCE CHICKEN OR VEAL CUTLETS

4 FRESH SAGE LEAVES

2 THIN SLICES PROSCIUTTO, CUT IN HALF CROSSWISE

I CUP FLOUR

SALT AND FRESHLY GROUND BLACK PEPPER

½ CUP VEGETABLE OIL

I TABLESPOON UNSALTED BUTTER

I TABLESPOON CHOPPED SHALLOTS

¼ CUP DRY WHITE WINE

I CUP BROWN SAUCE, PAGE 307

4 THIN SLICES FRESH MOZZARELLA (ABOUT I ½ OUNCES)

I RECIPE SPINACH IN GARLIC AND OIL, PAGE 232, DRAINED

1. Lay the cutlets on a work surface. Put 1 sage leaf on top of each and top the sage with prosciutto. Place plastic wrap over the cutlets and, using a mallet or small heavy frying pan, lightly pound the prosciutto until it adheres to the meat and the cutlets flatten a little. Remove the plastic wrap and discard it.

2. Spread the flour on a large plate and season lightly with salt and pepper. Coat the cutlets with flour and shake off any excess.

3. In a large sauté pan, heat the oil over medium-high heat. When the oil is hot, add the cutlets, prosciutto side down, for about 2 minutes or until they are lightly browned. Turn them over and cook the other side for about 2 minutes or until it is lightly browned. Transfer the cutlets to a plate and set them aside.

Continued

4. Discard any oil from the pan. Reduce the heat to medium and add the butter. When it is melted, add the shallots and cook them, stirring, for about 2 minutes or until they are browned and softened.

5. Add the wine and cook the shallots for about 30 seconds. Add the brown sauce and bring to a simmer. Add the cutlets and simmer them for about 3 minutes. Adjust the heat to maintain a simmer.

6. Meanwhile, preheat the broiler.

7. Remove the cutlets from the sauce and transfer them to a shallow ovenproof casserole that will fit under the broiler. Place the mozzarella on top of the cutlets.

8. Broil the cutlets for 2 to 3 minutes or until the cheese is melted.

9. Meanwhile, in a medium-sized sauté pan, heat the spinach over medium heat for about 5 minutes or until it is hot. Spread the spinach along the length of a large platter and spoon the sauce over the spinach. Place the cutlets on top of the spinach, season lightly with salt and pepper, and serve.

CHICKEN ALLA ROMANA

Every Italian American restaurant has a version of this chicken dish on the menu. When it came time to develop one for ours, one of our chefs from Brooklyn decided to bread chicken cutlets and pull the whole dish together with a perky lemon butter sauce. Dynamite! It's a one-stop meal—everything you need for a great family meal on a single platter.

Serves 2

5 LARGE RED POTATOES, CUT IN HALF

I SPANISH ONION, PEELED AND THINLY SLICED

3 TABLESPOONS GRATED ROMANO CHEESE

2 TABLESPOONS UNSALTED BUTTER, MELTED

I TEASPOON CHOPPED FRESH ROSEMARY

I TEASPOON CHOPPED FRESH OREGANO

I TEASPOON CHOPPED FLAT-LEAF PARSLEY

SALT AND FRESHLY GROUND BLACK PEPPER

I CUP ALL-PURPOSE FLOUR

4 LARGE EGGS

3 CUPS CARMINE'S BREAD CRUMBS, PAGE 283

FIVE 2-OUNCE CHICKEN CUTLETS

¼ CUP DRY WHITE WINE

I½ CUPS CHICKEN STOCK, PAGE 306

I½ TABLESPOONS CAPERS, RINSED AND DRAINED

4 TABLESPOONS UNSALTED BUTTER

2 TABLESPOONS CHOPPED ROASTED RED PEPPERS, PAGE 303

2 TABLESPOONS FRESH LEMON JUICE

I RECIPE SPINACH IN GARLIC AND OIL, PAGE 232, DRAINED

3 TO 4 SLICES FRESH MOZZARELLA

1. Preheat the oven to 350°F.

2. In a large bowl, mix together the potatoes, onions, grated cheese, melted butter, rosemary, oregano, and parsley. Season the potatoes with 1 tablespoon of salt and ½ teaspoon of pepper. Transfer them to a baking sheet and roast them for about 1¼ hours or until they are tender. Stir them occasionally during roasting. Set them aside.

3. Spread the flour on a large plate. Whisk the eggs in a shallow bowl. Spread the bread crumbs on a baking sheet.

4. One at a time, coat the chicken cutlets with flour, shaking off any excess. Dip them in the egg mixture and let any excess drip off. Coat them with bread crumbs. Set them aside on a plate.

5. In a medium-sized sauté pan, bring the wine to a boil over medium-high heat. Cook it for about 1 minute or until the liquid is reduced by half. Add the chicken stock and capers. Bring it to a boil and cook it for 2 minutes. Reduce the heat to a simmer and whisk in 3 tablespoons of the butter. Season the sauce to taste with salt and pepper. Stir in the red peppers and the remaining tablespoon of the butter. Add the lemon juice and season the sauce to taste with salt and pepper. Keep it warm.

6. Place the breaded chicken and the potatoes in a shallow baking pan. Spread the spinach in the bottom of another baking pan. Roast both pans for about 2 minutes or until the food is hot. Cover the chicken with the mozzarella and return the pan to the oven for 2 to 3 minutes or until the cheese melts.

7. Spread the spinach down the center of a large platter. Put the chicken on top of the spinach. Scatter the potatoes around the chicken. Pour the sauce over the chicken and serve.

CHICKEN SCARPARIELLO

Here it is, folks! Carmine's top-selling chicken dish in all its spicy, zesty, tasty magnificence. We don't think there is a better Chicken Scarpariello in the country. No. Make that the world! When Michael was developing this before the first Carmine's opened, he prepared several different versions for Artie to sample. After tasting them, Artie said, "Michael, it needs to be Carmine-ized!" This meant accentuating the tastes and working on the marinade to boost its flavors. Thus, the two men tasted, talked about, and tweaked this dish until it was perfected.

Serves 2 to 3

ONE 3½-POUND CHICKEN, CUT INTO 12 PIECES

1 TABLESPOON KOSHER SALT

2 TEASPOONS CHOPPED FRESH ROSEMARY

2 TEASPOONS CHOPPED FRESH OREGANO

2 TEASPOONS CHOPPED FRESH SAGE

FRESHLY GROUND BLACK PEPPER

3 LEMONS

1 CUP VEGETABLE OIL

2 TABLESPOONS UNSALTED BUTTER

4 TABLESPOONS COARSELY CHOPPED GARLIC

1 TABLESPOON FINELY CHOPPED SHALLOTS

¼ CUP DRY WHITE WINE

SALT

LEMON WEDGES, FOR GARNISH

1. Place the chicken pieces in a large bowl. Add the salt, 1 teaspoon of the rosemary, 1 teaspoon of the oregano, 1 teaspoon of the sage, and ½ teaspoon of black pepper. Squeeze the juice of 2 of the lemons over the chicken, toss it well, cover the bowl with plastic wrap, and refrigerate the chicken for at least 24 hours.

2. Preheat the oven to 400°F.

Continued

3. Remove the chicken from the marinade and pat it dry with paper towels. Discard the marinade.

4. In a large sauté pan, heat the vegetable oil over medium heat. When the oil is hot and starting to smoke, add the chicken pieces. Cook the chicken, without moving it, for 5 minutes or until it is golden brown. Turn it over and cook the other side, without moving it, for 5 minutes or until it is deep golden brown. Continue to cook for about 10 minutes more, or until it is all evenly browned.

5. Using tongs, transfer the chicken to a shallow roasting pan. Bake the chicken for 12 to 15 minutes or until it is cooked through.

6. Meanwhile, discard any oil in the sauté pan and wipe it clean with paper towels.

7. Heat 1 tablespoon of the butter in the sauté pan over medium heat. When it is melted, add the garlic, shallots, and remaining rosemary, oregano, and sage. Cook the mixture, stirring, for about 2 minutes or until the garlic and shallots start to brown.

8. Increase the heat and add the wine, stirring the bottom of the pan with a wooden spoon to deglaze it. Cook the sauce for about 2 minutes or until most of the wine has evaporated.

9. Stir in the remaining 1 tablespoon of butter. Season the sauce to taste with salt and pepper. Squeeze the juice of the remaining lemon into the sauce. It will not thicken.

10. Transfer the chicken to the sauté pan and mix the sauce and chicken well.

11. Place the chicken on a large platter, pour the sauce over it, and serve it garnished with lemon wedges.

CHICKEN CONTADINA

When our waiters carry this plate from the kitchen to the assigned table, they carry it waist high so other customers can get a glance and a whiff as it goes by. We get a lot of orders for this dish and our waiters get a lot of questions about it. A win-win situation, you might say. It's a crowd pleaser, for sure: a marriage of our Steak Contadina (but lighter) and Chicken Scarpariello (the wow of those flavors in the marinade). This is a perfect one-pot meal that just about screams Sunday dinner.

Serves 2 to 4

ONE 3-POUND CHICKEN, CUT INTO 12 PIECES

1 TABLESPOON KOSHER SALT

1 TEASPOON CHOPPED FRESH ROSEMARY

1 TEASPOON CHOPPED FRESH OREGANO

1 TEASPOON CHOPPED FRESH SAGE

FRESHLY GROUND BLACK PEPPER

JUICE OF 3 LEMONS

2 LARGE RUSSET POTATOES, SUCH AS IDAHO, CUT INTO ¼-INCH-THICK SLICES

1 CUP VEGETABLE OIL

4 FENNEL SAUSAGE LINKS (ABOUT 1 POUND TOTAL)

3 TABLESPOONS OLIVE OIL

SALT

2 SPANISH ONIONS, PEELED AND CUT INTO 6 WEDGES EACH

2 GREEN BELL PEPPERS, SEEDED, CORED, AND CUT LENGTHWISE INTO 6 EQUAL PIECES

2 RED BELL PEPPERS, SEEDED, CORED, AND CUT LENGTHWISE INTO 6 EQUAL PIECES

2 TABLESPOONS COARSELY CHOPPED GARLIC

10 FRESH BASIL LEAVES, SLICED

1 TABLESPOON CHOPPED FLAT-LEAF PARSLEY

6 SWEET OR HOT VINEGAR CHERRY PEPPERS WITH JUICE, CUT INTO QUARTERS, OPTIONAL

1. Place the chicken pieces in a large glass, ceramic, or other nonreactive bowl. Add the salt, the rosemary, the oregano, the sage, and about ½ teaspoon of black pepper. Pour the lemon juice over the chicken, toss it well, cover the bowl with plastic wrap, and refrigerate the chicken for 24 hours.

2. Preheat the oven to 400°F.

3. Place the potatoes in a bowl, cover them with cold water, and set them aside.

4. In a large ovenproof sauté pan, heat the vegetable oil over medium-high heat. When the oil is hot, add the sausages and cook them, turning occasionally, for 4 to 5 minutes or until they are lightly browned. Transfer the pan to the oven and bake them for about 10 minutes or until they are brown and firm. Set them aside. Reserve the pan juices in the sauté pan.

5. Remove the chicken from the marinade and pat it dry with paper towels. Discard the marinade.

6. Set the sauté pan with the pan juices over medium heat. When it starts to smoke, add the chicken and cook it without moving it for about 5 minutes or until it is deep golden brown. Turn it over and cook the other side, without moving it, for 5 minutes or until it is deep golden brown.

7. Transfer the sauté pan to the oven and bake the chicken for 15 to 20 minutes or until it is crispy. Set the chicken aside. Reserve the pan with any remaining pan juices.

8. Meanwhile, drain the potatoes and pat them dry with paper towels. In a large bowl, mix the potatoes with the olive oil and salt and pepper to taste. Place the potato slices in a single layer on a baking sheet and bake them for about 10 minutes or until they are crispy on top. With a spatula, turn the potato slices over and bake the other side for 10 minutes or until it is crispy. Set the potatoes aside.

9. Heat the sauté pan with the reserved pan juices over medium-high heat. When it is hot, add the onions and peppers. Increase the heat to high and stir in the garlic. Cook the onions and peppers, stirring occasionally, for about 5 minutes or until they start to brown. Reduce the heat to medium-low and cook them for about 12 minutes or until they are very tender. Stir in the basil and parsley. Transfer the onions and peppers to a colander to drain.

10. In a large bowl, toss together the sausage, chicken, potatoes, onions, and peppers. If desired, stir in the cherry peppers and their juice. Transfer the food to a platter and serve.

CHICKEN WITH LEMON BUTTER

Most Italian American restaurants have a version of this light, lovely lemon chicken on the menu. We toss lightly browned shallots into the dish, which rounds out the flavor of the sauce and makes it a perennial favorite with our guests.

Serves 2

1 CUP FLOUR

SALT AND FRESHLY GROUND BLACK PEPPER

SIX 2-OUNCE CHICKEN CUTLETS

¼ CUP OLIVE OIL

9 TABLESPOONS UNSALTED BUTTER

1 TABLESPOON FINELY CHOPPED SHALLOTS

¼ CUP DRY WHITE WINE

1 CUP CHICKEN STOCK, PAGE 306

1 TEASPOON CHOPPED FLAT-LEAF PARSLEY

JUICE OF 2 LEMONS, OR MORE TO TASTE

1 LEMON, HALVED, FOR GARNISH

1. Spread the flour on a plate and season it with salt and pepper.

2. Season the chicken cutlets with salt and pepper. Coat them with flour and shake off any excess.

3. In a large sauté pan, heat the olive oil over medium-high heat. When the oil is hot, carefully add the chicken. Cook it for about 2 minutes on each side or until it's golden brown all over. Set it aside on a plate to collect any accumulated juices.

4. Remove any oil from the pan. Reduce the heat to low and add 1 tablespoon of the butter. When it is melted, add the shallots and cook them for 2 to 3 minutes or until they are softened and lightly browned.

5. Add the wine, increase the heat to high, and cook it for about 30 seconds or until the liquid is reduced to 1 tablespoon. Add the chicken stock, bring it to a boil, and cook it for 2 to 3 minutes.

6. Reduce the heat to a low simmer and stir in the parsley. Whisk in the remaining 8 tablespoons of the butter, adding 1 tablespoon at a time and incorporating each one before adding the next. Adjust the heat to maintain a simmer.

7. Add the chicken and any accumulated juices to the pan. Add the lemon juice. Season it to taste with salt and pepper. Add more lemon juice, if desired.

8. Transfer the chicken to a platter and serve it with the lemon halves as a garnish.

STUFFED BRAISED CHICKEN LEGS AND FONTINA POTATO CROQUETTES

This is a tasty way to use a common and inexpensive ingredient: chicken legs. When served with our delectable and crispy potato croquettes, it gets even better. The chicken legs with the thighs attached (not just drumsticks) are stuffed with a heady amalgamation of mushrooms, cheese, and vinegar peppers for a hearty meal that fills the soul and the stomach. Ask your butcher to bone the legs and thighs; even the guy behind the meat window at the supermarket can do this for you.

Serves 2 to 4

4 BONED CHICKEN LEGS WITH THIGHS ATTACHED (ABOUT 2 POUNDS), SEE NOTE, PAGE 224

SALT AND FRESHLY GROUND BLACK PEPPER

1½ CUPS STUFFING MIXTURE FOR SAUSAGE-STUFFED MUSHROOMS, PAGE 28

¼ CUP GREEN PEAS, FRESH OR FROZEN AND THAWED

5 SPEARS FRESH ASPARAGUS, WOODY STEMS REMOVED, PEELED, AND CUT DIAGONALLY INTO 2-INCH PIECES

1 TABLESPOON OLIVE OIL

1 TABLESPOON UNSALTED BUTTER

½ ONION, PEELED AND SLICED

1 CLOVE GARLIC, PEELED AND THINLY SLICED

¼ CUP DRY WHITE WINE

4 CANNED PLUM TOMATOES, DRAINED

3 CUPS CHICKEN STOCK, PAGE 306

12 SMALL FRESH ROSEMARY SPRIGS

12 SMALL FRESH OREGANO LEAVES, CHOPPED

½ CUP BROWN SAUCE, PAGE 307

6 FONTINA POTATO CROQUETTES, PAGE 244

1. Spread the chicken legs open on a work surface, skin side down, and season them with salt and pepper.

2. Spoon about 1 tablespoon of the stuffing mixture into the pocket in the drumstick. Fold back any skin covering the thigh. Using your fingers or a small spoon, spread about 1 to 2 tablespoons of the stuffing over the thigh between the meat and skin. Carefully pull the skin up to cover the stuffing. Gently turn the leg over and reshape it, if necessary. Season the chicken skin with salt and pepper.

Continued

Repeat with the remaining chicken legs and transfer them to a plate, cover them with plastic wrap, and refrigerate them for at least 1 hour to chill the stuffing.

3. Preheat the oven to 400°F.

4. In a small pot of lightly salted boiling water, cook the peas for 2 minutes. Add the asparagus and cook the vegetables for 1 minute. Drain them and immediately submerge them in cold water. Drain them again and set them aside.

5. In a large ovenproof sauté pan, heat the olive oil over medium-high heat. When the oil is hot, add the chicken legs, stuffed side down, and then add the butter. When the butter is melted, baste the top of the chicken with the pan juices and cook it for about 2 minutes or until it begins to cook but is not browned. Scatter the onions around the chicken legs, stirring the onions to coat them with the oil mixture. Cook the onions for about 5 minutes or until they start to brown. Add the garlic and cook it for 1 to 2 minutes or until it is lightly browned.

6. Add the wine and cook it for 1 minute. Add the tomatoes, breaking them up with a wooden spoon. Add 2 cups of the chicken stock, the rosemary, and the oregano. The sauce will not be thick. Bring the liquid to a boil, occasionally basting the chicken.

7. Transfer the pan to the oven and bake it for 35 to 45 minutes or until the chicken skin is golden brown and crispy. Remove the pan from the oven and transfer the chicken to a baking sheet. Transfer the contents of the sauté pan to a large sauce pan.

8. Preheat the broiler.

9. Add the remaining 1 cup of the chicken stock to the saucepan over medium-high heat and bring it to a boil. Add the brown sauce, reduce the heat to low, and simmer it for 2 to 3 minutes. Season the sauce to taste with salt and pepper. It will look like a liquidy natural gravy. Remove the pan from the heat and add the peas and asparagus to the sauce.

10. Transfer the chicken legs to the broiler and broil them for 2 to 4 minutes or until they are crispy.

11. Spoon the sauce onto a platter. Place the chicken legs on top of the sauce. Serve the potato croquettes on the side.

NOTE: When the leg section is boned, there will be a cavity, or pocket, running the length of the drumstick, just the place for stuffing. The thigh portion will be butterflied with the skin on one side. Lay it skin side down to stuff it.

CRISPY ROMANO-CRUSTED CHICKEN BREAST WITH ARUGULA, RICOTTA SALATA, AND SMOKED MOZZARELLA SALAD

If you love the fresh, clean taste of mild chicken topped with a light, crisp salad dressed with vinaigrette, try this. The bread crumbs—one of our "star-making" ingredients—add crunch and flavor while the smoked mozzarella adds depth and just a breath of smokiness. We love this in the spring and summer.

Serves 2 to 3

SIX 2-OUNCE SKINLESS CHICKEN CUTLETS

SALT AND FRESHLY GROUND BLACK PEPPER

½ CUP ALL-PURPOSE FLOUR

4 LARGE EGGS

½ CUP GRATED ROMANO CHEESE

I TABLESPOON CHOPPED FLAT-LEAF PARSLEY

3 CUPS CARMINE'S BREAD CRUMBS, PAGE 283

GRATED ZEST OF I LEMON

½ CUP OLIVE OIL

2 LARGE BUNCHES ARUGULA

6 KALAMATA OLIVES

I LARGE RIPE FRESH TOMATO, CHOPPED

I SMALL RED ONION, PEELED AND THINLY SLICED

½ FENNEL BULB, TRIMMED AND THINLY SLICED

½ CUP DICED FRESH SMOKED MOZZARELLA

¼ CUP COARSELY GRATED RICOTTA SALATA, SEE NOTE, PAGE 226

ABOUT ¼ CUP CARMINE'S VINAIGRETTE, PAGE 287

I CUP ALL-PURPOSE RED SAUCE, PAGE 304

1. Season the chicken cutlets with salt and pepper.

2. Spread the flour on a plate. Whisk the eggs together with ¼ cup of the grated cheese and the parsley in a shallow bowl. Mix together the bread crumbs, the lemon zest, and the remaining ¼ cup of the grated cheese and transfer the mixture to a plate.

Continued

3. Coat the cutlets on both sides with flour and shake off any excess. Dip them in the egg mixture and let the excess drip off. Coat them on both sides with bread crumbs and transfer them to a platter.

4. In a large sauté pan, heat the olive oil over medium-high heat. When the oil is hot, add the chicken cutlets, one at a time, and cook them for 2 to 3 minutes or until the bottom is golden brown. Turn them and cook the other side for 3 to 4 minutes or until it is golden brown. Transfer the cutlets to paper towels to drain.

5. Preheat the oven to 400°F.

6. In a large bowl, toss together the arugula, Kalamata olives, tomatoes, onions, fennel, smoked mozzarella, and ricotta salata. Toss the mixture with ¼ cup of the vinaigrette, adding more if necessary. Season the salad to taste with salt and pepper.

7. Meanwhile, heat the red sauce in a small saucepan over medium-high heat for 2 to 3 minutes or until it is hot. Transfer the chicken cutlets to a baking sheet and bake them for 3 to 4 minutes or until they are warm.

8. Place the salad in the middle of a large platter. Arrange the chicken cutlets around the salad. Spoon 1 tablespoon of the sauce over each cutlet. Serve the remaining sauce on the side.

NOTE: Ricotta salata is a sheep's milk cheese that is not at all like the ricotta most Americans know. It's a pure white cheese with a dense, dry yet springy texture and a mild, agreeably salty flavor. It has been likened to feta cheese, although it is not exactly the same. Still, if you cannot find ricotta salata, use a good Greek feta in its place.

Appetizer

EGGPLANT PARMIGIANA	17.00
GARLIC BREAD	10.50
ZUPPA DI CLAMS	17.00
ZUPPA DI MUSSELS	15.00
STUFFED ARTICHOKE	13.50
STUFFED MUSHROOMS	12.00
SPIEDINI ALLA ROMANA	14.50
FRIED CALAMARI	24.50
FRIED ZUCCHINI	15.50
COLD ANTIPASTO	22.50
HOT ANTIPASTO	26.50
CARMINE'S SALAD	21.50
MIXED GREEN SALAD	18.50
CAESAR SALAD	20.50
PORTOBELLOS	
(PARMIGIANA OR GRILLED)	14.00
ROASTED PEPPERS W/ANCHOVIES	12.50
WITH MOZZARELLA	17.50
BAKED CLAMS	19.50

Vegetables & Sides

ESCAROLE	11.50
BROCCOLI	11.50
SPINACH	12.00
EGGPLANT PARMIGIANA	17.00
PEPPERS & ONIONS	11.50
SAUSAGE	10.50
MEATBALLS	11.00

Pasta

ANGEL HAIR, LINGUINE, PENNE, SPAGHETTI OR RIGATONI

CLAM SAUCE - RED OR WHITE	23.50
SHRIMP - RED OR WHITE	27.50
CALAMARI - RED OR WHITE	22.50
MIXED SEAFOOD - RED OR WHITE	P.A.
RAGU (ASSORTED MEATS)	25.50
POMODORO	22.50
GARLIC & OIL	21.50
RIGATONI & BROCCOLI	23.00
RIGATONI	
W/SAUSAGE & BROCCOLI	24.50
MEATBALLS	22.50
SAUSAGE	22.50
MARINARA	22.00
GIARDINIERA	23.50
RAVIOLI W/CHEESE	24.00
RIGATONI COUNTRY STYLE	25.50
MANICOTTI	24.00
LASAGNA	27.00
PENNE ALLA VODKA	25.50

Raw Bar

SHRIMP COCKTAIL	LG 21.00	SM 14.00
CLAMS ON THE HALF SHELL		
1/2 DOZ		11.00
DOZ		19.00

Chicken

CHICKEN SCARPARIELLO	25.50
CHICKEN CONTADINA	35.00
CHICKEN CUTLET	23.00
CHICKEN PARMIGIANA	24.00
CHICKEN MARSALA	24.00
CHICKEN SCALOPPINE	
W/LEMON & BUTTER	24.00
CHICKEN SALTIMBOCCA	26.00

Veal

VEAL CUTLET	24.00
VEAL PARMIGIANA	25.00
VEAL SCALOPPINE MARSALA	25.00
VEAL SCALOPPINE	
W/LEMON & BUTTER	25.00
VEAL SALTIMBOCCA	27.00

Seafood

SHRIMP MARINARA	28.50
SHRIMP SCAMPI	28.50
SHRIMP PARMIGIANA	28.50
SHRIMP FRA DIAVOLO	28.50
FRESH FISH OF THE DAY	P.A.
BROILED LOBSTER OREGANATA	P.A.
LOBSTER FRA DIAVOLO	P.A.

Beef

BROILED PORTERHOUSE STEAK	P.A.
PORTERHOUSE CONTADINA	P.A.
PORTERHOUSE PIZZAIOLA	P.A.
PORTERHOUSE	
W/PEPPERS & ONIONS	P.A.

House Specialties

CHICKEN CACCIATORE	MONDAY
RACK OF LAMB	TUESDAY
DOUBLE CUT	
VEAL CHOP	WEDNESDAY
OSSOBUCO	THURSDAY
CHICKEN ALLA ROMANA	FRIDAY
PRIME RIB CHOP	SATURDAY
FOUR PASTA SPECIAL	SUNDAY

Desserts

ITALIAN CHEESECAKE	9.00
BREAD PUDDING	14.00
CHOCOLATE CANNOLI	13.00
TIRAMISU	17.00
TARTUFO	6.50
STRAWBERRY SHORTCAKE	11.00
CHOCOLATE TORTA	11.00
FRESH FRUIT PLATTER	P.A.
TITANIC	23.00

6.
SIDE DISHES

Everything is cooked to order, and most dishes are "Carmine-ized," too. That means we make them bigger and bolder!

—MICHAEL RONIS, FOUNDING CHEF AND PARTNER

ESCAROLE IN GARLIC AND OIL ≈ SPINACH IN GARLIC AND OIL ≈ ESCAROLE AND BEANS ≈ BROCCOLI RABE ≈ GREEN BEANS, POTATOES, AND TOMATOES ≈ EGGPLANT PARMIGIANA ≈ FONTINA POTATO CROQUETTES ≈ CLASSIC BOILED POTATOES ≈ CREAMY POLENTA

ESCAROLE IN GARLIC AND OIL AND SPINACH IN GARLIC AND OIL

These dishes sound similar, but they are slightly different. Greens prepared this way—aglio e olio—celebrate the simplicity of good Italian cooking. With just a few top-notch ingredients, you can produce something deceptively delicious. When you buy escarole—which is sometimes called curly chicory—look for fluffy, ruffled leaves on good-looking heads. When you shop for the spinach, buy bunches with large, firm, curly leaves and avoid flat spinach leaves, if you can. If you buy it packed in a plastic bag, make sure the leaves look fresh and dry. Even if the package claims the spinach is clean, wash it again to ensure it's completely free of grit. Make sure all the greens are thoroughly washed and completely dry. For both, use superior olive oil—plain, blended, or extra virgin—and freshly chopped garlic.

ESCAROLE IN GARLIC AND OIL

Serves 2 to 4

2 HEADS ESCAROLE (ABOUT 2 POUNDS)

¼ CUP OLIVE OIL

1 TABLESPOON COARSELY CHOPPED GARLIC

SALT AND FRESHLY GROUND BLACK PEPPER

½ CUP CHICKEN STOCK, PAGE 306

1 LEMON, HALVED

1. Trim off the base of each head of escarole. Cut each head of escarole in half lengthwise and then cut each half into thirds crosswise. Wash and dry the escarole. Transfer it to a large bowl and set it aside.

2. In a large sauté pan, heat the olive oil over medium-high heat. When the oil is hot, add the garlic and cook it, stirring, for about 1 minute or until it is golden brown. Take care not to let the garlic burn.

3. Add the escarole, season it to taste with salt and pepper, and sauté it, using a large fork to toss it in the oil, for about 2 minutes or until it starts to wilt. Cover the pan and cook it for 30 to 40 seconds. Remove the cover and cook it, stirring, for 1 minute.

Continued

4. Add the chicken stock, cover the pan, increase the heat to high, and cook the escarole for 1 minute. Reduce the heat to a simmer, cover the pan, and cook it for 3 to 4 minutes, adjusting the heat to maintain a simmer. Remove the cover and taste the escarole, seasoning it to taste with salt and pepper.

5. Transfer the escarole and its juices to a large bowl and serve it with the lemon halves as a garnish.

SPINACH IN GARLIC AND OIL

Serves 2 to 4

¼ CUP OLIVE OIL

2 TABLESPOONS COARSELY CHOPPED GARLIC

2 POUNDS FRESH SPINACH, STEMS REMOVED

SALT AND FRESHLY GROUND BLACK PEPPER

1 LEMON, HALVED

1. In a large sauté pan, heat the olive oil over medium-high heat. When the oil is hot, add the garlic and cook it, stirring, for about 1 minute or until it is golden brown. Take care not to let the garlic burn.

2. Add the spinach and, using a large fork to toss it in the oil, sauté it for 2 to 3 minutes or until it starts to wilt. Cover the pan and cook it for 30 seconds. Remove the cover, stir the spinach, and season it to taste with salt and pepper. Stir it again. Transfer the spinach to a large bowl and serve it with the lemon halves as a garnish.

ESCAROLE AND BEANS

When you soak and then cook dried beans, rather than relying on canned, the final dish tastes better and the beans clearly have a more pleasing texture and bite. It is not the least bit difficult to cook dried beans, but it does require some advance planning. We toss our cooked beans with escarole and prosciutto and very good olive oil. If you add some cooked macaroni and Italian sausage, this dish can be a main course. We like this almost more when it's made one day and eaten the next. It's just great!

Serves 4

½ CUP DRIED CANNELLINI OR WHITE NORTHERN BEANS

1 HEAD ESCAROLE (ABOUT 1 POUND)

¼ CUP OLIVE OIL

2 CLOVES GARLIC, PEELED AND SLICED

½ TEASPOON HOT RED PEPPER FLAKES, OPTIONAL

SALT AND FRESHLY GROUND BLACK PEPPER

¼ CUP CHICKEN STOCK, PAGE 306

2 THIN SLICES PROSCIUTTO, SLICED, OPTIONAL

1 TABLESPOON CHOPPED FLAT-LEAF PARSLEY

1. In a large bowl, combine the beans with enough cold water to cover them by 2 inches. Soak the beans for at least 8 hours or overnight. Drain and refresh the water 2 to 3 times during soaking, if possible. Drain the beans and transfer them to a large saucepan.

2. Add cold water to cover the beans by 2 inches, bring them to a boil over medium-high heat. Lower the heat to a simmer, cover the pan, and cook the beans for 15 minutes. Remove the cover and cook them for 20 to 25 minutes, skimming any foam from the surface. Increase the heat to high and cook them for 40 to 45 minutes or until most of the liquid has evaporated and the beans are tender but not mushy. Set the beans aside to cool.

3. Remove the base of the escarole and separate the leaves. Stack the leaves and cut them into ½-inch-wide strips crosswise. Wash them thoroughly in cold water. Spin them dry or dry them with paper towels.

Continued

4. In a large sauté pan, heat the olive oil over medium-high heat. When the oil is hot, add the garlic and cook it for about 2 minutes or until it is lightly browned. Remove the garlic with a slotted spoon and set it aside on paper towels to drain.

5. Add the escarole and red pepper flakes, if using, to the pan. Stir the escarole constantly for 4 minutes or until it is just wilted. Add the beans and any remaining cooking liquid, season the mixture to taste with salt and pepper, and stir it well.

6. Add the chicken stock, prosciutto, if using, and parsley. Bring it to a simmer, cover the pan, and cook it for about 10 minutes to give the flavors a chance to blend. Adjust the heat to maintain a simmer. Transfer the vegetables to a bowl and serve.

BROCCOLI RABE

This is cooked in the time-honored Italian American way of sautéeing the broccoli rabe until its fibrous structure breaks down and it turns soft. At the same time, its intrinsic flavor infuses this simple dish. We think this is the best way to cook this pleasingly bitter cousin of the turnip—no, it's not related to broccoli. Buy bright green, fresh-looking broccoli rabe (also called rapini, broccoli raab, broccoli rape, broccoli di rape, Chinese broccoli, and turnip broccoli) and let it turn a darker, duskier green as it cooks. It's really wonderful and bursting with good Carmine's-style flavor.

Serves 2 to 4

2 LARGE BUNCHES BROCCOLI RABE (ABOUT 2 POUNDS), TRIMMED

¼ CUP OLIVE OIL

1 TABLESPOON COARSELY CHOPPED GARLIC

PINCH OF HOT RED PEPPER FLAKES

SALT AND FRESHLY GROUND BLACK PEPPER

¼ CUP CHICKEN STOCK, PAGE 306

1 LEMON, HALVED, FOR GARNISH

1. In a large pot of lightly salted boiling water, blanch the broccoli rabe for about 3 minutes after the water has resumed the boil. Drain it, immediately submerge it in ice-cold water, drain it again, and gently squeeze out any excess water. Set it aside.

2. In a medium-sized sauté pan, heat the olive oil over medium-high heat. When the oil is hot, add the garlic and cook it, stirring, for about 2 minutes or until it is golden brown. Take care not to let the garlic burn. Add the red pepper flakes and stir it for 30 seconds.

3. Add the broccoli rabe and sauté it, using a large fork to toss it in the oil, for 3 to 4 minutes, or until it is very hot. Season it to taste with salt and pepper.

4. Add the chicken stock, raise the heat to high, and bring it to a boil. Reduce the heat to a low simmer and cook the broccoli rabe, stirring, for about 4 minutes or until it is tender. Transfer it to a bowl and serve it with the lemon halves as a garnish.

GREEN BEANS, POTATOES, AND TOMATOES

Because we are committed to the spirit of Italian American home cooking, what some people call "grandmother's cooking," we cook these vegetables together until they are soft and yielding and their flavors become one. Cooking vegetables to this degree may not be stylish in today's culinary world, but for side dishes such as this, it's the only way to go. This does not mean the veggies are overcooked—far from it. They are stewed just until the dish is warm, enticing, and delicious.

Serves 4

1 LARGE RUSSET POTATO, PEELED AND CUT INTO 1-INCH CUBES

1 POUND FRESH GREEN BEANS, TRIMMED

¼ CUP OLIVE OIL

¼ CUP DICED RED ONIONS

1 CLOVE GARLIC, PEELED AND COARSELY CHOPPED

2 CUPS CANNED ITALIAN PLUM TOMATOES, DRAINED AND COARSELY CHOPPED

8 TO 10 FRESH OREGANO LEAVES

1 BAY LEAF

SALT AND FRESHLY GROUND BLACK PEPPER

1. Place the potatoes in a medium-sized pot, add enough lightly salted cold water to cover them by 2 inches, and bring it to a boil over high heat. Reduce the heat to medium and simmer the potatoes for about 20 minutes or until they are just tender. Drain them in a colander and rinse them under cold water. Set them aside.

2. In a large pot of lightly salted boiling water, blanch the green beans for about 5 minutes or until they are tender. Drain them and immediately submerge them in cold water. Drain them again and set them aside.

3. In a large sauté pan, heat the olive oil over medium heat. When the oil is hot, add the onions and cook them, stirring, for about 2 minutes or until they are lightly browned. Add the garlic and cook the mixture, stirring occasionally, for 2 minutes. Take care not to let the garlic burn.

Continued

4. Add the green beans, tomatoes, oregano, and bay leaf. Season the vegetables to taste with salt and pepper. Mix them well and simmer them for 5 minutes. Add the potatoes and mix them in well. Simmer the vegetables for 5 minutes, or until the green beans are very tender and the dish is heated through. Transfer the vegetables to a bowl and serve.

EGGPLANT PARMIGIANA

When most Americans think of Italian food, this earns a spot at the top of the list. It's exactly the kind of gutsy dish that makes people happy, and not necessarily because of the eggplant! The eggplant, which should be firm and smooth with a crisp green cap, is a perfect vehicle for the cheese and marinara sauce. Our big, bold version is one of the hallmarks of our success and—along with Chicken Scarpariello, Carmine's Garlic Bread, and our Titanic dessert—has earned us our spot on New York's culinary map.

Serves 4 to 5

1 TO 2 EGGPLANTS (ABOUT 1½ POUNDS TOTAL)

2 TO 3 CUPS ALL-PURPOSE FLOUR

2 TO 3 CUPS VEGETABLE OIL

6 LARGE EGGS

1¾ CUPS GRATED ROMANO CHEESE

1 TABLESPOON CHOPPED FRESH FLAT-LEAF PARSLEY

½ TEASPOON SALT

4 CUPS CARMINE'S MARINARA SAUCE, PAGE 288

2½ CUPS GRATED MOZZARELLA CHEESE

1. Cut the ends off the eggplant and discard them. Cut each eggplant into ¼-inch-round slices.

2. Spread the flour out on a large plate.

3. Coat each slice of eggplant with flour and shake off any excess. Stack the eggplant slices on top of each other.

4. Meanwhile, in a deep heavy saucepan or high-sided skillet, heat about 2 cups of the vegetable oil over medium-high heat until a deep-frying thermometer registers 350°F.

5. In a shallow bowl, whisk the eggs together with ½ cup of the grated Romano cheese, the parsley, and the salt. Dip the eggplant, a slice at a time, in the egg mixture and let any excess drip off.

Continued

6. Deep-fry the eggplant slices, 2 to 4 at a time, for about 3 minutes or until they are golden brown and tender. Remove them with a slotted spoon and place them on paper towels to drain and cool.

7. Preheat the oven to 350°F.

8. Spread 1 cup of marinara sauce over the bottom of an 8-by-4-inch nonstick loaf pan. Arrange a layer of eggplant slices over the sauce. They can slightly overlap each other, if necessary. Spread 3 to 4 tablespoons of marinara sauce over the eggplant. Sprinkle ½ cup of the mozzarella and 1 tablespoon of the Romano cheese over the sauce. Repeat layering the eggplant, marinara sauce, mozzarella, and Romano cheese to the top of the pan or ½ inch below the rim. End with a layer of eggplant and about ¼ cup of marinara sauce spread over the top of it. Sprinkle 1 heaping tablespoon of the Romano cheese on top of the sauce. Cover the top tightly with aluminum foil and place the pan on a baking sheet.

9. Bake the eggplant for about 1 hour or until it is hot and the sauce is bubbling. Let the pan sit at room temperature for about 1 hour or until the eggplant is cool enough to serve.

10. Put a platter on top of the loaf pan and, holding the platter and pan securely, invert the pan to release the eggplant. Cut it into slices and serve it with warm marinara sauce and grated Romano cheese on the side.

FONTINA POTATO CROQUETTES

Try these tasty little croquettes with any meat dish and you will think you are tasting a little bit of heaven! They are that good. The croquettes are a bit labor intensive, but a little work never hurt, especially when there's such a tasty reward.

Makes 12 to 14

3 RUSSET OR ALL-PURPOSE POTATOES (1 TO 1½ POUNDS), PEELED AND DICED

4 TEASPOONS UNSALTED BUTTER

7 OUNCES FONTINA, DICED

7 LARGE EGGS

¾ TO 1 CUP GRATED ROMANO CHEESE

1 TABLESPOON CHOPPED FLAT-LEAF PARSLEY

SALT AND FRESHLY GROUND BLACK PEPPER

FLOUR

4 CUPS CARMINE'S BREAD CRUMBS, PAGE 283

1 CUP VEGETABLE OIL

1. Place the diced potatoes in a large pot. Add enough lightly salted cold water to cover them by 2 inches and bring it to a boil over high heat. Reduce the heat to medium and simmer the potatoes for 12 to 15 minutes or until they are fork-tender. Immediately drain them in a colander.

2. Transfer the potatoes to a bowl and mash them with a fork or potato masher or put them through a ricer. Add the butter and, using a wooden or metal spoon, stir the potatoes until they are smooth. Add the fontina and stir the potatoes well until the cheese has melted into them. Stir in 1 egg and then stir in the Romano cheese and parsley. Season the potatoes to taste with salt and pepper. Refrigerate them for 20 to 30 minutes or until they are very cold and firm enough to roll without crumbling. It's important that the potatoes be cold, so don't rush this step.

3. Pinch off the potato mixture into pieces of about 2 to 3 tablespoons each. Place the pieces on a lightly floured surface and sprinkle them with flour.

4. Working with a piece at a time, roll the potato between your palms to form a

ball. Lay the balls on the floured surface (add more flour if needed) and roll each one into a log about 3 inches long and ¾ inch wide.

5. Transfer the logs to a baking sheet lined with plastic wrap and refrigerate them for about 1 hour to chill them. (If they are not chilled, the bread crumbs will not adhere to the rolls.)

6. Preheat the oven to 400°F.

7. Whisk the remaining 6 eggs in a large shallow bowl. Spread the bread crumbs out on a large plate.

8. Remove the potato croquettes from the refrigerator. Dip each croquette in the egg mixture, then roll it in the bread crumbs, and return it to the baking sheet.

9. In a large nonstick sauté pan, heat the vegetable oil over medium-high heat. When the oil is hot, cook 6 to 7 potato croquettes at a time (do not crowd the pan) for about 45 seconds or until the bottoms are golden brown. Using a spatula, turn the croquettes to brown them on all sides. Drain them on paper towels and repeat the process to cook all the croquettes.

10. Transfer the croquettes to a baking pan and bake them for 5 to 8 minutes or until they are heated through. Serve them at once. If you want, let them cool and freeze them for later use.

CLASSIC BOILED POTATOES

Makes 12 potatoes

12 SMALL YUKON GOLD POTATOES OR OTHER ALL-PURPOSE POTATOES, PEELED

SALT AND FRESHLY GROUND BLACK PEPPER

Put the potatoes in a large pot. Add enough cold water to cover the potatoes by 3 inches. Add 1 teaspoon of salt to the water. Bring it to a boil over high heat. Reduce the heat to medium and simmer the potatoes, uncovered, for 20 to 25 minutes or until they are just tender. Remove them from the heat, drain them, and serve them hot, seasoned to taste with salt and pepper.

CREAMY POLENTA

When it comes to Italian sides, soft, warm polenta has to be everybody's favorite comfort food. It's an ideal accompaniment to just about any main course with sauce or gravy because it is the ultimate "sopper-upper" for all the good flavors sliding over the plate or lingering in the bottom of the bowl. Serve it with the stuffed pork fillet on page 191 but also with beef, chicken, or fish. The list happily goes on and on!

Serves 6 or 7

5 CUPS WATER

2 ½ CUPS CHICKEN STOCK, PAGE 306

¼ CUP EXTRA-VIRGIN OLIVE OIL

SALT

2 BAY LEAVES

2 CUPS MEDIUM-GROUND YELLOW POLENTA

I CUP GRATED ROMANO CHEESE

8 TABLESPOONS (½ CUP) BUTTER

1. In a medium-sized saucepan, heat the water, the chicken stock, the olive oil, 1 tablespoon of salt, and the bay leaves to boiling over high heat. Add the polenta in a slow, steady stream, whisking constantly until all the polenta is smooth and lump-free. It should still be boiling rapidly.

2. Reduce the heat to low and simmer the polenta slowly, whisking almost constantly along the sides and up from the bottom of the pan, for about 30 minutes or until the polenta is shiny and pulls away from the sides of the pan. Adjust the heat to maintain the simmer.

3. Stir in the cheese and butter and season the polenta to taste with more salt, if needed. Stir it well and remove it from the heat. Remove and discard the bay leaves. Serve the polenta in a bowl or on a platter.

7.
CARMINE'S DESSERTS

We anticipated the first Carmine's would be a neighborhood restaurant, but never dreamed that eighteen years later it would become a New York City icon.

—ALICE CUTLER, PRESIDENT AND PARTNER

CHOCOLATE BREAD PUDDING ≈ CHOCOLATE TORTA ≈ TITANIC ICE CREAM SUNDAE ≈ CARMINE'S TIRAMISU ≈ HOMEMADE TARTUFO ≈ STUFFED BRIOCHE WITH MASCARPONE AND CHOCOLATE ≈ CHOCOLATE PANNACOTTA ≈ STRAWBERRY AND ASSORTED BERRY CAKE ≈ ESPRESSO ZABAGLIONE ≈ PINE NUT COOKIES ≈ SPICE COOKIES WITH LEMON ICING ≈ JAM COOKIES

CHOCOLATE BREAD PUDDING

This bread pudding got its start in a Brooklyn kitchen, where a Sicilian grandmother made it for her grandson. We hired that grandson, whose name is John, and one day when we asked him to make bread pudding, he made it the only way he knew how. It was our lucky day! We added the chocolate and tweaked it a little, but essentially this is John's grandma's recipe, and today it's one of our bestsellers. If you have leftovers, which we doubt you will, slice it cold the next day and cook it like French toast. There's nothing better than dessert for breakfast!

Serves 6 or more

¾ CUP GOLDEN RAISINS

7 LARGE EGGS

3 CUPS HEAVY CREAM

1 CUP GRANULATED SUGAR

3 TABLESPOONS PURE VANILLA EXTRACT

2 TEASPOONS GROUND CINNAMON

ONE 2-POUND LOAF DAY-OLD RUSTIC PEASANT OR COUNTRY BREAD

½ CUP UNSALTED BUTTER, AT ROOM TEMPERATURE

1 CUP SEMISWEET CHOCOLATE CHUNKS OR CHIPS

SWEETENED WHIPPED CREAM OR VANILLA ICE CREAM, FOR SERVING, OPTIONAL

1. In a small bowl, cover the raisins with cold water and soak them for about 1 hour. Drain them and set them aside. (The raisins can soak while you proceed with the rest of the recipe.)

2. To make the custard, in a large bowl, whisk together the eggs, cream, sugar, vanilla, and cinnamon. Set it aside.

3. Trim the crust from the bread (reserve the crust for another use, such as bread crumbs) and cut the bread into 4-by-2-inch rectangles about ¾ inch thick. Lightly toast the bread slices in a toaster, a toaster oven, the oven, or broiler. While the toast is warm, spread each side generously with butter.

Continued

4. Make the bread pudding in a large loaf pan, about 10 by 5 by 3 inches. Place enough of the bread slices in the bottom of the pan to cover it completely, making sure they fit snugly. Scatter a quarter of the raisins and a quarter of the chocolate chips over the bread. Top it with another layer of bread slices. Keep layering the pudding until there are 4 layers and all the raisins, chocolate, and bread are used. The top layer should be raisins and chocolate.

5. Gently pour the custard over the pudding so that it sinks down to the bottom and covers the top of the pudding. With the back of a spoon or spatula, press down on the bread to compact the pudding and distribute the custard. Cover the pan tightly with plastic wrap and then with aluminum foil.

6. Refrigerate the pudding for at least 2 hours or for up to 12 hours. The longer (12 hours) the better.

7. Preheat the oven to 350°F. Position a rack in the center of the oven. Put a deep roasting pan on the rack, large enough to hold the loaf pan easily.

8. Remove the foil and plastic wrap. Discard the plastic wrap and replace the foil over the pan. Put the pudding in the roasting pan and add enough hot water to the roasting pan to come half to three-quarters of the way up the sides of the loaf pan.

9. Bake the pudding for about 1½ hours or until a skewer poked through the foil comes out clean. If it does not come out clean, return the pudding to the oven for 15 to 30 minutes longer, or until it's done. Let the pudding cool, unwrapped, for 1 hour before serving.

10. Invert a serving platter over the pudding and, holding the platter in place over the loaf pan, turn it upside down to release the pudding onto the platter. Immediately turn the pudding upright. Serve slices with whipped cream or ice cream, if desired.

NOTE: The pudding can be made up to a day ahead of time, refrigerated, and then reheated in a 350°F. oven for about 15 minutes or until it is hot in the center.

CHOCOLATE TORTA

The only word for this dessert is decadent. If you are one of those people who don't think dessert is dessert unless it's chocolate, you've met your match! The torta is best served at room temperature. When you touch it, your finger should leave a small indentation. If it doesn't, let the torta sit out for a little longer. It will be a great test of your patience, but the wait will be worth it!

Serves 8 to 10

10 OUNCES SEMISWEET CHOCOLATE CHUNKS OR CHIPS

1¼ CUPS UNSALTED BUTTER, AT ROOM TEMPERATURE, CUT INTO SMALL PIECES

3 LARGE EGGS

½ CUP PLUS 2 TABLESPOONS GRANULATED SUGAR

¼ CUP FRESHLY BREWED ESPRESSO OR OTHER STRONG COFFEE, REFRIGERATED UNTIL COOL

2 TABLESPOONS COFFEE-FLAVORED LIQUEUR, SUCH AS KAHLUA OR TIA MARIA, OPTIONAL

1 TABLESPOON PURE VANILLA EXTRACT

CONFECTIONERS' SUGAR, FOR SERVING

SWEETENED WHIPPED CREAM, FOR SERVING

SLICED STRAWBERRIES, FOR SERVING

1. Preheat the oven to 300°F.

2. In the top of a double boiler over barely simmering water, melt the chocolate and butter. Whisk the chocolate and butter together until they are thoroughly combined. Remove the mixture from the heat and set it aside. Alternatively, melt the chocolate and butter in a microwave-safe container. Microwave on high power for 1 to 2 minutes or until the butter melts and the chocolate looks shiny. Stir until blended.

3. In the bowl of an electric mixer fitted with the whisk attachment and set on medium-high speed, beat the eggs for about 1 minute or until they are frothy. Add the sugar and beat the mixture for about 1 minute or until it is well mixed.

Continued

4. Add the espresso, liqueur, if using, and vanilla extract and mix it well.

5. With the mixer running on low speed, pour the still-warm chocolate into the bowl and mix it well.

6. Pour the chocolate mixture into an 8-inch-round cake pan that is at least 2 inches deep. The mixture should come nearly to the rim. Cover the pan with aluminum foil.

7. Transfer the cake pan to a larger pan and set it on the middle rack of the oven. Pour hot water into the larger pan to come about three-quarters of the way up the sides of the smaller pan. Bake the torta for about 1 hour or until the center is firm.

8. Carefully lift the torta pan from the water bath and put it on a wire rack. Remove the foil and let the torta cool at room temperature for at least 1 hour. Cover it again and refrigerate it for at least 1 hour and up to 5 hours. Remove the torta from the refrigerator a few hours before serving to let it reach room temperature.

9. To serve, slice the torta in the pan and put a slice on a serving plate. Dust it with confectioners' sugar and serve it with whipped cream and strawberries on the side.

NOTE: When it gets very cold, the torta gets as thick and dense as a chocolate bar. If you plan to eat it on the day you make it, let it chill for 2 hours and then serve, to be sure it is the right consistency. If it stays in the refrigerator longer, let the torta come to room temperature on the countertop, which could take up to 3 hours depending on how cold the torta is and how warm your kitchen is. You can also warm up a cold torta by microwaving it in 15-second intervals. Warming should take only 30 to 40 seconds overall.

TITANIC ICE CREAM SUNDAE

This gigantic sundae, made with six whopping scoops of ice cream, whipped cream, caramelized fruit, hot fudge sauce, and—get ready—an entire Chocolate Torta, gives you bang for your buck! Leo, a waiter at the 44th Street Carmine's, came up with the idea in response to a table that asked for "at least one of everything!" on the dessert menu. Leo and a pastry chef put their heads together, and the glorious Titanic was the result. It's been on the menu ever since—our Titanic is unsinkable!

Serves 8 to 10

FOUR ½-INCH-THICK SLICES PINEAPPLE, FRESH OR CANNED, DRAINED

3 TABLESPOONS UNSALTED BUTTER

2 TABLESPOONS PACKED LIGHT BROWN SUGAR

¾ CUP JARRED FUDGE SAUCE

2 CUPS HEAVY CREAM

½ CUP CONFECTIONERS' SUGAR

I TABLESPOON PURE VANILLA EXTRACT

I CHOCOLATE TORTA, PAGE 253

3 SCOOPS CHOCOLATE ICE CREAM

3 SCOOPS VANILLA ICE CREAM

5 LARGE STRAWBERRIES, CORED AND SLICED

2 BANANAS

3 TABLESPOONS CHOPPED ROASTED HAZELNUTS, SEE NOTE, PAGE 258

4 FERRARA WAFER SWIRLS WITH CHOCOLATE OR ANOTHER LOG-SHAPED WAFER COOKIE

1. Preheat the oven to 350°F.

2. Cut the pineapple slices in half and then cut each half into quarters. Lay the pieces on a parchment-paper-lined baking sheet so that they do not touch. Dot them with butter and sprinkle them with brown sugar. Bake them for about 45

Continued

minutes or until they are caramelized and a little crispy. Remove them from the pan and set them aside to cool for at least 15 minutes.

3. Pour the fudge sauce into the top of a double boiler or small saucepan and set it over barely simmering water. When it is hot, remove it from the heat, cover it, and set it aside in a warm spot in the kitchen to keep it warm. Alternatively, heat it in the microwave.

4. In the bowl of an electric mixer fitted with the whisk attachment, whisk the cream, confectioners' sugar, and vanilla for 2 to 3 minutes or to medium-firm peaks.

5. Place the torta on a large platter. Place a scoop of chocolate ice cream on each end of the torta. Place a scoop of vanilla ice cream next to each scoop of chocolate ice cream. Place the third scoop of vanilla ice cream in the center of the torta and top it with the third scoop of chocolate ice cream. Gently push the scoops together so they adhere and the top scoop is firmly anchored to the bottom one.

6. With a rubber spatula, spread the whipped cream over the torta and ice cream. Work swiftly and steadily. As you work, slope the cream on the sides as it goes toward the ice cream scoops next to the torta. The shape of the cake should be similar to a football or the dessert's namesake ocean liner.

7. Arrange the strawberry slices and the pineapple pieces over the cake.

8. Cut the bananas in half lengthwise and then in half again lengthwise so that each is in 4 long, thin slices. Arrange the bananas around the cake on the platter.

9. Drizzle the hot fudge sauce quickly over the cake and banana and sprinkle it with the hazelnuts. Insert the cookies into the cake to resemble smokestacks and serve immediately.

NOTE: To roast hazelnuts, spread the nuts in a small, dry roasting pan and roast them in a 350°F oven for 10 to 15 minutes, shaking the pan several times, or until the nuts look golden beneath the skins and are fragrant. Wrap the nuts in a kitchen towel until they are cool. Transfer them to a sieve and rub them back and forth to remove any loose skins. If you roast skinless hazelnuts, simply let them cool on a plate.

CARMINE'S TIRAMISU

Tiramisu means "pick me up." We think it should mean "sit down and dig in" because the dessert is more apt to make you want to stay at the table for as long as you can, savoring every bite of the creamy, custardy confection. It's something like an English trifle in conception: a homey dessert made with cake and a creamy fillings. Just as they do in Italy, we use superrich mascarpone as well as whipped cream and then, for the Carmine's flourish, top the pudding with a shower of chocolate shavings. No wonder all our guests stay in their seats for this dessert.

Serves 6 to 8

ZABAGLIONE

6 LARGE EGG YOLKS

6½ TABLESPOONS GRANULATED SUGAR

¾ CUP MARSALA WINE

TIRAMISU

I CUP HEAVY CREAM

½ CUP CONFECTIONERS' SUGAR

I TEASPOON PURE VANILLA EXTRACT

8 OUNCES MASCARPONE, SEE NOTE, PAGE 261

2 TABLESPOONS MARSALA WINE

2 CUPS FRESHLY BREWED COLD ESPRESSO OR INSTANT ESPRESSO COFFEE

¼ CUP COFFEE-FLAVORED LIQUEUR, SUCH AS KAHLÚA OR TIA MARIA

ONE 18-OUNCE PACKAGE LADYFINGERS

4 OUNCES BITTERSWEET CHOCOLATE

TO MAKE THE ZABAGLIONE

1. In the top of a double boiler, off the heat, whisk the egg yolks for about 1 minute or until they become frothy and begin to thicken. Add the granulated sugar and whisk it for about 1 minute or until the sugar is incorporated into the eggs. Add the Marsala and whisk it for 1 minute.

Continued

2. Meanwhile, fill the bottom of the double boiler partway with water and bring it to a simmer over medium heat, making sure the water level stays well below the base of the top of the double boiler.

3. Set the egg mixture over the simmering water and whisk it for 6 to 8 minutes or until the zabaglione is slightly thickened. Remove it from the heat and continue to whisk it in the top of the double boiler for about 2 minutes or until it starts to cool.

4. Transfer the top of the double boiler to a larger bowl filled with ice cubes and cold water. Whisk the zabaglione for 2 more minutes to cool it, taking care no ice water gets into the custard. Remove it from the ice bath, cover it with plastic wrap, and refrigerate it for at least 2 hours or overnight. (If it's easier, transfer the mixture to a bowl.)

TO MAKE THE TIRAMISU

1. In the bowl of an electric mixer fitted with a wire whisk, whisk the heavy cream on medium-high speed for about 2 minutes or until it is slightly thickened. Add the confectioners' sugar and vanilla extract, increase the speed to high, and whisk it for 3 to 4 minutes until the cream thickens a little more. Add the mascarpone and Marsala and whisk it for 2 to 3 minutes or until the cream is as thick as sour cream.

2. Using a rubber spatula, fold the zabaglione into the whipped cream just until it is incorporated. Do not overmix.

3. In a shallow pan, combine the coffee and liqueur. Dip 2 ladyfingers in the coffee just until they are lightly saturated. Lay them in a 9-by-11-inch glass dish or a bowl of similar size. Repeat the process until ladyfingers cover the bottom of the dish. You will only use about half the ladyfingers.

4. Using a rubber spatula, spread half of the cream mixture over the ladyfingers, filling the pan halfway. Using a vegetable peeler, cover the cream with strips of shaved chocolate.

5. Lay another layer of coffee-flavored ladyfingers over the cream and then top it with the rest of the cream. Cover it with shaved chocolate and refrigerate it for at least 2 hours and up to 24 hours to chill.

NOTE: Mascarpone is a rich, smooth, soft cow's milk cheese made from cream, with a texture similar to sour cream. It's sold in tubs at Italian markets and good cheese counters and usually is used in desserts and other sweet preparations.

HOMEMADE TARTUFO

If you are lucky enough to watch tartufo being made in Rome, as Michael has, you will witness lovely lopsided ice cream balls being liberally coated with chocolate shavings. We add an outer shell of chocolate, just to make the tartufo a little more sinfully wicked. If the hand-rolled ice cream ball is not perfect, the dessert is even more charming. The dessert really is very easy, but does take time. You will get the hang of it immediately once you read the recipe all the way through. To make this in advance, freeze the finished tartufo on a cookie sheet for 8 to 10 hours and store it in a resealable plastic bag in the freezer until you are ready to serve it. For a crowd, make two or three tartufos.

Serves 4

14 OUNCES BITTERSWEET CHOCOLATE

4 MARASCHINO CHERRIES, STEMS REMOVED

1 PINT VANILLA ICE CREAM

4 TEASPOONS SLICED ALMONDS, TOASTED, SEE NOTE, PAGE 263

1 PINT HARD-FROZEN CHOCOLATE ICE CREAM

2 TABLESPOONS TASTELESS VEGETABLE OIL

1. Place 4 freezer-safe coffee cups or small bowls that are 3 to 3½ inches in diameter in the freezer for at least 20 minutes to get cold.

2. Divide the chocolate in half. Chop half into small chunks and leave the rest whole.

3. Pat the cherries dry with paper towels.

4. Take the cups from the freezer and place them on a freezer-safe tray or shallow pan. Working steadily and efficiently, place ½ cup of vanilla ice cream in each of the 4 cups. With your fingers or a small rubber spatula, press the ice cream into the cup to form a rounded bottom and fill the cup halfway up with no air pockets. You may have to return the ice cream to the freezer several times for a few minutes to keep it hard.

5. Push a cherry into the middle of each cup so that half the cherry is submerged in the ice cream. Sprinkle about 1 teaspoon of the toasted almonds around each

cherry. Cover the cups with plastic wrap and return them to the freezer for about 15 minutes.

6. Take the cups from the freezer. Put ½ cup of chocolate ice cream into each cup and use your fingers or a rubber spatula to push the chocolate ice cream into the vanilla ice cream so there's no air between them. Be sure to add enough chocolate ice cream to fill the cups to the rim. Freeze them for at least 20 minutes to harden the ice cream.

7. Let the ice cream molds sit on the counter for about 5 minutes. Gently remove the ice cream balls from the cups by running a small rubber spatula around the chocolate and then sliding it under the ball to lift it out of the cup. Set the ice cream balls on a parchment-paper-lined pan and return them to the freezer for about 5 minutes to harden.

8. Meanwhile, using the largest holes on a box grater, grate the remaining chocolate onto a parchment-paper-lined baking sheet. Take the ice cream balls from the freezer and roll them in the chocolate until they are completely covered. Set them on the parchment-paper-lined pan and return them to the freezer for at least 4 hours and up to 24 hours.

9. In the top of a double boiler set over simmering water, combine the chopped chocolate and the oil and melt the chocolate, stirring occasionally. When it is melted, transfer it to a small bowl. Use a rubber spatula to scrape down the sides of the bowl. Alternatively, melt the chocolate with the oil in a microwave-safe container. Microwave on high power for 1 to 1½ minutes or until the chocolate looks shiny. Stir it until the chocolate and oil are blended and smooth. Let the chocolate cool for about 15 minutes or just to room temperature.

10. Gently pierce an ice cream ball with a large fork and dip the bottom of the ball into the melted chocolate. Spoon the melted chocolate over the top of the ice cream ball, letting it drip down the sides until the ball is completely covered. With a fork, gently slide the ice cream ball back onto the parchment-lined pan. Repeat this with the remaining 3 ice cream balls. Freeze them for at least 4 hours or overnight before serving.

NOTE: To toast sliced almonds, spread them in a shallow baking pan and toast them in a preheated 400°F. oven for 4 to 6 minutes, shaking the pan from time to time, or until they darken a shade and are fragrant. Watch carefully because they can burn in seconds. Cool them on a plate.

STUFFED BRIOCHE WITH MASCARPONE AND CHOCOLATE

This dessert is all about the ingredients, and when you have them assembled, this is a show-stopping finish to a meal. Think of these as brioche-French toast sandwiches filled with mascarpone and chocolate and sauced with melted vanilla ice cream! A perfect union of sweet, creamy, rich flavors and textures.

Serves 2 to 4

½ CUP MASCARPONE

5 TABLESPOONS CONFECTIONERS' SUGAR

3 TABLESPOONS WHOLE MILK

GRATED ZEST OF ½ LEMON

GRATED ZEST OF ½ ORANGE

FOUR 5-BY-5-INCH SLICES BRIOCHE, CRUSTS REMOVED, EACH ABOUT ½ INCH THICK

6 TABLESPOONS COARSELY GRATED SEMISWEET CHOCOLATE

2 LARGE EGGS

2 TABLESPOONS SUGAR

1 TEASPOON PURE VANILLA EXTRACT

3 TABLESPOONS UNSALTED BUTTER

1 GENEROUS SCOOP VANILLA ICE CREAM

1. Preheat the oven to 400°F.

2. In a small bowl, stir the mascarpone with a spatula or wooden spoon for about 3 minutes or until it is very creamy. Add 4 tablespoons of the confectioners' sugar, the milk, and the lemon and orange zest and stir it to mix the ingredients.

3. Using a butter knife, spread the mascarpone over each slice of bread to the thickness of a quarter. Take care not to tear the bread.

4. Sprinkle about 3 tablespoons of grated chocolate over 2 slices of the bread, keeping the chocolate near the center of the bread so it won't seep out when the sandwiches are cooked. Top them with the other 2 slices of bread, mascarpone side down, and press them gently together.

5. In a shallow dish, whisk together the eggs, sugar, and vanilla extract. Dip the sandwiches in the batter so that one side is well saturated. Turn them and saturate the other side.

6. In a large nonstick skillet, heat the butter over medium heat. When it foams, put both sandwiches in the sizzling butter and cook them for about 3 minutes a side or until the bread is lightly browned on both sides. Lift the sandwiches from the skillet and transfer them to an ovenproof plate or tray. Bake them for 2 to 3 minutes or until they are crispy.

7. Meanwhile, in a small bowl, stir the ice cream until it liquefies and can be spooned like a sauce.

8. Put a sandwich on each of 2 serving plates, or cut the sandwiches in half and put each half on a serving plate for 4 servings. Spoon the melted ice cream around the sandwiches. Sift the remaining confectioners' sugar over the sandwiches and serve.

FOR THE LOVE OF CHOCOLATE

OUR CUSTOMERS LOVE OUR CHOCOLATE DESSERTS. WHETHER THEY ORDER OUR TARTUFO, BREAD PUDDING, OR TORTA, THE SMILES ON THEIR FACES ARE EQUALLY WIDE AND HAPPY. CHOCOLATE IS AN ELUSIVE INGREDIENT—OR IS IT A FOOD?—THAT IS UNLIKE ANY OTHER AND YET IS FAMILIAR TO EVERYONE. AND WE MEAN EVERYONE! TODDLERS TO GRANDMOTHERS LOVE THE STUFF.

NOT ALL CHOCOLATE IS ALIKE AND BY THIS WE MEAN FROM TYPE TO TYPE AS WELL AS FROM BRAND TO BRAND. WHEN A RECIPE CALLS FOR SEMISWEET CHOCOLATE, YOU CANNOT SUBSTITUTE UNSWEETENED OR MILK CHOCOLATE, AND VICE VERSA. THE RECIPE WILL NOT WORK.

WE USE ONLY SEMISWEET AND BITTERSWEET CHOCOLATE FOR OUR DESSERTS, AND THESE TWO CHOCOLATES ESSENTIALLY ARE INTER-CHANGEABLE. TOGETHER, THEY ALSO ARE KNOWN AS "DARK CHOCOLATE": ACCORDING TO THE STANDARDS OF IDENTITY RECOGNIZED BY ALL CHOCOLATE MAKERS, BOTH SEMISWEET AND BITTERSWEET CHOCOLATE MUST CONTAIN MORE THAN A THIRD CHOCOLATE LIQUEUR (WHICH IS NOTHING MORE EXOTIC THAN PURE CHOCOLATE WITH NO SUGAR OR OTHER FLAVORING). CHOCOLATE MAKERS ADD SUGAR AND FLAVORINGS SUCH AS VANILLIN TO THE LIQUOR, AND THEY ALSO MIX IT WITH VARIOUS AMOUNTS OF FAT. THE BEST CHOCOLATE USES ONLY COCOA BUTTER FOR ADDED FAT, ALTHOUGH SOME CHOCOLATE MANUFACTURERS SUBSTITUTE VEGETABLE FAT FOR SOME OR ALL OF THE COCOA BUTTER. CONNOISSEURS WILL TELL YOU IT'S THE COCOA BUTTER THAT CONTRIBUTES MOST SIGNIFICANTLY TO THE GLORIOUS "MOUTH FEEL" WE GET FROM A GREAT CHOCOLATE.

OUR FAVORITE BRAND OF DARK CHOCOLATE IS GHIRARDELLI, AND IF YOU FIND IT IN THE MARKET NEAR THE BAKING INGREDIENTS OR IN THE CANDY AISLE, GRAB IT. IT'S A DOMESTIC BRAND, MADE IN CALIFORNIA. OTHER DOMESTIC CHOCOLATES, SUCH AS SCHARFFEN BERGER, ARE GOOD, TOO. YOU WON'T GO WRONG WITH BAKER'S, HERSHEY, OR NESTLÉ SEMI- OR BITTERSWEET CHOCOLATE EITHER. EUROPEAN BRANDS ARE EXCELLENT, TOO. TRY CALLEBAUT, LINDT, OR VALRHONA. THEY MIGHT COST A LITTLE MORE BUT THEY TASTE WONDERFUL.

CHOCOLATE PANNACOTTA

We couldn't be happier that it's so easy to find Nutella in our markets nowadays. That thick, nutty spread gives this simple custard amazing flavor. We also dressed it up with chocolate, always a crowd-pleaser. Nearly every Western culture has a simple creamy pudding and this one is Italy's finest. Of course, we Carmine-ized it so it's better than any other version you've ever tried!

Serves 4

PANNACOTTA

3 LARGE EGG YOLKS

⅓ CUP GRANULATED SUGAR

½ CUP HEAVY CREAM

½ CUP MILK

4 TABLESPOONS (2 OUNCES) SEMISWEET CHOCOLATE CHIPS, MELTED

2 OUNCES NUTELLA (ABOUT ¼ CUP)

1 TEASPOON PURE VANILLA EXTRACT

GRATED ZEST OF ¼ ORANGE

TOPPING

¼ CUP CHILLED HEAVY CREAM

1 OUNCE SEMISWEET CHOCOLATE, COARSELY GRATED

TO MAKE THE PANNACOTTA

1. Preheat the oven to 350°F.

2. In the bowl of an electric mixer fitted with the paddle attachment, beat the egg yolks and sugar for about 4 minutes until the mixture is lemon colored and creamy. Add the cream, milk, melted chocolate, Nutella, vanilla, and orange zest. Beat it until it is well mixed.

3. Put 4 espresso or similar-sized cups in a small roasting pan or casserole. Skim any foam from the surface of the custard with a large spoon and then spoon the custard into the cups, dividing it evenly. Add enough hot water to come three-quarters of the way up the sides of the cups, cover the pan loosely with aluminum

Continued

foil, and bake the custards for 40 to 45 minutes or until the centers are set. Check the custards after 40 minutes. If the centers shake and look liquid, bake them for another 5 minutes or so.

4. Carefully remove the casserole from the oven so that no water splashes into the custards. Let the custards cool in the water bath for about 10 minutes. Using a kitchen towel or pot holder, lift the cups from the pan and transfer them to a small metal tray or pan. Refrigerate the custards for at least 2 hours and up to 24 hours.

TO MAKE THE TOPPING AND ASSEMBLE THE DISH

1. In the bowl of an electric mixer fitted with the whisk attachment, beat the heavy cream until soft peaks form. It might be easier to whip the cream by hand, using a wire whisk. Dollop the whipped cream on top of each custard, garnish it with grated chocolate, and serve.

STRAWBERRY AND ASSORTED BERRY CAKE

When summer berries are at their best, make shortcake! We use an assortment of berries and a syrup made from the strawberries, which is used to moisten and flavor our homemade pound cake. Store-bought pound cake works well, too. Who can wait for a cake to bake when you want nothing more than to pile it with layers of berries and clouds of whipped cream?

Serves 6 to 7

STRAWBERRY SYRUP

2 CUPS WATER

½ CUP SUGAR

6 STRAWBERRIES, SLICED

POUND CAKE

1½ CUPS CAKE FLOUR (NOT SELF-RISING)

½ TEASPOON BAKING POWDER

¼ TEASPOON BAKING SODA

1 CUP GRANULATED SUGAR

1 CUP UNSALTED BUTTER, AT ROOM TEMPERATURE

¼ TEASPOON SALT

3 LARGE EGGS

¼ CUP BUTTERMILK

1½ TEASPOONS PURE VANILLA EXTRACT

WHIPPED CREAM AND ASSEMBLY

2 CUPS HEAVY CREAM

½ CUP CONFECTIONERS' SUGAR

1 TEASPOON VANILLA

1 PINT STRAWBERRIES, SLICED

1 PINT BLUEBERRIES

1 PINT RASPBERRIES

¼ CUP PISTACHIO NUTS, CHOPPED

7 TEASPOONS AMARETTO

TO MAKE THE SYRUP

1. In a small saucepan, bring the water, sugar, and sliced strawberries to a boil and boil the mixture for about 10 minutes or until the liquid is slightly reduced and

Continued

thickened and is the consistency of very thin syrup. Transfer the syrup to a blender and blend it until it is smooth. Refrigerate the syrup for 1 hour.

TO MAKE THE CAKE

1. Preheat the oven to 325°F. Butter a 6-by-4-by-4-inch loaf pan with softened butter and then coat it with flour. Tap out the excess flour.

2. Sift together the flour, baking powder, and baking soda into the bowl of an electric mixer fitted with the paddle attachment. Add the sugar, butter, and salt and beat it for about 1 minute. Add the eggs and mix it for about 2 minutes or until the ingredients are incorporated. Add the buttermilk and the vanilla and beat it until the batter is smooth and completely lump-free.

3. Pour the cake batter into the buttered and floured pan and cover the pan with aluminum foil. Bake it for about 1 hour and 20 minutes. After 1 hour and 5 minutes, insert a toothpick into the center of the cake. If is comes out with batter clinging to it, bake the cake for another 10 to 15 minutes or until a toothpick inserted in the center comes out clean. Set the pan on a wire rack and let the cake cool for about 20 minutes. Turn it out of the pan and turn it upright on a plate. Set it aside for about an hour before serving, or cover it with plastic wrap and set it aside at room temperature for 3 to 4 hours until you are ready to serve it. If you want to keep it longer, refrigerate the wrapped cake for up to 5 days. Double wrap it and freeze it for up to a month.

TO MAKE THE WHIPPED CREAM AND ASSEMBLE THE DISH

1. In the bowl of an electric mixer fitted with the whisk attachment, whip the heavy cream and the confectioners' sugar for about 3 minutes until the cream thickens. Add the vanilla and whip it until soft peaks form. Refrigerate the whipped cream while assembling the cake.

2. Sliced the cake into pieces about ½ to ¾-inch thick. Dip a slice of cake into the syrup, turning the cake to coat both sides, and let the cake sit in the syrup for about 30 seconds or until it absorbs the syrup but does not get soggy. Put each slice on a dessert plate and top it with about 3 tablespoons of whipped cream. Add 3 to 4 slices of strawberries and some of the blueberries and raspberries, 3 more tablespoons of whipped cream, some of the blueberries and raspberries, 2 tablespoons of whipped cream, and more berries. Sprinkle it with chopped pistachio nuts and drizzle a little Amaretto over the top. Drizzle it with any leftover syrup and serve immediately.

ESPRESSO ZABAGLIONE

Zabaglione is an icon in the world of Italian desserts. It can be served warm and liquid as a sauce—very similar to crème anglaise—or you can serve it as a pudding, as we do here. Be patient when you make the custard to avoid curdling. Cook the eggs slowly and let them cool completely before folding in the whipped cream. Serve this in the prettiest stemmed glassware you have so that everyone will fall in love with the smooth custard and your creative presentation.

Serves 4 to 5

¾ CUP HEAVY CREAM

6 LARGE EGG YOLKS

½ CUP GRANULATED SUGAR

½ CUP FRESHLY BREWED ESPRESSO, CHILLED, OR OTHER STRONG COFFEE

¼ CUP MARSALA WINE

2 TO 3 TABLESPOONS COARSELY SHAVED SEMISWEET CHOCOLATE

10 PINE NUT COOKIES, PAGE 274, FOR SERVING

1. In the bowl of an electric mixer fitted with a chilled whisk attachment, whip the cream on medium-high speed until it thickens. Set it aside in the refrigerator to chill for at least 1 hour and up to 24 hours.

2. In the top of a double boiler set over simmering water on medium heat, whisk the egg yolks for 20 seconds. Add the sugar, espresso, and wine slowly to the mix. Whisk the mixture for 12 to 15 minutes or until it is thickened and shiny.

3. Set the top of the double boiler into a larger bowl half filled with ice cubes and cold water. Whisk the zabaglione for 6 to 7 minutes or until it is cool. Remove it from the ice bath and refrigerate it for at least 10 minutes and up to 1 hour or until it feels very cold. (If it's easier, transfer the custard to a bowl.)

4. Remove the custard from the refrigerator and fold all but about a heaping tablespoon of whipped cream into it. Divide the custard among 4 or 5 wineglasses or small, pretty bowls. We like to use martini glasses. Refrigerate the zabaglione for at least 4 hours.

5. Top each with a little whipped cream and shaved chocolate and serve them with the cookies.

PINE NUT COOKIES

If you serve these cookies with espresso after dinner, with or without the zabaglione, they will disappear in a flash. They are terrific in an assortment, too, with our lemony spice cookies and anything made with chocolate! Pine nuts, also called pignoli, pignolia, and piñon are the seeds of pine trees, found nestled in the cones, and are integral to the cooking in the regions where they grow, such as the Mediterranean, the American Southwest, the Middle East, and parts of China. They are wonderful in sweet baked goods and also delicious in classic pesto.

Makes 14 to 16 cookies

10 OUNCES UNSWEETENED ALMOND PASTE, CRUMBLED INTO PEBBLE-SIZED BITS

½ CUP GRANULATED SUGAR

1 TABLESPOON BEATEN EGG WHITE (ABOUT HALF A LARGE EGG WHITE)

½ TEASPOON PURE VANILLA EXTRACT

2 TABLESPOONS TOASTED PINE NUTS, SEE NOTE, PAGE 275

1. Preheat the oven to 300°F. Line a baking sheet with parchment paper and butter the parchment paper.

2. In the bowl of an electric mixer fitted with a paddle attachment, mix the almond paste and sugar on low speed for about 3 minutes or until they are well combined.

3. Add the egg white and vanilla extract and mix them on low speed for about 3 minutes or until a smooth dough is formed.

4. Pinch off about 1 tablespoon of the dough and form it into a ball. On a work surface, roll the dough into balls and then flatten them slightly. Transfer the balls to the parchment-paper-lined baking sheet, leaving about 2 inches between them. You will have 14 to 16 balls.

5. Put a sheet of parchment paper on top of the cookies, set a baking sheet on top of the parchment paper, and press lightly to flatten the cookies slightly. Remove the baking sheet and the parchment paper. Alternatively, top the cookies with waxed paper and flatten each with the bottom of a glass.

6. Press about 6 to 8 pine nuts into the center of each cookie and bake them for 40 to 45 minutes or until they are lightly browned.

7. Transfer the cookies to a wire rack to cool for 20 minutes. Store them in a container with a tight-fitting lid for up to 2 days.

NOTE: To toast the pine nuts, spread them in a single layer in a dry frying pan. Toast them over medium heat for 3 to 4 minutes, shaking the pan gently, or until they darken a shade and are fragrant. Cool them on a plate.

SPICE COOKIES WITH LEMON ICING

These cookies delight your senses, as with every bite the cool lemon icing meets the warmth of the spices. They crumble in your mouth, which makes them perfect to munch with cocoa in the winter and iced tea or lemonade in the summer.

Makes about 3 dozen cookies

½ CUP (1 STICK) UNSALTED BUTTER, SOFTENED

½ CUP GRANULATED SUGAR

1 EGG

½ CUP RAISINS

GRATED ZEST OF ½ ORANGE

GRATED ZEST OF ½ LEMON

1½ TABLESPOONS FRESH ORANGE JUICE

1½ TEASPOONS PURE VANILLA EXTRACT

½ TEASPOON GROUND CINNAMON

1½ CUPS PLUS 2 TABLESPOONS ALL-PURPOSE FLOUR

½ TEASPOON BAKING POWDER

¼ TEASPOON BAKING SODA

1½ CUPS CONFECTIONERS' SUGAR

4 TO 5 TABLESPOONS FRESH LEMON JUICE (2 TO 3 LEMONS)

1. Preheat the oven to 300°F. Line a baking sheet with parchment paper and butter the parchment paper to prevent sticking.

2. In the bowl of an electric mixer fitted with the paddle attachment, beat the butter and sugar for about 3 minutes or until the mixture is pale yellow. Add the egg and mix them on low speed for about 30 seconds until they are combined. Using a wooden spoon, stir in the raisins, orange and lemon zest, orange juice, vanilla extract, and cinnamon and mix them until the batter is well blended. The best way to stir these items in is to turn the machine on and off and mix the batter in spurts to blend it well.

3. Whisk together the flour, baking powder, and baking soda in a bowl and add the flour mixture to the batter on low speed until the ingredients are thoroughly combined.

4. Turn the dough out onto a lightly floured surface and shape it into a tight ball. Wrap it with plastic wrap and refrigerate it for at least 10 minutes.

5. Meanwhile, in a small bowl, whisk together the confectioners' sugar and 4 tablespoons of the lemon juice for about 2 minutes or until the mixture becomes a smooth glaze. Set it aside.

6. Pinch off about 1½ to 2 tablespoons of dough, roll it into a ball, and flatten it slightly. Transfer each one to the parchment-paper-lined baking sheet. Repeat the process with the rest of the dough. Leave about 2 inches between the cookies.

7. Bake the cookies for about 40 minutes or until they are lightly browned. Remove them from the oven and transfer them to a wire rack to cool.

8. Whisk the lemon glaze for about 10 seconds or until it is smooth. Add a few drops of lemon juice if the glaze is too thick. Dip the top, rounded side of each cookie into the glaze to cover it. Let any excess drip off. Transfer the cookies to a platter, glazed side up, and refrigerate them for 10 minutes before serving.

JAM COOKIES

The key to these sweet little jam-filled log cookies is to fill the crevices while the cookies are still warm so that the jam melts into them. We use strawberry jam, but your favorite can be substituted. Or try several different jams for a colorful cookie tray. Almond paste is easy to find in most supermarkets. It is sold in plastic-wrapped logs or in 6- to 8-ounce cans. Once opened, it must be wrapped tight and refrigerated. It will last up to a month. Almond paste should not be confused with marzipan, which is sweeter.

Makes 14 to 16 cookies

10 OUNCES UNSWEETENED ALMOND PASTE, CRUMBLED INTO PEBBLE-SIZED BITS

½ CUP GRANULATED SUGAR

1 TABLESPOON BEATEN EGG WHITE (ABOUT HALF A LARGE EGG WHITE)

¼ TEASPOON PURE VANILLA EXTRACT

6 TABLESPOONS STRAWBERRY JAM

1. Preheat the oven to 300°F. Line a baking sheet with parchment paper and butter the parchment paper to prevent sticking.

2. In the bowl of an electric mixer fitted with the paddle attachment, mix the almond paste and sugar for 2 minutes on low speed until they are well blended. Add the egg white and vanilla extract and mix them on low speed for about 2 minutes or until a smooth dough is formed.

3. Pinch off about 1 tablespoon of the dough and form it into a ball. On a work surface, roll the dough into a log 2 to 2½ inches long. Transfer the log to the baking sheet. Repeat the process with the remaining dough. You will have 14 to 16 logs.

4. Leave about 2 inches between the logs on the baking sheet. With the tip of a small sharp knife, make an incision along the length of the logs, starting and ending about ⅛ inch from the ends and cutting only about halfway through the logs.

5. Transfer the cookies to the oven and bake them for about 35 minutes.

6. Remove the cookies from the oven and, using the back of a small spoon, widen the crevices a little to make a narrow alley or gully. Work quickly so the cookies

don't cool and harden. Using a small spoon, spread the strawberry jam along the crevice in each log. Return the cookies to the oven for about 10 minutes or until the filling seeps into the crevices.

7. Transfer the cookies to a wire rack to cool. Store them in a tightly sealed container for up to 2 days.

8.
BASIC RECIPES

We rely on old-fashioned values and service.

—JEFFREY BANK, CEO AND PARTNER

The volume of food we produce rivals that of any national chain, yet ours tastes just like your Italian grandmother made for you at Sunday dinner.

CARMINE'S BREAD CRUMBS ≈ TOASTED BREAD CRUMBS ≈ CASINO BUTTER ≈ GARLIC BUTTER ≈ CARMINE'S VINAIGRETTE ≈ CARMINE'S MARINARA SAUCE ≈ BOLOGNESE SAUCE ≈ BRACIOLE ≈ PEPPERS AND ONIONS ≈ CARMINE'S MEATBALLS ≈ SAUSAGE FOR RAGU AND HERO SANDWICHES ≈ ROASTED RED PEPPERS ≈ ALL-PURPOSE RED SAUCE ≈ CHICKEN STOCK ≈ BROWN SAUCE ≈ BEEF STOCK

CARMINE'S BREAD CRUMBS

Do you want to know one of our best-kept secrets? It's our fresh bread crumbs seasoned with fresh garlic, parsley, and top-quality cheese. No frills, just a good, carefully made ingredient that makes so many of our dishes sing with joy and flavor! This is a good way to use up day-old or slightly stale bread, but not so stale that it's hard.

Makes about 4 cups

6 SLICES WHITE BREAD, WITH CRUSTS, TORN INTO LARGE PIECES

½ CUP GRATED ROMANO CHEESE

2 TABLESPOONS PLUS 1 TEASPOON FINELY CHOPPED GARLIC

2 TABLESPOONS CHOPPED FLAT-LEAF PARSLEY

1 TEASPOON DRIED OREGANO

SALT AND FRESHLY GROUND BLACK PEPPER

1. In the bowl of a food processor fitted with a metal blade, process the bread until it is coarsely ground. Add the cheese, garlic, parsley, and oregano and pulse the mixture until the bread crumbs are finely ground.

2. Season the bread crumbs to taste with salt and pepper and pulse the mixture just to mix in the seasonings.

3. Use the bread crumbs immediately or refrigerate them in an airtight container for 3 to 4 days.

TOASTED BREAD CRUMBS

When a recipe calls for toasted bread crumbs, these fit the bill perfectly.

Makes about 1 cup

3 SLICES WHITE BREAD, WITH CRUSTS

3 TABLESPOONS OLIVE OIL

1 TEASPOON FINELY CHOPPED GARLIC

2 TABLESPOONS GRATED ROMANO CHEESE

½ TEASPOON CHOPPED FLAT-LEAF PARSLEY

1. Cut the bread into large chunks. In the bowl of a food processor fitted with a metal blade, pulse the bread until the crumbs are very fine. Set them aside.

2. In a small nonstick sauté pan, heat the olive oil over medium-high heat. When the oil is hot, add the garlic and cook it, stirring, for about 1 minute or until it is golden brown. Take care not to let the garlic burn.

3. Add the bread crumbs and mix them well with the oil and garlic. Cook them for about 30 seconds and then stir them well. Reduce the heat to medium or medium-low and cook them for 4 to 5 minutes, stirring occasionally, or until they are golden brown and crispy.

4. Transfer the bread crumbs to a shallow bowl and let them cool for 20 minutes at room temperature.

5. Stir in the grated cheese and parsley and mix them well.

6. Use the bread crumbs immediately or refrigerate the bread crumbs in a tightly covered container at room temperature for 3 to 4 days.

CASINO BUTTER

Makes 2 cups

4 OUNCES BACON, CHOPPED

½ MEDIUM-SIZED ONION, PEELED AND FINELY CHOPPED

½ RED PEPPER, SEEDED, CORED, AND FINELY DICED

½ GREEN PEPPER, SEEDED, CORED, AND FINELY DICED

I CUP UNSALTED BUTTER, AT ROOM TEMPERATURE

2 TABLESPOONS CHOPPED FLAT-LEAF PARSLEY

2 TABLESPOONS FRESH LEMON JUICE

2 TEASPOONS WORCESTERSHIRE SAUCE

I TEASPOON SALT

⅛ TEASPOON FRESHLY GROUND BLACK PEPPER

8 DROPS HOT SAUCE, SUCH AS TABASCO

1. In a small skillet over medium heat, cook the bacon, turning it, for 5 to 6 minutes or until it is crispy. Drain it on paper towels and set it aside. Leave the bacon fat in the pan.

2. Add the onions and peppers to the bacon fat in the skillet and sauté them for 7 to 8 minutes or until they are tender. Remove them from the heat and set them aside.

3. In a medium-sized bowl, beat the butter with a wooden spoon for about 3 minutes or until it is creamy. Stir in the vegetables, crumbled bacon, parsley, lemon juice, Worcestershire sauce, salt, pepper, and hot sauce and mix it well. Taste it and adjust the seasoning, if necessary.

4. Transfer the butter to a small bowl, cover it with plastic wrap, and refrigerate it for at least 1 hour. The butter will keep for up to 1 month.

GARLIC BUTTER

This may be a little more complicated to make than some garlic butters, but it has a depth of flavor that we find essential for so many of our recipes. Of course we spread it on our garlic bread, but we use it in other dishes, too, where its rich goodness takes everything up a notch. Without a doubt, this, like our bread crumbs, is an ingredient we rely on to make our food special. It's easy to make and well worth having on hand.

Makes 1 ¼ cups

1 CUP SALTED BUTTER, AT ROOM TEMPERATURE

12 FRESH OREGANO LEAVES, CHOPPED

2 TABLESPOONS FINELY CHOPPED GARLIC

2 TABLESPOONS GRATED ROMANO CHEESE

2 TABLESPOONS GARLIC POWDER

1 TABLESPOON OLIVE OIL

1 TABLESPOON DRIED OREGANO

1 TABLESPOON CHOPPED FLAT-LEAF PARSLEY

1 TEASPOON ONION POWDER

1. In a medium-sized bowl, beat the butter, using a rubber spatula or wooden spoon, for about 3 minutes or until it is very soft. Mix in the remaining ingredients until they are well blended.

2. Transfer the garlic butter to a glass dish, cover it, and refrigerate it. It will keep in the refrigerator for up to 1 month. Let the butter come to room temperature before using it.

CARMINE'S VINAIGRETTE

What makes our vinaigrette special? We think it's two acids: the marriage of imported red wine vinegar with lemon juice, both bolstered by great olive oil. We use this on a number of our salads and to jazz up other foods, too.

Makes about ½ cup

JUICE OF ½ LEMON

2 TABLESPOONS IMPORTED RED WINE VINEGAR

PINCH OF DRIED OREGANO

SALT AND FRESHLY GROUND BLACK PEPPER

¼ CUP EXTRA-VIRGIN OLIVE OIL

In a small bowl, whisk together the lemon juice, vinegar, oregano, and salt and pepper to taste. Slowly whisk in the olive oil until it is well blended. Use the dressing right away or store it in a covered container in the refrigerator for up to 10 days. Whisk it before using it.

CARMINE'S MARINARA SAUCE

We use this versatile sauce in so many of our recipes that we always have it ready and waiting. You will want to, too.

Makes about 5 cups

THREE 26- TO 28-OUNCE CANS ITALIAN PLUM TOMATOES (WE USE SAN MARZANO)

¼ CUP OLIVE OIL

¼ CUP COARSELY CHOPPED GARLIC (FROM ABOUT 12 CLOVES GARLIC)

12 FRESH BASIL LEAVES, SLICED

2 TEASPOONS CHOPPED FLAT-LEAF PARSLEY

1 TEASPOON SALT

FRESHLY GROUND BLACK PEPPER

1. Drain the tomatoes in a colander set in a large bowl for 5 minutes. Reserve the tomato liquid.

2. In a large pot, heat the olive oil over medium heat. When the oil is hot, add the garlic and cook it, stirring, for about 5 minutes or until it is golden brown. If the garlic starts to cook too quickly, reduce the heat.

3. Add the basil, parsley, salt, and pepper to taste. Cook the mixture for 30 seconds. Add the tomatoes, increase the heat to high, and cook them for about 5 minutes, using a wooden spoon or long-handled fork to break them up, or until the tomatoes boil. Reduce the heat and simmer the sauce for about 10 minutes or until the tomatoes break down.

4. Add the reserved tomato liquid. Increase the heat to high and bring the sauce to a boil. Boil it for about 12 minutes or until it starts to thicken. Stir it occasionally and scrape the bottom of the pan to prevent the sauce from burning.

5. Transfer the sauce to a bowl and set it aside for about 1 hour or until it cools to room temperature. Transfer it to a tightly covered storage container and refrigerate it for up to 1 week or freeze it for up to 1 month.

BOLOGNESE SAUCE

Make 7 cups

¼ CUP OLIVE OIL

2 TABLESPOONS FINELY CHOPPED GARLIC

½ ONION, FINELY CHOPPED

4 TABLESPOONS FINELY CHOPPED CELERY

4 TABLESPOONS FINELY CHOPPED CARROTS

I POUND COARSELY GROUND BEEF

½ POUND SWEET OR HOT FENNEL SAUSAGE, CASING REMOVED

2 TABLESPOONS CHOPPED FRESH BASIL

2 TABLESPOONS CHOPPED FLAT-LEAF PARSLEY

I BAY LEAF

½ TEASPOON CHOPPED FRESH ROSEMARY

½ TEASPOON CHOPPED FRESH OREGANO

SALT AND FRESHLY GROUND BLACK PEPPER

I ½ CUPS DRY RED WINE

ONE 26- TO 28-OUNCE CAN ITALIAN PLUM TOMATOES, DRAINED AND COARSELY
   CRUSHED

2 CUPS CHICKEN OR BEEF STOCK, PAGES 306 AND 308 RESPECTIVELY

I CUP GRATED ROMANO CHEESE

2 TABLESPOONS UNSALTED BUTTER

1. In a large pot, heat the olive oil over medium heat. When the oil is hot, add the garlic and stir it. Increase the heat to high, add the onions, and cook the mixture, stirring, for about 1 minute or just until it is fragrant. Add the celery and cook it, stirring, for 1 minute. Add the carrots, and cook it, stirring, for 1 minute longer to soften the vegetables slightly.

2. Add the beef and sausage and use a wooden spoon or long-handled fork to break up the meat so that it will cook evenly. Cook the mixture for 5 to 7 minutes

Continued

or until the meat is browned. Stir it occasionally after the first 2 or 3 minutes of cooking.

3. Add the basil, parsley, bay leaf, rosemary, oregano, 1 tablespoon of salt, and ½ teaspoon of pepper. Reduce the heat to medium and cook the mixture, stirring, for 2 to 3 minutes.

4. Add the wine, increase the heat to high, and bring the mixture to a boil. Boil it for about 3 minutes or until the red wine is reduced to ¼ cup. Add the tomatoes and stock and return it to a boil. Reduce the heat and simmer it for about 50 minutes until it is well blended. Increase the heat to high and boil it for 10 minutes or until some of the liquid evaporates and it is a slightly thickened consistency.

5. Season the sauce to taste with salt and pepper. Remove it from the heat and stir in the grated cheese and butter. Serve the sauce immediately, ladled over cooked pasta.

6. To store the sauce, transfer it to a bowl, and cool it to room temperature. Transfer it to a tightly covered storage container and refrigerate it for up to 1 week or freeze it for up to 1 month.

CANNED TOMATOES ARE GREAT!

AS YOU COOK THROUGH CARMINE'S FAMILY-STYLE COOKBOOK, YOU WILL NOTICE THAT WE OFTEN USE CANNED TOMATOES. WHY NOT FRESH? THE ANSWER IS BOTH SIMPLE AND COMPLICATED. THE SIMPLE EXPLANATION IS THAT CANNED TOMATOES ARE EASY TO USE AND ALWAYS AVAILABLE; THE MORE COMPLICATED ONE IS THAT THERE ARE TIMES WHEN THEY WORK BETTER THAN FRESH TOMATOES IN DISHES THAT CALL FOR THEIR INTENSE FLAVOR AND FIRM TEXTURE. ALSO, WHEN FRESH TOMATOES ARE OUT OF SEASON AND ALL YOU CAN FIND ARE HARD, PALE-COLORED SPECIMENS WITH DRY, MEALY FLESH, CANNED TOMATOES CLEARLY ARE SUPERIOR IN TERMS OF FLAVOR, TEXTURE, AND ENJOYMENT.

THE BEST CANNED TOMATOES COME FROM SAN MARZANO, ITALY. THESE ARE WHAT WE USE AT CARMINE'S. LOOK FOR THEM IN THE SUPERMARKET AND STOCK UP. IF YOU CAN'T FIND THEM, BUY ANOTHER BRAND IMPORTED FROM ITALY OR USE YOUR FAVORITE DOMESTIC BRAND. CANNED TOMATOES KEEP FOR AGES, SO IF YOU HAVE ROOM, ALWAYS HAVE SEVERAL LARGE CANS ON HAND. BUY CANS OF WHOLE PEELED TOMATOES WITH NO SEASONING—THE LESS PROCESSING THEY'VE BEEN THROUGH, THE BETTER THEY WILL TASTE.

BRACIOLE

This Italian American dish is made with stuffed rolls of thinly sliced pork and then simmered in a red sauce, or "gravy" as many people call it. We use it in a number of dishes, including the Ragu Pasta on page 130. It could also be served as a side dish, or spooned over a roll for a juicy sandwich. Italian Americans often pronounce this "BRAZ-uhl."

Makes 3 to 4 braciole and 6 cups sauce

BRACIOLE

THREE TO FOUR 4-OUNCE SLICES PORK BUTT OR SHOULDER

10 OUNCES DAY-OLD ITALIAN BREAD (8 TO 14 SLICES)

½ CUP OLIVE OIL

2 TEASPOONS CHOPPED GARLIC

½ CUP CHOPPED SPANISH ONION

2½ OUNCES CHOPPED PROSCIUTTO

8 FRESH BASIL LEAVES, CHOPPED

2 TABLESPOONS CHOPPED FLAT-LEAF PARSLEY

1 TEASPOON SALT

¼ TEASPOON FRESHLY GROUND BLACK PEPPER

¼ CUP GRATED ROMANO CHEESE

SAUCE AND ASSEMBLY

10 CUPS CARMINE'S MARINARA SAUCE, PAGE 288

2 TABLESPOONS OLIVE OIL

½ LARGE ONION, PEELED AND THINLY SLICED

2 CLOVES GARLIC, PEELED AND CHOPPED

3 TABLESPOONS CHOPPED FRESH BASIL

2 TABLESPOONS CHOPPED FLAT-LEAF PARSLEY

SALT AND FRESHLY GROUND BLACK PEPPER

TO PREPARE THE BRACIOLE

1. Using the flat side of a cleaver, a mallet, or a small heavy frying pan, flatten each piece of meat so that it is about ⅛ inch thick, 9 inches long, and 6 inches wide. Refrigerate the meat until needed.

2. Tear the bread into chunks and place them in a large bowl. Add enough water to cover the bread and gently push it into the water. Weight the bread with a small plate to keep it submerged and set it aside to soak for 30 minutes.

3. Remove the plate and tear the bread into small pieces. Let the bread soak for another 10 minutes.

4. Drain the bread in a colander and squeeze out as much of the water as possible. Transfer the bread to a large bowl and set it aside.

5. In a small sauté pan, heat the olive oil over medium-high heat. When the oil is hot, add the garlic and cook it, stirring, for 30 seconds. Add the onions, increase the heat to high, and cook the mixture, stirring, for 2 to 3 minutes or until the onions and garlic are golden brown. Reduce the heat to medium-high, add the prosciutto, and cook it, stirring, for 3 to 4 minutes or until the prosciutto is crispy. Add the basil leaves and the parsley, stir the mixture, and then season it with the salt and pepper.

6. Add the contents of the pan to the bread and, using a large spoon, mix them together until they are thoroughly combined. Fold in the grated cheese. Cover the stuffing and refrigerate it for about 40 minutes to make the braciole easier to work with.

7. Spread the meat on a work surface and spoon about ¼ cup of stuffing into the center of each piece of flattened meat. Spread it to leave about 1½-inch borders on the 2 long sides of the meat. Fold the borders over the stuffing and, starting at a short end, roll each piece tightly. Tie each roll with kitchen string. Use it right away or refrigerate it until needed.

TO MAKE THE SAUCE AND ASSEMBLE THE DISH

1. In a 3-quart pot, bring the marinara sauce to a simmer. When it simmers, remove it from the heat.

2. Heat a large sauté pan over medium heat for 3 minutes. When the pan is hot, add the olive oil and let it heat for 1 minute.

3. Meanwhile, season all sides of the braciole with salt and pepper. Place the braciole in the pan and cook them for about 2 minutes or until the bottoms are golden brown. Turn them and cook them for another 2 minutes or until the braciole are golden brown on all sides. Put the browned braciole in the marinara sauce.

Continued

4. In the same sauté pan, cook the onions over medium heat for about 10 minutes or until they are browned and caramelized. Add the garlic and cook the mixture for about 4 minutes or until the garlic browns. Add it to the sauce and bring the sauce to a boil over medium-high heat. Add the basil and parsley and season the sauce to taste with salt and pepper.

5. Reduce the heat to medium-low and simmer the braciole in the sauce for 2 to 2½ hours or until the meat is tender and the tines of a fork easily pierce it without tearing it.

6. Serve right away or let the braciole and sauce cool to room temperature. Transfer it to a tightly covered storage container and refrigerate it for up to 1 week or freeze it for up to 2 months.

PEPPERS AND ONIONS

Makes about 4 cups

¼ CUP OLIVE OIL

6 CLOVES GARLIC

2 LARGE SPANISH ONIONS, EACH PEELED AND CUT INTO 6 WEDGES

2 RED BELL PEPPERS, SEEDED, CORED, AND CUT INTO 6 LENGTHWISE PIECES

2 GREEN BELL PEPPERS, SEEDED, CORED, AND CUT INTO 6 LENGTHWISE PIECES

SALT AND FRESHLY GROUND BLACK PEPPER

8 BASIL LEAVES, SLICED

1 TABLESPOON CHOPPED FRESH FLAT-LEAF PARSLEY

1. In a large sauté pan, heat the olive oil over medium heat. When the oil is hot, add the garlic and cook it for 1 to 2 minutes or until it is brown. Using a slotted spoon, remove the garlic and set it aside on paper towels to drain.

2. Add the onions and peppers. Season them to taste with salt and pepper. Sauté them, stirring occasionally, for 4 to 5 minutes or until they start to brown. Return the garlic to the pan and add the basil and parsley. Reduce the heat to medium, cover the pan, and cook the mixture, stirring occasionally, for about 15 minutes or until the peppers have softened and both the peppers and onions are caramelized. Use the peppers and onions right away or transfer them to a lidded container and refrigerate them for up to 3 days.

CARMINE'S MEATBALLS

These meatballs are one of our trademark dishes—and could be just about the greatest meatballs ever made! From day one, customers have told us that the meatballs are as good as their grandmother's. High praise, indeed! We hope every one of our guests almost believes a little old Italian grandmother is in our kitchen cooking Italian American dishes as she always has. Make these to use as we do in Carmine's Family-Style Cookbook *or however you and your family like meatballs: simmered in your favorite marinara sauce, lightly sautéed with peppers and sausage, chopped up and scrambled with eggs, rolled into small nuggets and served with toothpicks for cocktail parties. There are nearly endless ways to use meatballs this good.*

The best way to mix all these ingredients is with your hands so that you literally can fold them into the meat, but don't be rough. Once you have made these a few times, you will get the feel for them. Another key is to brown the meatballs and then cook them in the sauce to let the flavors blend.

Makes about 12 meatballs and 6 cups sauce

1½ POUNDS GROUND BEEF, SUCH AS CHUCK WITH 20% FAT

½ POUND GROUND VEAL

2 LARGE EGGS, BEATEN

¼ CUP CARMINE'S BREAD CRUMBS, PAGE 283

3 TABLESPOONS CHOPPED FLAT-LEAF PARSLEY

2 TABLESPOONS CHOPPED FRESH BASIL

1 TABLESPOON SALT

1 TEASPOON FINELY CHOPPED GARLIC

½ TEASPOON FRESHLY GROUND BLACK PEPPER

4 SLICES FIRM WHITE BREAD, CRUSTS REMOVED

1 CUP MILK

1 CUP GRATED ROMANO CHEESE

2 TEASPOONS OLIVE OIL

1 LARGE SPANISH ONION, PEELED AND THINLY SLICED

1 TABLESPOON CHOPPED GARLIC

10 CUPS CARMINE'S MARINARA SAUCE, PAGE 288

1. In a large mixing bowl, use your hands or a wooden spoon to mix together the beef, veal, and eggs. Add the bread crumbs, parsley, basil, salt, garlic, and pepper and mix it well.

Continued

2. Tear the bread into pieces and transfer it to a mixing bowl. Add the milk and let it sit for 5 to 7 minutes or until the milk is nearly absorbed. Add the bread to the meat and use your hands or a wooden spoon to mix it well. Stir in the grated cheese.

3. Cover the bowl with plastic wrap and refrigerate it for 45 minutes to 1 hour or until the meat mixture is firm.

4. Using an ice cream scoop, remove chunks of meat and roll them between dampened palms into meatballs, each weighing about 3 ounces. Refrigerate the meatballs for at least 10 minutes before proceeding with the recipe.

5. To sauté the meatballs, heat one teaspoon of the olive oil in a large sauté pan over medium-high heat. When the pan is hot, add the meatballs and cook them for about 10 minutes, turning them until they are browned on all sides. Transfer them to a platter and set them aside.

6. In the same pan, heat the remaining teaspoon of the olive oil over medium-high heat. Add the onions and garlic and sauté them for 8 to 10 minutes or until they are browned.

7. Meanwhile, in a large pot large enough to hold the meatballs, heat the marinara sauce over medium-high heat for 6 to 8 minutes or until the sauce starts to boil. Stir in the onions and garlic.

8. Add the browned meatballs and any accumulated juices and cook them over medium heat for about 45 minutes. Do not cover them while cooking. Remove them from the heat and set them aside for about 45 minutes or until they have had ample time to mellow and the flavors of the sauce and meat intermingle.

9. To store the meatballs, let them cool in the sauce. Transfer them to a tightly lidded storage container and refrigerate them for up to 1 week or freeze them for up to 1 month.

SAUSAGE FOR RAGU AND HERO SANDWICHES

Italian American recipes often are composed of several different sauces and preparations that, on their own, seem to be finished dishes. These sausages are a case in point for the latter. We call for them in two of our most popular dishes: Sausage and Pepper Hero, page 77, and Ragu Pasta, page 130. If you want, you can eat them as cooked here for a simple, delicious meal.

Makes 12 sausages

½ CUP OLIVE OIL

TWELVE 3-OUNCE FENNEL OR HOT
   ITALIAN SAUSAGE LINKS

8 FRESH BASIL LEAVES, SLICED

1½ TEASPOONS CHOPPED FLAT-LEAF
   PARSLEY

1½ TEASPOONS CHOPPED GARLIC

1½ SPANISH ONIONS, PEELED AND
   THINLY SLICED

10 CUPS CARMINE'S MARINARA SAUCE,
   PUREED, PAGE 288

SALT AND FRESHLY GROUND BLACK
   PEPPER

1. In a large sauté pan, heat the olive oil over medium-high heat. When the oil is hot, add the sausages. Cook them for 3 to 4 minutes, turning them occasionally to brown the sausages on all sides. Using tongs, remove the sausages from the pan and set them aside on a platter.

2. Add the basil, parsley, and garlic to the pan and sauté it for about 1 minute. Add the onions, reduce the heat to medium, and cook the mixture, stirring occasionally, for about 5 minutes or until the onions soften. Transfer the contents of the sauté pan to a pot large enough to hold the marinara sauce.

3. Add the marinara sauce to the pot and stir it well. Put the sausages and any accumulated juices in the pot and mix it well. Adjust the heat so that the sauce simmers, uncovered, and cook it for about 45 minutes to 1 hour or until the sausages are tender and cooked through. Adjust the heat to maintain a simmer. Season the sauce to taste with salt and pepper.

4. Set the sausage in the sauce aside at room temperature to cool. Transfer it to a tightly lidded storage container and refrigerate it for up to 1 week or freeze it for up to 1 month.

ROASTED RED PEPPERS

Makes 4 roasted peppers

4 LARGE RED BELL PEPPERS

SALT AND FRESHLY GROUND BLACK PEPPER

1 TABLESPOON CHOPPED GARLIC

¼ CUP OLIVE OIL

10 FRESH BASIL LEAVES, THINLY SLICED

1 TABLESPOON CHOPPED FLAT-LEAF PARSLEY

1. Char the peppers over a grill or gas flame or under a broiler until they are blackened on all sides. Put the peppers in a large bowl, cover it with plastic wrap, and set it aside for about 45 minutes so that the peppers cool. Peel the skins off the peppers; they will slide right off with your fingertips. If you need to, scrape stubborn patches off with a small knife. It is not necessary to get every fleck of charred skin off the peppers.

2. Cut the peppers lengthwise through one side. Discard the stems, seeds, and ribs. Pat the peppers dry with paper towels.

3. Spread the peppers open on a work surface. Season them lightly with salt and pepper. Rub the chopped garlic into both sides of the peppers. Drizzle them with a little olive oil and then sprinkle the basil and parsley over them.

4. Stack the peppers on top of each other on a dish. Drizzle them with any remaining oil. Cover the dish and refrigerate the peppers overnight or for up 4 days.

ALL-PURPOSE RED SAUCE

What can we say about this full-flavored red sauce? We use it in the recipe for Crispy Romano-Crusted Chicken Breast on page 225, but you can use it for so many more preparations. Try it over grilled beef, on top of pizza or pasta, or to make a hero better than ever.

Makes 2 cups

1 CUP CARMINE'S MARINARA SAUCE, PAGE 288

6 RED BELL PEPPERS

¼ CUP OLIVE OIL

1 TO 2 SERRANO PEPPERS

2 CLOVES GARLIC, PEELED AND SLICED

6 TO 8 FRESH BASIL LEAVES, SLICED

½ TEASPOON FRESH THYME LEAVES

1 TEASPOON RED WINE VINEGAR

SALT AND FRESHLY GROUND BLACK PEPPER

1. In a small pot, bring the marinara sauce to a boil over medium-high heat. Reduce the heat and simmer it for about 10 minutes or until the sauce is reduced to ½ cup. Set it aside to cool.

2. In the bowl of a food processor fitted with a metal blade, puree the cooled sauce until it is smooth. Set it aside.

3. Meanwhile, preheat the oven to 450°F.

4. Roast the red peppers, turning them occasionally, for about 25 minutes or until they are blackened on all sides. Put the peppers in a bowl, cover it with plastic wrap, and set it aside for about 45 minutes. Rub the charred skin off the peppers. Cut the peppers lengthwise through one side. Discard the stems, seeds, and ribs. Coarsely chop the peppers and set them aside.

5. In a small sauté pan, heat the olive oil over low heat. When the oil is hot, add the serrano peppers, and cook them, turning the peppers occasionally, for about 5 minutes or until they are browned on all sides and softened. Remove them from the oil, using a slotted spoon, and drain them on paper towels. Cut the peppers in

half and remove the ribs and seeds. Coarsely chop them and set them aside. Reserve the oil in the sauté pan.

6. Add the garlic to the oil in the sauté pan. Cook it over low heat for about 1 minute or until it is lightly browned. Add the marinara sauce, bring it to a simmer over medium heat, and cook it for about 2 minutes. Stir in the basil and thyme.

7. Return the sauce to the food processor and add the red peppers, serrano peppers, and vinegar. Process it until it is smooth. Season it to taste with salt and pepper.

8. Transfer the sauce to a tightly lidded storage container and refrigerate it for up to 1 week or freeze it for up to 1 month.

CHICKEN STOCK

While we always think homemade stock is best, we recognize that not everyone has time to make it. If you do, this recipe is tops. If not, use canned broth, preferably low-sodium.

Makes 2 quarts

2 POUNDS CHICKEN BONES, OR ONE 3-POUND CHICKEN CUT INTO 8 PIECES

12 SPRIGS FRESH FLAT-LEAF PARSLEY

2 MEDIUM CARROTS, PEELED AND CUT INTO 2-INCH PIECES

2 LARGE RIBS CELERY WITH THE LEAVES, CUT INTO 4-INCH PIECES

1 LARGE ONION, PEELED AND CUT IN HALF

1 TEASPOON BLACK PEPPERCORNS

1 BAY LEAF

3 QUARTS WATER

1. Rinse the chicken bones or chicken pieces under cold water and place them in a large stockpot.

2. Add the parsley, carrots, celery, onions, peppercorns, and bay leaf. Add the water.

3. Bring the stock to a boil over medium heat. Boil it for 15 minutes, skimming off any froth that rises to the surface. Reduce the heat to low and simmer it gently, partially covered, for 2 hours. Adjust the heat to maintain a simmer. Remove the cover, raise the heat to medium, and boil it for 10 minutes.

4. Strain the stock through a fine-mesh sieve into a large bowl. Discard the bones and vegetables. (The skinned chicken pieces can be reserved for other uses.)

5. Cool the stock by putting the bowl in a larger bowl or a sink filled with cold water and ice cubes. When it is at room temperature or cooler, remove the bowl, cover it, and refrigerate it until the stock is cold. Scrape off any fat congealed on the surface of the stock.

6. Transfer the stock to tightly lidded storage containers and refrigerate it for up to 3 days or freeze it for up to 2 months.

BROWN SAUCE

This easy-to-make sauce is bolstered by a good beef stock. We have a recipe for beef stock and if you have time, make your own. If not, use low-sodium beef broth. We use this in several recipes, including Stuffed Braised Chicken Legs and Fontina Potato Croquettes, page 223, and Chicken or Veal Marsala, page 207.

Makes 1 ¾ quarts

½ CUP UNSALTED BUTTER

1 RIB CELERY, CUT INTO 1-INCH PIECES

½ ONION, PEELED AND CHOPPED

½ CARROT, PEELED AND CHOPPED

FEW SPRIGS FRESH THYME

6 CUPS BEEF STOCK, PAGE 308

½ CUP ALL-PURPOSE FLOUR

SALT AND FRESHLY GROUND BLACK PEPPER

1. In a large saucepan, melt the butter over medium heat. When the butter is hot, add the celery, onion, carrots, and thyme and cook them for 4 to 5 minutes or until the vegetables are tender and golden brown.

2. Meanwhile, in a large pot set over medium-high heat, bring the beef stock to a boil.

3. Sprinkle the flour over the vegetables and stir them continuously for about 5 to 6 minutes or until the flour is absorbed.

4. Add 3 cups of the hot stock to the flour mixture and whisk it until it is combined. Add the rest of the stock and whisk it well. Reduce the heat to low and gently simmer it for 1 hour, skimming off any fat from the surface and making sure the liquid does not boil.

5. Strain the sauce through a fine-mesh sieve into a bowl. Season it to taste with salt and pepper and set it aside. Or transfer it to a tightly lidded storage container and refrigerate it for up to 1 week or freeze it for up to 3 months.

BEEF STOCK

Makes 6 to 7 cups

3 POUNDS BEEF BONES, CUT INTO SMALL CHUNKS

2 RIBS CELERY, CUT INTO 1-INCH PIECES

1 LARGE CARROT, CUT INTO 1-INCH PIECES

1 ONION, CUT INTO 1-INCH PIECES

½ SMALL LEEK, RINSED WELL AND CUT INTO 1-INCH PIECES, OPTIONAL

½ CUP TOMATO PASTE

6 PEPPERCORNS

3 BEEF BOUILLON CUBES

2 CLOVES GARLIC

¼ BUNCH FLAT-LEAF PARSLEY

FEW SPRIGS FRESH THYME

1 SMALL BAY LEAF

1. Preheat the oven to 450°F.

2. Rinse the bones under cold water to remove any blood.

3. Spread the celery, carrots, onions, and leeks, if using, in a large roasting pan and place the bones on top. Spread the tomato paste over the bones. Roast it for 30 to 40 minutes, stirring occasionally, or until the bones are nicely browned.

4. Transfer the bones and vegetables to a large stockpot. Add the peppercorns, bouillon cubes, garlic, parsley, thyme, and bay leaf.

5. Set the roasting pan over medium-high heat and stir in about ½ cup of water. When the water boils, scrape the browned bits off the bottom of the pan to deglaze it. Pour the deglazed liquid into the stockpot. Add enough cold water to cover the bones by 2 to 2½ inches.

6. Bring the stock to a boil over medium heat. Reduce the heat and simmer it for 2 to 3 hours or until it is fully flavored. Adjust the heat to maintain a simmer.

7. Strain the stock through a fine-mesh sieve into a large bowl. Discard the bones and vegetables.

8. Cool the stock by putting the bowl in a larger bowl or a sink filled with cold water and ice cubes. When it is at room temperature or cooler, remove the bowl, cover it, and refrigerate it until the stock is chilled. Scrape off the layer of congealed fat from the surface.

9. Transfer the stock to a tightly lidded storage container and refrigerate it for up to 3 days or freeze it for up to 6 months.

ACKNOWLEDGMENTS

This book was inspired by Artie Cutler's nineteen-year journey. Artie was a legend in the restaurant industry, a visionary, who not only predicted culinary trends, but showed incredible foresight in aquiring real estate and in developing markets. The list of just some of his restaurants, many of which may be familiar, best exemplify that vision: Murray's Sturgeon Shop, Dock's Oyster Bar & Seafood Grill, Haru, Ollie's Noodle Shops, Columbia and Times Square Bagels, Monsoon, Virgil's BBQ, Artie's Deli, Gabriela's, and the flagship of our company and subject of this book, Carmine's.

Sadly, Artie left us too soon, before he could see the culmination of all his dreams. After Artie's death, his wife, Alice, took over as president, majority shareholder, and keeper of Artie's vision. Since I joined the company nine years ago, Alice has become not only the most amazing partner I could ask for, but a dear friend and mentor. Words cannot adequately express the respect and affection I hold for her and her family. With her support and confidence, she has allowed me, as CEO, to make decisions that have brought the company and brand to ever higher levels, an accomplishment I feel certain would make her husband proud.

Although my official title is CEO of the Alicart Restaurant Group, I feel more like the conductor of the world's greatest culinary orchestra. As with all thriving collaborations, true success cannot come without the hard work and dedication of all members of the ensemble. Currently, our orchestra has about a thousand players; at the request of the editor, I will only mention a few significant people, without whom these achievements and this book would not be possible:

Carl Milner, Alice's brother, joined the company after Artie passed away, helping take control and organize the more than twenty-nine various business ventures Artie had been involved in. Not content to just be a restaurateur, Artie was an avid horseracing and boxing fan. He owned trotters with family friend Jeff Gural, and also invested in a prizefighter with Jeff Baynon and Tom Cavallaro. Carl selflessly uprooted himself to stand by his sister's side, and in turn helped to restore order in the company. Today Carl remains active and is involved in Gabriela's.

Michael Ronis, founding chef and partner, has shown that his passion for food knows no bounds. His talent is quite evident throughout the pages of this amazing book. He has grown into the role of elder statesman, training and allowing our younger staff to step into strong supervisory positions.

Chief Operating Officer Gary Bologna, and Executive Chef Glenn Rolnick, both partners, are truly the eyes and ears of the restaurants. Together, their synergy, dedication, and passion make them the best partners anyone could ask for. They, along with Alice, are the heart and soul of this company and I am so grateful for their support. I'd like to thank their wives, Roberta and Karen, respectively, for their encouragement as well. Their generosity and patience, especially during new restaurant openings, have allowed us to grow as we have.

Though I mention the following people only briefly—much the way credits roll by too fast at the end of a movie—do not underestimate their importance. They are the true operators of our restaurants. The majority of them have been with the company for many, many years, and it is with great pride that we watch their professional and personal growth:

Assistant Director of Operations Michael Honea; Corporate Sous Chef Chris O'Neil; GM and Associate Partner Michael Connolly, Carmine's 44th St.; GM and Associate Partner Carl Delponte, Carmine's 91st St.; Beverage Director James Yacyshyn; Director of Banquets Penny Kaplan; Director of Training Bea Stein; the chefs of Carmine's, Jeff Gotta, Louis Javier, Joe Delgado, Anthony

Penn, and Terry Natas. Thank you to Nat Milner, managing partner of Gabriela's, for keeping that brand alive, going on its fourteenth year.

Leading our accounting staff at Alicart is Drew Kuruc, along with Theresa Chang and her entire staff. A special thanks to Amanda Wetzstein, my former administrative assistant, who has since moved on to southern, greener pastures, and is sorely missed.

Without St. Martin's Press and editor Elizabeth Beier's passion, you would only be eating at a Carmine's and not cooking Carmine's recipes at home today. Thank you also to her assistant, Michelle Richter; production editor, Bob Berkel; interior designer, James Sinclair; production manager, Cheryl Mamaril; and cover designers, David Rotstein and Steve Snider.

Mary Goodbody is a true professional in every sense who worked tirelessly with Michael Ronis to translate corporate recipes into household recipes that still match the flavor of Carmine's.

Thanks to Michael Psaltis of Regal Literary for his guidance, and to Alex Martinez, whose pictures are so incredible that my kids tried to literally eat this book.

Also thanks to Stuart Newman and Roy Tumpowsky, two of our trusted advisors, and to Dr. Jane Sullivan, of Sullivan and Associates, whose advice has always been insightful and valuable.

In my more than twenty years in the hospitality industry, I can honestly say that the Alicart Restaurant Group has assembled one of the best teams in the business, and the family-style portions you experience at Carmine's seem to emanate from our staff's family-style attitude toward each other.

My love for my wife, Karen, daughter, Sarah, and son, Andrew, inspire me to work hard every day, and together they make a fabulous focus group for Carmine's.

Thank you to my mother and father for the values they instilled in me and my sister and also cookbook author Lauren Bank Deen and brother Dr. Michael Bank, who remind me that family is everything.

I hope you enjoy exploring these recipes in the comfort of your home with your family, and that you are able to visit Carmine's to share a fabulous meal with *our* family.

JEFFREY BANK

CEO AND PARTNER OF THE ALICART RESTAURANT GROUP

INDEX